A Dictionary of Scots Words and Phrases in Current Use

A Dictionary of Scots Words and Phrases in Current Use

James A.C. Stevenson

HIPPOCRENE BOOKS, INC.
New York

First published 1989 by The Athlone Press Ltd, London.
Copyright © James A.C. Stevenson 1989
Copyright © Iseabail Macleod 1989

Paperback edition 1998 by Hippocrene Books, Inc.

For information, address:
HIPPOCRENE BOOKS, INC.
171 Madison Avenue
New York, NY 10016

Cataloging-in-Publication data available from the Library of Congress.

ISBN 0-7818-0664-X

Printed in the United States of America.

To Christine

Contents

Foreword		ix
Acknowledgements		x
A Key to Varieties of Scots		xi
A Note on Pronunciation		xiii
I	People Titles and Labels Parts of the Body	1
II	Human Attributes Behaviour	16
III	Health Appearance Dress	34
IV	Eating and Drinking	49
V	Communication Speech Sound	68
VI	Movement Commotion Violence	79
VII	Law Administration	91
VIII	Education Religion The Supernatural	104
IX	Festivals Local Customs Music and Dance	117
X	Sports and Games	133
XI	Countryside Nature Time and Weather	149
XII	Fishing Farming Industry Crafts and Gear	167
XIII	Construction House Household	181
XIV	Grammar Words Number and Quantity	199
XV	Miscellany	214
Bibliography		245
Index		246

Foreword

Scots is a living language. This short dictionary examines many of its most widely-used words and expressions. Some of these are peculiarly Scottish and communicate much about Scotland's unique culture and society. Others have found their way outside Scotland into general English.

Entries range from examples of Scots slang (e.g. *bampot*) or dialect (e.g. *quine*) to words and phrases – some of them to all appearances standard English – which refer to characteristic features of modern Scottish society (e.g. *ceilidh, Old Firm, children's hearings*).

Entries are arranged in fifteen sections, each of which deals with some aspect of everyday life in Scotland. A key is provided to indicate the various contexts (colloquial, literary, etc.) in which the words are commonly used (see page xi). Examples of actual usage in contemporary writing, newspapers, periodicals and conversation are included to illustrate the meanings of words.

Many features of a full-scale dictionary are missing. For these the reader must turn to the *Concise Scots Dictionary* or to the *Scottish National Dictionary*. Many of the unidentified quotations used come from the pages of the *Scottish National Dictionary*; if it did not exist, a work like this would be a thankless, if not an impossible, task.

Acknowledgements

Very special thanks are due to Iseabail Macleod, formerly Senior Editor of *The Concise Scots Dictionary*, and now Editorial Director of the Scottish National Dictionary Association. Her help in deciding policy for this dictionary, and her careful reading of and comments on all the entries, have been invaluable.

Meg Duguid read the whole manuscript, and made many helpful suggestions. My wife has always been ready to give an informed opinion when asked to do so.

I am grateful to Bob Hodgart, Adam Hogg and Bob Williams, who either read part of the manuscript or made useful suggestions when called upon for help; and also to various Scots, some of them overheard in queues or on buses, who have unwittingly furnished me with up-to-date quotations. Thanks also to Mrs Elizabeth Glass, who typed the manuscript with good-humoured efficiency.

I must not forget to finish with the statutory *mea culpa*: the faults of this book are attributable to me alone.

A Key to Varieties of Scots

General Scots Words or phrases which are widely used among Scots and have no precise English equivalent e.g. ashet, girn, leet.

Colloquial Scots The vocabulary, idiom and grammar of native speakers of Scots e.g. wur, forby, speir.

Occasional Scots Words and phrases, mostly from colloquial Scots, sometimes used by Scots whose usual speech is standard English e.g. peelie-wallie, laldie, stravaig.

Dialect Scots Words used only by speakers of a particular regional dialect, such as north-eastern Scots e.g. loon, quine.

Localised Scots Words used in several different districts of Scotland e.g. disjaskit, skeerie, cundy.

Learned or **literary Scots** Words known chiefly through their use by writers and scholars e.g. shenachie, leed, makar.

Technical Scots Words pertaining to a trade e.g. hutch, skew.

Many words defy classification and are not categorized.

Note on Pronunciation

For a full account of the sounds of Scots see *The Concise Scots Dictionary*, which also gives the pronunciation of every Scots word. Note however the following, which occur frequently:
-ch after a vowel is pronounced gutturally as in the name of the composer *Bach* e.g. *loch, fecht.*
ei is pronounced like *ee* in English *sleep* e.g. *teind, deil.*
ou is pronounced like *oo* in English *pool* e.g. *fou, behouchie.*

laird (l)

I

People   Titles and Labels
Parts of the Body

bairn Colloquial Scots for a child (boy or girl). In 1987 someone on Radio Scotland recalled feeling envy of 'the better-aff *bairns*' at school. *Bairn* and its diminutive *bairnie* are frequently used in occasional Scots, sometimes in a derogatory way of an adult: 'He's nothing but a big *bairnie*.' See also JOCK TAMSON'S BAIRNS (I), WEAN (I).

bampot A 'crazy character', an idiot. An example of recent Scots slang. Especially popular with the young, but the 1988 GENERAL ASSEMBLY (VIII) of the Church of Scotland was called on by one delegate to pay more heed to 'the gifts of the *bampots*,' those usually dismissed as cranks or eccentrics. Presumably from English *barmpot*, first recorded about 1950; *barm* is the froth of fermenting liquid, and is the origin of *barmy*, daft. Scots must have failed to hear the English *r*.

behouchie An inoffensive reference to the backside. Colloquial Scots. A child may be threatened with 'a skelp on the *behouchie*' (see SKELP, VI). First recorded some sixty years ago; believed to be a combination of *behind* and *hough* (see HOCH, IV). Also found in the form *bahookie*.

bidie-in An unmarried partner, of either sex. Dialect (the term originated in Aberdeenshire) and occasional Scots. A letter to a paper in 1987 referred to 'the delightful colloquial term of *bidey-in* to describe an unmarried wife.' To BIDE (XV) in a place is to live there.

bladderskite, bletherskate see BLETHER (V).

body Often pronounced more like *buddy*. In English *body* is used to mean a person, but not so widely as in Scots. One Burns song starts 'Gin (if) a *body* meet a *body* Comin thro the rye,' and this usage prevails, even when speaking of oneself: 'Can you no leave a *body* alone?' In the statement 'Lipton's tea is better than any other *buddy's*' (*Scots Mag.*, 1982), *any other body* stands for *anyone else*. Linked with an adjective it may sometimes suggest disdain – 'That daft *body*.' Earlier this century an old lady said of the French, 'Wha could understand thae (those) jabberin *buddies*?' The *Scottish National Dictionary* points out that the form *buddy* is 'never used for the human body, dead or alive.'

brither Colloquial Scots usage for *brother*. In at least one Edinburgh school in the 1930s it was replaced among the boys by another, now obsolete, term for a brother, *billy*, which probably derived from English *bully*.

chiel, chield Scots form of *child*, now nearly always used in the sense of a young man, a lad. Literary Scots, and rarely heard in speech except in north-eastern Scots dialect. In 1957 someone recalled that on a fair day 'the young *chiels* used to buy [the bonny lassies] sweeties' (*Tocher*, no. 40). In 1987 the visit of a Canadian writer to Scotland was announced in a headline adapted from a line by Burns: 'Canadian *chiel* amang us, takin' notes' (*Scotsman*). See also LAD (I).

clan A community united under a single chief and, increasingly since the 17th century, by acceptance of a common surname. The *clan* was based on the belief (once a reality) that all its members were descended from a common ancestor – hence the name *clan*, as *clann* is the Gaelic word for children. The *clan* system in Scotland was destroyed in the aftermath of the 1745 Jacobite rising, but *clan societies* still exist in many parts of the world. The closeness of the ties binding members of a *clan* together is reflected in the standard English word *clannish*. *Clan* came from Gaelic into Lowland Scots in the 15th century, and passed from there into standard and general English. See also TARTAN (III).

dochter Scots form of *daughter*. Like the other 'family' words, it is heard only in colloquial Scots.

ee Colloquial Scots for *eye*. 'Keep yer *ee* on the ba' is a maxim in ball games of every kind. The usual plural of *ee* is *een*, though *ees* is sometimes heard.

eediot, eejit Scots forms of *idiot*, also heard in other parts of the British Isles. A well-known sportsman, namesake of a local politician, was recently asked if he didn't get fed up with 'being taken for that *eejit*' who had made the headlines in the day's papers.

faither Scots form of English *father*. Until the 17th century *fader* was the usual form in Scots, and it is still heard in parts of north-east Scotland and in Shetland. Colloquial Scots.

fit Scots form of English *foot*. Colloquial Scots, and in daily use in both literal and figurative uses – 'a sair (sore) *fit*' or 'the *fit* o the class.' Also an element in many compounds, of which the best known is *fitba* (football). In the 19th, and into the 20th, century the foot was in the popular mind associated with the bringing of good or bad luck – a belief that is preserved to some extent in traditions associated with a FIRST-FOOT (IX).

fowk is the Scots form of standard English *folk*. It is often used for the inhabitants of a place collectively: 'Glesca *fowk*'. When referring to relatives, it is usually singular – 'my *fowk*', or 'my folk', where in England *folks* is more usual.

freen(d) The form of *friend* commonly used in colloquial Scots: the *d* is more often absent than present. The word can also be used to mean a relative. Though this sense is now rare, you may still hear in the north-east of Scotland '*to be freen(s) wi* (or *to*)' meaning to be related to.

gab see GOB (I)

Gael A Highlander, or more specifically a Gaelic speaker. Makes up a good title for a summer variety show, as in 'Gaels of Laughter' (it is pronounced like *gales*). During the annual MOD (IX) newspapers tend to carry headlines like '*Gaels Assemble in Oban.*' From the Gaelic word for a Highlander.

gillie A male servant or attendant. At one time, a *gillie* waited on a Highland chief; he is now an attendant on a 'sportsman' – that is, one whose main interest in the Highlands is hunting, shooting and fishing, and who is glad of local and often expert knowledge. One may still see advertisements inviting applications for the job of *gillie* on a fishing river or grouse moor. From Gaelic *gille*, a lad or servant.

gob The mouth, also sometimes the beak of a bird. Colloquial Scots, but also known in English dialect and slang. The alternative Scots form, **gab**, can also mean the mouth, as in 'Haud (hold) yer *gab!*' 'Shut up!' *Gob*, first recorded in Scots in the 16th century, is perhaps from Gaelic *gob*, beak, mouth. *Gab* is not to be confused with English *gab* (glib talk), which has a different origin. Curiously enough, the first recorded example of 'gift of the gab' is from a 17th-century Scottish poet who attributed to Job a 'good gift of the *gob.*'

gomerel A stupid person, a fool. General Scots, but also common in northern English dialect. 'How could you be such a *gomerel?*' Glasgow *gommy*, in the same sense, is presumably a shortened version of *gomerel*. The word may come from 18th-century Scots *goam*, to fail to notice, itself from northern English *gome*, of Norse origin. The Scots adjective *goamless*, formed in the present century, means stupid: it has perhaps been influenced by English *gaumless* (now usually spelt *gormless*), which has the same meaning.

gutser A 'greedy pig'. This unattractive 20th-century term began in north-eastern Scotland, but seems to be spreading. It probably derives from the Scots use of *guts* as a verb for to eat greedily: so does *gutsie* in the Scots sense of greedy, whereas English colloquial usage means plucky.

hairy A prostitute, or a woman who behaves like one. In recent use, softened into a slighting way of referring to a young woman. Colloquial Scots, originating in Glasgow. In *No Mean City*, a novel about Glasgow gang-life in the 1920s and 1930s, the shawl is described as the badge of 'the *hairy*, the very uniform of the poor class women slum dwellers' (1935). A modern Glasgow folk song tells of a night out in the life of *Hairy* Mary, who falls into the clutches of a 'hard man'.

haun Scots form of hand. To be *haunless* or *handless* is to be awkward, clumsy or unskilled. General Scots. In the literal sense of without hands it was common to older Scots and Middle English, but is obsolete in standard English, though sometimes used for slow or incompetent in English dialect. *Near hand*, almost, nearly, is a much older idiom, dating from the 14th century. Someone in a hurry 'rushed out barefoot and *near haun* naked' (*Scotsman*, 1988). A hand's turn is heard only in such negative statements as 'He didna dae (didn't do) *a haun's turn* all day,' he did no work at all. First recorded in the 19th century.

heid Colloquial Scots form of *head*. In constant use among football addicts, who appreciate a good *heider: heiders* is a variant of football, and consists largely in *heiding* the ball. The headmaster of a school may be known unofficially as the *heidie*. At the other end of the scale, someone regarded as a 'nut-case' may be called a *heidbanger* by his fellows. A recent letter to the *Scotsman* described the 'loony Left' as '*heidbangers*' (1987).

hen A colloquial Scots term of address for a woman or girl. 'Here y'are, *hen.*' Still widely used as a term of endearment. In small Edinburgh shops, where fifty years ago it was almost universally used, it has now given way to the unisex 'dear'. A small girl I knew used to refuse to enter certain local shops because she was greeted as '*hen*' by the shopkeepers.

hersel see HIMSELF (I).

hert is the colloquial Scots pronunciation of *heart.* The word is given wider currency by the popularity of the *Herts,* the short title for an Edinburgh football team. Their full name is Heart of Midlothian, the name given at one time to the old TOLBOOTH (XIII) prison, which was demolished in 1827. The spot where it once stood in the High Street, near St Giles Cathedral, is marked by a heart-shaped arrangement of stones in the street.

high heid yin General Scots for a very important person; one in authority. It suggests a healthy degree of mockery for YIN (XIV, one) who thinks himself better than, and so looks down on, others. At a public function, there is usually special provision for 'the *high heid yins.*' See also HEID (I).

himsel(f) An oblique way of referring to the principal person in any particular circumstances – the master of a house, a farmer, an employer, and so on. 'Is *himsel*' inside?' It is also sometimes, with mock respect, used for the devil. A woman in a position of authority may likewise be referred to as **hersel**. General Scots.

hunker The *hunkers* are the backs of the thighs, or hams. Colloquial and occasional Scots. To sit *on one's hunkers,* or to *hunker doon* (down), is to adopt a squatting position. As is well known, this is hard to do for very long. Hence the common expression for being in great trouble: 'He's really doon *on his hunkers.*' Perhaps derives from an Old Norse word for to squat. Recorded in Scots since the 18th century, first as a verb meaning to sit on one's haunches.

hurdie Usually plural, *hurdies*, the buttocks, hips or haunches of a human being or animal. Someone has gone on record as having a boil of his left *hurdie*. Colloquial Scots, but not often heard nowadays. *Hurdie* has been in Scots since the 16th century; it is of unknown origin.

hure (ordinarily pronounced as if two syllables) is the Scots equivalent of English *whore*. The pronunciation *hoo-er* was correct in England until the 19th century: it is also widely heard in Ireland.

janitor The caretaker of a building, especially of a school or college, who takes charge of the keys and supervises the cleaning of the building. The *jannie* of a school is a person to be conciliated. This sense of *janitor* is also found in American English.

jessie An insulting name, like *cissy*, given to a man regarded as effeminate, or to a boy who does not come up to the macho standards demanded by his mates: 'He's just a big *jessie*.' General Scots. Jessie is a pet form of Janet, and was very common as a name in Scotland earlier this century.

Jimmy An egalitarian way of addressing a stranger: rather like Australian *mate*. 'Have you the right time, *Jimmy*?' Colloquial Scots.

Jock Tamson's bairns General Scots expression of common humanity, often heard in the form '*We're a' Jock Tamson's bairns*', we are all human beings. When someone asked who Jock Tamson was, he was answered: 'Weel, he's God.' In the 1970s a popular folk song group called themselves 'Jock Tamson's bairns'.

keelie Originally, a male city slum–dweller, regarded by the better off with mixed fear and contempt. The word was used in both Edinburgh and Glasgow, but even in the former the *Glesca keelie* was regarded as a breed apart. Now *keelie* is used almost exclusively in Glasgow, of those who are rough, tough, ready for trouble and not always waiting till they are attacked. Jack House, who dedicated his book *The Heart of Glasgow* (1965) to 'the salt of the earth – the *Glesca keelie*', sees behind these aggressive qualities humour, courage and durability. *Keelie* is from Gaelic *gille*, GILLIE (I).

lad, laddie Frequently used as in English for a young man or youngster, though the phrase *lad o pairts* (a boy of promise) is distinctively Scots, and frequently appears in letters to the papers about Scottish education. Some Glasgow school-children, asked in 1986 to discuss co-education, almost invariably preferred '*laddies* and *lassies*' to 'boys and girls'. At one time *lad* meant a bachelor. Though this usage is now rare it survives as an honorary title at various local festivals in which a young unmarried man is chosen to represent the whole community. In Galashiels he is called the 'Braw *Lad*', in Musselburgh the 'Honest *Lad*', and so on. His consort may be known as the LASS (I). See also CHIEL (I).

laird is a Scots form of LORD (VII), but now only in the restricted sense of a landed proprietor. In modern times the two words have been quite differently applied. It is not used in titles of the nobility, and no one would talk about the Laird's prayer. A *laird* was at first a lesser landowner holding his lands directly from the king, then (more loosely) a landowner of even a very small estate, sometimes a single farm. The latter might then be known as *the Laird of Dumbiedykes* (as in Scott's *Heart of Midlothian*), or more simply as *the Laird*, and might be addressed as *Laird*. *Laird* is from *lard*, the northern Middle English form of *lord*. It is general Scots.

lass as in English means a girl or young woman. It can also be used for daughter ('Jock Wilson's *lass*') or girl-friend. **Lassie** can be used in all these senses, and today is commoner than *lass*, though *lass* is preferred in even slightly formal contexts: 'Come on in, *lass*.' Both words are used to address female animals, as in 'Doon, *lass*!' to a dog. In local festivals since the beginning of this century a '*lass*' has been chosen to take her place alongside the 'LAD' (I) as the lord and lady of a day. In hospital in Kirkcaldy in 1961 I was visited by the Lang Toon (Long Town) *Lad* and *Lass*, and presented with an apple by one of them.

loon The north-east equivalent of LAD (I). Though most used in dialect, it is widely known and understood, in references to the '*loons* and quines' of the north east, to mean 'lads and lasses', or young people in general: 'The quines and *loons* of Aberdeen are in luck this week' (1986). See also QUINE (I). In the north-east and parts of the east *loon* is used for a young working-man, particularly one working on a farm, but also specially for the youngest member of a gang of workmen – the one who is expected to do the odd jobs.

In earlier use, *loon* was a term of abuse: an early English traveller in Scotland described it as 'a name of reproach, as a villain or such like' (1548). It first appeared in Scots about 1500, and had various senses, all of them discreditable. But alongside these senses the more neutral one of a boy or youth gradually gained ground, and it has outlived them. *Loon* was used in northern Middle English for a worthless person. Scots and English both probably derive from a Dutch word for a fool.

lug An ear. Colloquial and occasional Scots; also found in northern English dialect. *Lug* displaced the word *ear* in Scots in the 15th and 16th centuries, just as in the present century *ear* has been regaining the ground once lost. It is possible that in earliest use *lug* referred to inanimate things: the first recorded instance in Scots in 1494 mentions the *lugs* or flaps of a cap. With reference to ears, *lugs* was at first concerned only with their external appearance as curiously formed appendages sticking out from the heads of humans and some animals. The human *lug* invited punishment – a tug, a blow, and worst of all a nail driven through it to fasten its owner to a place of punishment.

Lug has often been applied to a handle, as of a mug or teapot, and frequently to pairs of handles – the *lugs* of a drinking bowl. An object with such projections may be

called *luggit* – a *luggit* QUAICH (XII) or a *luggit* bonnet (a cap
with ear-flaps). A person with very prominent ears may have
to answer to the nickname *luggie.* Lug is of Scandinavian
origin, and is connected with the English verb *lug,* pull or
drag.

man, *Sc* **mon** A husband (as well as a man in other senses).
Colloquial Scots; also used in this sense in English dialect.
'Ma *man's* aff wark (off work).' The diminutive *mannie* can be
used to a boy, 'Ma *mannie* (my little man)', but not to an
adult unless you are trying to put him down. Followed by
the Christian name of the person addressed *man* suggests
mild rebuke or resignation: '*Man* Wullie, whit fur (why) did
ye dae that?'

messan is an insult. In 'you dirty (wee) *messan*' the
seriousness of the insult depends on the age or status of the
person addressed. Localised Scots. First recorded in Scots in
the 15th century, in a reference to 'little dogs and *messans*
with their bells.' It then meant a small pet dog, but by the
18th century it was used only of mongrels, or of people for
whom one felt contempt. From Gaelic *measan,* a lap-dog.

mither Colloquial Scots form of *mother.* In Shetland and
parts of the north-east *midder* is also heard. In 1985 a series of
television programmes on Scots language was called 'The
Mither Tongue.'

mon see MAN (I).

neb The nose. Colloquial Scots, but being displaced by *nose.*
One may have a 'big *neb*' or a 'lang *neb*': a poem by Robert
Garioch is about a war between the '*lang-nebs* and the Big
Heid Clan,' in which he was taken for one of 'thae *lang-nebbit*
folk' (about 1950). A busybody may be spoken of as a *neb,*
because he wants to *neb* into the private affairs of others. To
be *nebbie* is to be inquisitive. When first recorded in Scots in
the 14th century, *neb* applied to the beak of a bird rather than
the nose of a human, and this sense is still heard in Scots. This

was also the meaning of the Old English word from which *neb* was derived.

nieve The closed or clenched fist. When you shake hands you give someone your *nieve*, or if you are rowing you grip the oar in your *nieve*. In one version of an 'ancient rhyme' 'Neevy neevy nick nack, Which haun (hand) will you tak?' the *neevy* is derived from *nieve*, and alludes to the hand being closed on something – a 'prize' to be won, or a coin that settles a pecking-order. *Nieve* came to Scots from northern Middle English before 1400. It is of Old Norse origin.

nyaff A term of abuse or contempt aimed at someone's smallness and insignificance. Colloquial Scots. 'A *nyaff* can mean a small, trouble-making, good-for-nothing exhibition-ist' (*Scots Mag.*, 1982). In moments of extreme irritation *nyaff* can be applied to an objectionable person of any size. *Nyaff* came into Scots in the 19th century as a verb to describe first the yapping of a small dog, and then human chatter. It is probably imitative of the sound made by an excitable small dog.

oxter The armpit or the inside of the upper arm. General Scots, but also found in English and Irish dialect. An account of the death of an infant about 1600 tells how the mother woke to find 'the bairn in her *oxter* (child in her arm)' was dead. A person 'wi his heid (head) under his *oxter*' is downcast or depressed. *Oxter* was also applied to the underside of the shoulder of an animal. *Oxter*, which first appeared in Scots early in the 15th century, is recorded in northern Middle English from the 16th century. It is probably of Old English origin.

pinkie General Scots for the little finger. Also used in parts of the United States. One of my sons used to recite with gusto a poem beginning, 'You've hurt your finger, puir wee man. Your *pinkie*? Dearie me!' When I was at school in the 1930s if two boys found themselves in agreement one of them might hold up his *pinkie* crooked, and the other would

in response link with it his similarly bent *pinkie*. This, though
I did not know it at the time, was once called *cleeking pinkies*
(see CLEEK, XII), and was an old way of sealing a bargain.
Pinkie is a diminutive of *pink*, which was used in 17th century
Scots for any very small thing: it is connected with Dutch
pink, which has little finger as one of its meanings.

quine A Scots variant of *quean*, which is now rare or obsolete
in both Scots and English. Burns on occasion used *queans* for
young women. *Quine* is widely used, especially in country
areas, in the north-east of Scotland for a girl, a young
unmarried woman. It is frequently linked with LOON (I, lad)
in references to *loons and quines*, which may mean either
young men and women or boys and girls, according to
context. It and its diminutive *quinie* are also used for a
daughter. I have recently given a lift to a woman going into
Aberdeen 'to see ma *quinie*'.

runt A small thick-set person. Though now rare in this sense
in Scots, the word has flourished in American English in such
insults as 'a sawn-off little *runt*.' This phrase recalls the
original sense of *runt*, an old tree-stump (now rare in
Scotland). The most common Scots meaning is now the stalk
of a cabbage or kail plant when it has dried and hardened (see
also KAIL, XII). *Runt* is also used in parts of Scotland to refer to
someone gnarled in both looks and manners – often a cross-
grained old woman. The origin of *runt*, first recorded in
Scots in the 16th century, is doubtful.

Sassenach Originally Gaelic *Sassunach*, Saxon, and applied
to all speakers of English or Lowland Scots: the novelist
Smollett wrote in 1771 that 'the Highlanders have no other
name for the people of the low country but *Sassenaugh* or
Saxons.' Given wider currency by writers like Scott, who
used it to give colour to the speech of his Highland
characters. In modern times it is frequently used by Scots
when speaking of the English in a light-hearted or jocu-
lar way – 'a Sassenach scribe' (1986), or: 'The Scots face
the *Sassenachs* at Hampden on Saturday.' A Liverpudlian

legitimately wearing a London Scottish kilt was asked by an inebriated but patriotic Scot, 'What's a *Sassenach* like you wearing a kilt for?' (1970).

scaffie A street sweeper. A slightly disguised shortening of English *scavenger*, and still widely used in colloquial Scots. Even the sophisticated refuse lorry of today is sometimes referred to as the *scaffie* or *scaffie cairt* (cart).

shenachie A teller of old Gaelic stories and traditions. The word is learned or literary Scots, since it deals largely with a feature of Gaelic society in the past. A *shenachie* was a member of a clan chief's household, and it was his duty to record clan history and genealogy, and to recite these when called upon to do so. In the 1963 *Proceedings of the British Academy* one scholar was described as 'a born *shenachie* had his lot been cast in the Middle Ages.' The word is a phonetic rendering of the original Gaelic, which has the same range of meaning. The first syllable, which bears the main stress, represents *sean*, the Gaelic for old.

skinnymalink(ie) A very thin person or animal. General Scots. A real *skinnymalink* may be taunted with the rhyme '*Skinnymalinkie* long-legs'. A shortened form is used by the poet Robert Garioch to describe a skinny policeman: 'a *skinnylinky* copper' (*c* 1930). There is a Scots word *linkie* for a deceitful person, but here the *linkie* is perhaps used for sound rather than sense.

southron Scots variant of *southern*, and pronounced like it, but with *-ren* for *-ern*. In books on Scottish history read in schools sixty years ago, the English were often referred to as the *Southron*. The word is still in literary use, and is sometimes used in contentious letters to the papers. In 1988 a reviewer found one new book full of 'overweening *Southron* smugness' (*Scotsman*). If not derogatory, it is slightly less than friendly.

stookie Scots form of English *stucco*, plaster of paris.

Recorded in this sense since 1796; a child whose limb is in plaster will still display 'my *stookie*' with some pride. From that beginning, *stookie* developed in Scots the sense of a plaster statue: people on a formal occasion may be described as standing around like *stookies*. People who stand thus still in company are suspected of lacking wit or self-assurance, and may be addressed as *stookie*: 'Come on, *stookie*, get a move on.' *Stookies* is a children's game. Players are in turn swung around, then suddenly released. When they come to rest, they must try to maintain the posture and expression of face then adopted until that 'round' of the game is finished. On the borderline between general and colloquial Scots.

teuchter A Highlander, especially a Gaelic-speaking one. General Scots. The word is meant to be derogatory: it carries about the same degree of dislike or disdain as does SASSENACH (I) when used with hostile intent. The *Buchan Observer* in 1986 condemned those who saw in the national MOD (IX) nothing more than 'a *teuchter* jamboree.' The word is in some places, especially in the north-east, used equally slightingly of any one from a country area. A Dundee man may speak of 'a Perthshire *teuchter*'. *Teuchter* came into use only in the 20th century; it is of uncertain origin.

thrapple The throat, gullet or windpipe of a person or animal. General Scots. It is nowadays relatively unusual to threaten to take somebody 'by the *thrapple*' and choke him. If you drink something that is too hot you may feel it all the way down your *thrapple*; to *weet* (wet) your *thrapple* is to take a drink to refresh yourself. In the past the adam's apple was referred to as the *knot o the thrapple*; a more modern dialect name is the *thrapple-bow*. Older Scots had *throppill* for the windpipe in 1375; so had Middle English, but the word is now dialect only in English, and then used chiefly of horses. The origin of *throppill* is uncertain, but it may be from an Old English *throt bolla*, adam's apple.

tot A small child, was originally Scots, but is now general English. First recorded in Scots in the 18th century; of unknown origin. From it developed the general English meaning of a small amount of drink, as in a *tot* of rum. From *tot* came the Scots adjective *tot(t)ie*, very small, tiny. The smallest child in a primary class may be identified by others as 'the *tottie* boy' until his name is known. *Tottie* is sometimes given as a pet- or nickname to a child or small person.

wame The Scots form of English *womb*; it is also sometimes used in the sense of womb in north English dialect. In colloquial Scots today it means the belly or stomach. To have 'a sair (sore) *wame*' is to have stomach-ache. A greedy person may be told, 'Yer ee (eye) is bigger nor (than) yer *wame*.'

wean A child, from infancy till about the age of twelve. Pronounced to rhyme with *rain*. 'The *wean*'s fine' may refer to health or behaviour. *Wean* was first recorded in Scots in the 17th century, and is associated more with the Glasgow area (cf. BAIRN (I), which is mainly used in the east). It is made up of the two words *wee* and *ane* (one) run together. In some parts where it is less common, especially the north-east, it is pronounced more as two syllables (*wee-un*), with the stress on the *wee-*.

wife often ha the same meaning as in standard English. In colloquial Scots *the wife* is common for *my wife*, but in general Scots *wife* is still frequently used in its older sense of a woman, married or unmarried, generally of mature years. It is faintly disrespectful or disparaging, and is now less common than *wifie*, the diminutive: 'The wee *wifie* in the corner shop.' *Auld wife* is sometimes applied to a man who seems to possess some of the less amiable qualities attributed to a *wifie* – fussiness, a tendency to gossip, etc.

II

Human Attributes   Behaviour

blate Timid, shy, diffident. Colloquial Scots. A man may be '*blate* wi the lasses', and a girl may tell him not to be so *blate* – if 'she's no *blate*'. An 18th century song written after the 1745 Jacobite rising accused a general of being 'na *blate*' to be first to bring news of his defeat. A Scots proverb holds that 'a *blate* cat makes a prood moose (proud mouse).' In the north-east, crops may be described as *blate*, or backward, if they are slow to grow in the spring. The origin of *blate* is uncertain: it may go back to Old English. It was first recorded in Scots in the 15th century.

by-ordinar Unusual, extraordinary. Now chiefly literary Scots. At one time it was regarded as *by-ordinar* to have stayed at school till the age of 15. A person distinguished in some special way may be described as a *by-ordinar* man or woman. This compound word was formed in the 17th century: the *by-* here means out of.

bubble To weep; a 'cry'. General Scots. In my schooldays a recipient of the BELT (VI) used to be watched curiously by his classmates to see if he was *bubbling* or not. In 1987 a homesick girl confessed that now and then she had 'a wee *bubble*'.

canny has had over the centuries a wide range of meanings, but the sense in which it is best known is exemplified in the phrase 'a *canny* Scot' – that is, someone who looks three times before he leaps, especially where money is concerned. One may be asked to be *canny* when washing up the best china, or even when buying a new dress. To *gang* (go) *cannily* is to be careful. One of Burns's songs begins 'Bonnie wee thing, *cannie* wee thing:' here the virtue praised is not frugality but gentleness. But a man described as *canny* was more likely to be skilled at what he was doing; a pub in Edinburgh, properly known as the Volunteer Arms, is still widely referred to as the '*canny* man'. A woman too might be seen as a '*canny* body'.

The skill displayed might go beyond the natural. What was *no canny*, or **uncanny**, was supernatural, and in some cases a *canny man* or *canny woman* (or WIFE, I) was believed to have supernatural powers. But when the skill was confined to bringing a child into the world, a *canny wife* was, and in some areas still is, a midwife (cf. French *sage femme*); the moment of childbirth was known as the *canny moment*. *Canny*, though general Scots, is also common in northern English dialect. It is probably connected with *can*, which as a noun meant knowledge or skill. See also CA CANNY (XV).

carnaptious Quarrelsome. General Scots, but not in common use. Its impressive sound and length is often balanced by a noun which brings the phrase back to earth – 'You *carnaptious* auld . . . ' (you may make your choice). Apparently from Scots *knap*, a bite, in this sense obsolete except in dialect: the *car–* is intensive, giving a literal meaning of very apt to bite or snap.

chore To steal. Localised Scots. In 1980 a teacher preparing for a class outing was taken aback to hear some of the boys discussing the chances of 'doing some *choring*' in town. First recorded in 1923, in gipsy speech: in the Borders, someone was accused of '*chorin* a yarrie (egg)'.

conceit in the sense of a person's opinion of himself has been obsolete in English since the 18th century, but has remained in general Scots, usually in the phrase to have *a good conceit of oneself*. The phrase was used by Burns in one of his letters:

'Lord, send us a good conceit o' oursel' (1788). Early in 1988 one sports writer claimed that the Welsh have 'a good *conceit* of their rugby' (*Scotsman*).

couthie Pleasant, agreeable. Colloquial and occasional Scots. Frequently applied to behaviour, especially that felt to be typically Scottish. In 1986 a folk-singer was praised for having a 'warm and *couthy*' voice. A person may possess a *couthie* and friendly way of greeting others, and visitors to his (or her) home may be sure that a *couthie* welcome will await them. *Couthie* can also be used of places, in the sense of cosy or comfortable: in 1980 a writer in the *Scots Magazine* referred to a '*couthie* corner of Dundee High Street'. *Couthie*, like UNCO (XIV), goes back to the Old English word *cūth*, older Scots *couth*, known or familiar (cf. general English *uncouth*).

crabbit Scots form of English *crabbed*, but meaning in a bad temper as well as bad-tempered by nature: 'Dinna be sae *crabbit*' alongside 'She's a *crabbit* auld (old) thing.' General Scots.

daft Common in general Scots to express various mental states between folly and madness. In English in dialect use, but most English people understand the word. A distinctively Scots use is in the phrase *daft on* or *daft aboot* (about), 'crazy' about a person or thing, excessively keen on. Jock can be *daft aboot* (or *on*) Morag, or vice versa: either of them may be *daft on* golf. Often used negatively to convey dislike: 'I'm no *daft aboot* his singing.' *Daftie* is more restricted in sense – it means a fool or an imbecile, except when used (as in colloquial English) as a term of general abuse.

disjaskit Depressed. Localised Scots. A person can look, or be, *disjaskit*, downcast, though this can sometimes suggest tiredness or exhaustion as well. 'He was fair *disjaskit* when he cam hame' after work. Things too can be *disjaskit* in the sense of worn out or run down. In 1816 Scott wrote of a '*disjasked-*looking road,' and a group of untidy or badly dressed people can be described as *disjaskit*. The origin of the word is uncertain.

donnert Stupid, dull. Colloquial Scots. Often applied to old people when they are no longer as quick in the UPTAKE (II) as they once were: 'I'm auld and *donnart*,' or 'I'm gettin gey (very) *donnart*.' Also used as a noun for a fool or blockhead of any age. From the rare or obsolete verb *donner*, to daze or stun.

douce Respectable, quiet. General Scots, but now more common on the literary or very literate level. A woman was recently described as 'a *douce*, church-going body.' Nowadays frequently applied to places or communities noted for their sedateness: 'the *douce* South Side of Glasgow' (1986). 'Comely Bank [in Edinburgh] used to be a *douce* place. Now it is alive with cars and people' (1987). *Douce* when first recorded in Scots in the 16th century meant sweet or pleasant. It came from Middle English, and ultimately from French (*douce* is the feminine of *doux*, sweet, gentle).

dour Unyielding, unbending: humourless. General Scots, and pronounced to rhyme with French *pour*, not English *sour*. The '*dour Scot*' has become a cliché, but is probably accepted by many Scots as being a just and not altogether uncomplimentary appraisal. *Dour* to do something means to be reluctant or slow: fish may be '*dour* to bite', or a fire may be *dour* (to light). This sense is now localised or dialect Scots. *Dour* has been in Scots since the 14th century. Its origin is doubtful, but it may come from French *dur* or Latin *durus*, hard.

drouth Scots form of standard English *drought*, but the sense of dry weather is now virtually obsolete. In the sense of thirst, it is still general Scots: 'I have a great *drouth* on me' can delicately propose a visit to the nearest bar. Someone whose thirst is overwhelming may come to be known as a *drouth*, a drunkard. *Drouthy* is thirsty, and can convey the suggestion that someone is subject to a constant thirst for strong drink. Tam o' Shanter and his 'ancient trusty *drouthy* crony' (1791) had been 'fou (drunk) for weeks thegither (together).'

easy-osy Easy-going to a fault. General Scots. An *easy-osy* foreman will not get the best out of the men working with him, and if one of the men tends to be *easy-osy*, rather lazy, then he will slacken off at the job. In 1987 a football team was criticised for being 'too *easy-osy* on the ball' in one of their matches. An *easy-osy* job is one that can be done without too much effort. *Easy-osy* is a 19th century formation from *easy*: the *osy* emphasises the sense by partially echoing the sounds of *easy*.

eident Diligent; always busy. Rarely heard in colloquial Scots, but used in literary and occasional Scots, perhaps because it conveys moral approval. A good housekeeper can be described as *eident*. First recorded in Scots in the 14th century: it is of Old Norse origin, and came to Scots through northern Middle English.

fantoosh Flashy, showy, fashionable. Occasional Scots. It is more *fantoosh* to shop in certain streets. Fancy cakes have been described as *fantoosh*. In 1986 a doctor, prescribing for a patient, said, 'We'll give you something more *fantoosh* later on.' Coined, according to the *Scottish National Dictionary*, during the First World War, after obsolete English slang *fanty-sheeny*, from the Italian for a puppet, but some may suspect that it is directly from French *fantoche* (a puppet).

feart Afraid. Colloquial Scots. A child can be '*feart* o the dark', or '*feart for* (or *at*) one of his teachers', despite claims that he's 'nae *feart.*' If he admits to his fear, then he is a *feartie*, a *feardie* or a *feardie-gowk*, a coward. *Nae fears!* is the Scots equivalent of standard English *no fear!* – Certainly not!

feckless Ineffective, weak, spiritless. Used to be a great favourite with sports writers: '*Feckless* display by home side.' Scott observed that human beings were 'peer (poor) *feckless* bodies.' Now acceptable standard English. *Feckless* is from Scots *feck*, a reduced form of *effect* in which both the first syllable and the final consonant have been lost.

fleein Very drunk, but happy. General Scots. Somebody who '*gets fleein*' on Hogmanay may try to greet every passer-by with incoherent good-will. At one time, it was possible to be *fleein* with rage, but this usage seems to have died out. The common factor was excitability and lack of self-control. *Flee* is the Scots form of *fly*.

footer To fiddle or trifle. General Scots. A visitor to the opera in 1987 complained that 'Madame Butterfly kept *footering* about with her kimono.' A child may be told to 'stop *footering* about and get on with your homework', and his mother may blame him for being 'a wee *footer*', or for being *footerie*, not getting on with the job in hand. *Footerie* can be used of the job itself if it calls for much attention to small details: assembling the parts of a plastic model of a sailing ship is an exceedingly *footerie* job. *Footer* was first recorded in Scots in the 18th century. It may be connected with obsolete English *fouter* (a term of contempt), or it may be directly from French *foutre*, to have sexual intercourse.

forfoch(t)en Exhausted, played out. Colloquial and occasional Scots. The saying 'I'm *sair* (or *fair*) *forfochen*' has survived largely because of its expressive quality. It came into Scots from Middle English as a derivative of *fight*, and meant exhausted by fighting. Only in Scots did it develop the sense of tired out.

fou Scots form of *full*; colloquial and occasional Scots. At one time *fou* was used, as is *full*, for well-fed, but now *to be fou* usually means to be drunk. The *fou* form developed quite late – in the late 17th century *full* was still the usual spelling. But by the 18th century one could become '*roarin fou*.' By itself, *fou* does not suggest the freedom from inhibition conveyed by FLEEIN (II): it records that a drinker has exceeded his capacity. Very drunk indeed is *fou as a puggie* (a monkey), which seems unfair to monkeys.

fushionless Lacking in vital power. Colloquial and occasional Scots. When a person is called *fushionless*, he is considered to be deficient in spirit, energy and initiative: all that one can feel for him is sympathy. He is 'a puir (poor) *fushionless* body.' When used of things, *fushionless* conveys the same idea of insipidity: it may be said of food, drink, words, actions, speeches. In 1931 someone found standard English *fushionless* when compared with his local Scots dialect. This adjective derives from the noun *fushion* (pronounced to rhyme with *Russian*), now rare and largely confined to north-east Scotland. It names the quality so lacking in *fushionless* persons or things. Towards the end of the Second World War there was no *fushion* in beer; when a man is ill, he may seem to have lost all his *fushion* – power, energy, even 'guts'. *Fushion* goes back to an Old Scots *foisoun*, abundance, first recorded in 1375. The word came, through Middle English, from old French *foison*.

fykie Difficult to please. Colloquial and occasional Scots. Someone you work for may be *fykie*, fussy over details or trifles, and an invalid can be *fykie* about his or her food. A job involving close attention to detail can be a *fykie* one, tiring and sometimes boring. An earlier meaning, now localised Scots, is fidgety. The noun *fyke* could mean restlessness, the fidgets; and the verb to *fyke*, first recorded in the 16th century, meant to fidget. Both noun and verb are rare. *Fyke* is probably of Old Norse origin.

gall(o)us Wild but likable. It may be that words are more likely to deteriorate than to improve in meaning: if so, *gallous* is an exception. Originally it meant villainous, wicked: but even a *gallous* underdog had to do something to boost his confidence, and *gallous* came to mean cheerfully brash, impertinent even in the face of authority. It can also be applied to things or events, so long as a balance is maintained between admiration and outrage: it is now widely used in this way in the Glasgow area by the young as an expression of general but enthusiastic approval. A '*gallus* haircut' is 'right up-to-the-minute and very stylish.' *Gallousness* is a quality on which Glaswegians above all pride themselves. It has been claimed as one of the qualities that helped Glasgow Celtic to win the European Cup in 1967, and the Glasgow sense of humour has been described as '*gallous* humour' (1986). It was a quality apparently possessed by the jazz musician Count Basie: an enthusiast thought of him as a natural Glaswegian because his '*gallousness* stuck out a mile' (1987). Cheek is perhaps the best single-word equivalent; and scatty has something of the flavour of *gallous*. *Gallous* is ultimately the same word as *gallows* – hence the early association with villainy. See also GALLUSES (III).

girn To complain in a whining manner, to grumble. General Scots. 'John's wife is aye (always) *girnin* aboot something.' Some people enjoy 'a good *girn*', and a person who is continually complaining is soon recognised as a *girner*, and will sometimes be asked, 'What are you *girnin* at noo?' An older sense was to twist the face in pain or anger. Burns noted that hanging caused the victim to '*girn* and gape.' It was in this sense that *girn* was first recorded in Scots in 1375, and in which it is also common in English dialect. *Girn* is the same word as standard English *grin* – the *i* and the *r* have changed places.

glaikit Foolish, not 'all there.' Colloquial and occasional Scots. An insult to which, like certain rude gestures, there is no satisfactory answer. One unfortunate was described as having 'a permanent *glaikit* look on his face.' A *glaik* is a foolish or stupid person. In older Scots the noun was found only in the plural form, *glaiks*, and meant deception or trickery. At some stage the emphasis must have shifted from the deception practised to the person deceived or fooled. The origin of *glaik(it)* is unknown.

gollop To gulp (food) down, to swallow greedily. Colloquial Scots. 'Don't *gollop* your dinner.' Also a noun: 'he ate his supper in *gollops*,' in large, hastily-swallowed portions. Probably a development from English *gulp*.

greet To weep, shed tears. In English, only in dialect and poets affecting dialect, but universal in colloquial Scots.

Differs from *greet* (to salute) in having *grat* or *gret* as its past tense, though the two verbs may go back to a common root. In 1986 a mother lamented, 'When I knew I was pregnant, I could do nothing but *greet.*' What was worse, once born the baby '*gret*, and *gret*, and *gret*.' And a student confessed that, on hearing her exam results, 'I just *grat.*' A *greetin face* is a person who always looks unhappy, as if about to weep: 'a good defender has to be a bit of a *greetin face*' (B.B.C. football commentator, 1987).

grue To react with revulsion, as by shuddering, shivering, or otherwise displaying disgust or horror. Colloquial and occasional Scots. Some may *grue* at the mere sight of blood. When faced with unpalatable food, a child may *grue* by wrinkling up its face in distaste. A sudden fright or shock may 'gar one's flesh *grue*', make the blood run cold (see GAR, XIV). *Grue* was first recorded in Scots as *grow* in 1375. It came from a northern English word that was probably of Old Norse origin.

hochmagandy (also spelt *hough-*; the stress is on the first and third syllables) Sexual intercourse. Literary Scots. First recorded about 1700 in a reference to playing 'at *houghmagandy.*' In 1785 Burns noted that 'Many jobs ... may end in *houghmagandie.*' Modern dictionaries of Scots describe it as 'a ludicrous formation', and a writer in the *Listener* in 1985 felt that 'the very shape of the word gives the impression of something improper.' Probably connected with *hough*, the upper part of the leg. See also HOCH (IV).

jalouse (stress on *-louse*, pronounced like *lose*) To suspect. Occasional Scots, and quite often used in literary Scots. 'I *jaloused* that the man was an innocent drop-out from society' (*Scots Mag.*, 1985). It derives from the French *jalouser*, to regard with jealousy, and so has the same origin as *jealous*.

joukerie-pawk(e)rie Deceit, trickery, hanky-panky. It is hard to believe that this word, first recorded in Scots in the late 17th century, is not the origin of *jiggery-pokery*, which became current in England two centuries later. *The Scotsman* in 1958 suspected that there had been some *'jukery-pokery'* in the 'demarcation of constituencies.' *Joukerie* is from JOUK (VI) and *pawkerie* is from *pawk* (see PAWKIE, II).

kittle Capricious, fickle. Now chiefly localised or dialect, though the saying 'Women are *kittle* cattle' is widely known. *Kittle cattle* is applied to both human beings and animals who are reckoned to be unpredictable or hard to deal with. Not only women are accused of being *kittle*: in the past it has been applied to, among others, ratepayers and farmers. *Kittle*, when first used in Scots in the 16th century, meant to tickle; it is still heard in this sense in Scots. *Kittle* people were ticklish: it is from this that there developed the sense of easily upset, and later of fickle. *Kittle* is of Scandinavian origin, and is also found in eastern English dialect.

moolie Mean, tight-fisted. Localised Scots. 'Ye'll get naethin oot o that *moulie* auld devil.' This sense developed in the 19th century; the older meaning of mouldy is also heard. From an older Scots verb for to grow mouldy.

pawkie has gained a foothold in English by seemingly describing the Scot on his own terms: the *'pawkie* Scot' is held to be quietly shrewd, and CANNY (II) enough to be able to do well in situations where others may find themselves in difficulty. In general Scots today *pawkie* is more often used of what is reckoned to be a typically Scottish sense of humour, seen as dry, quiet, even sly, but down-to-earth and critical of what are regarded as false values. *Pawkie* was first recorded in Scots in the 17th century in the senses of crafty or stubborn – both senses preserved into the 19th century. It developed from a noun *pauk* (a crafty or wily trick), the origin of which is unknown. Both *pauk* and *pawkie* are found in modern north English dialect, the first in the sense of insolence, the latter meaning stubborn or scrupulous.

pech To gasp for breath, to breathe heavily after exercise. General Scots. 'With a bit o *pechin* and pantin, we got [the wardrobe] back on the cart' (*Scots Magazine*, 1985). The verb may also refer to the action causing heavy breathing: 'We *peched* up to the monument above Comrie' (1987). *Pech* can also mean a pant or a gasp, and *oot o pech*, or *pecht*, means out of breath. 'It's a sair (sore) *pech* to the top o the hill' laments the difficulty of climbing without running short of breath. *Pech* was first recorded in Scots in the early 15th century. Its origin is uncertain; probably the sound was intended to echo the meaning. There was also a *pech* in northern Middle English.

perjink referring to a person's appearance suggests smartness or neatness, usually in dress. 'She's awfae (very) *perjink* the day' suggests an unusual degree of care for one's appearance. Other senses of *perjink* view this care as fussiness or primness. As a judgment on character, *perjink* suggests priggishness: you have to be careful how you speak when Mrs X is there, 'she's that *perjink*.' Fussy behaviour, as of someone who is regarded as house-proud, can also be described as *perjink*. *Per-* here means very, too. The origin of *jink* is not known; it may be that the sound was believed to fit the intended meaning.

pernicketie (stress on *-nick-*) A person who is *pernicketie* is fussy, too precise, about details; a job which is *pernicketie* demands fussy attention to detail. The work of compiling a dictionary has been described as *pernicketie*, and the longer one does such work, the more *pernicketie* one becomes, especially about the work of other people. As early as 1826 some people were *pernicketie* about their food, and in 1926 someone was accused of being a *pernicketie* old maid. This useful word is general Scots. It was first recorded in Scots in the 19th century, and has now been accepted into standard English. Of unknown origin.

plowter To mess about in water or in thin mud. General Scots. After rain a child in 'wellies' can obtain great pleasure from wading through puddles, especially with a stick in hand – in short, *plowtering*. It is less pleasant on a country outing to have to '*plowter* through the clabber (mud)' (Radio Scotland, 1987) after heavy rain. Before the days of washing machines there was a temptation to *plowter* in the rich mixture of water and soap-suds. Perhaps this gave rise to the expression *plowter aboot*, to mess about, act purposelessly instead of working. *Plowter* was formed in the 19th century from *plowt*, to submerge in liquid, also to splash through mud or water. *Plowt* is probably an example of onomatopoeia: it is now used only in dialect.

puggled Tired out, exhausted. General Scots. In 1986 an amateur gardener called to his neighbour, 'I haven't been working as long as you, and I'm *puggled* already.' Probably an extension of meaning of English forces slang *puggled*, very drunk.

radge Wild, 'crazy.' Colloquial Scots, but now more often heard from young people, among whom it may be a grudging compliment. 'Jock's right *radge*. He threw an orange at a police-car.' Can also be a noun – a 'crazy character' may be described as a *radge*. First recorded in 1894, of a '*radgy* horse.' It comes from *rage*, which in Middle English could mean mad. In Scots it may have been influenced by the gipsy words *raj* and *rajy*, which have the same origin and meaning.

ram–stam In a headlong or unrestrained way. 'He went at the job *ram-stam*, and was finished in no time.' General Scots. In the earliest recorded example the word was *ram-tam*: someone in 1735 'ran *ram-tam*' into a loch. The first element is probably English *ram* (the animal): the origin of the second is unknown.

red–handed is a coinage of Sir Walter Scott's that has been widely adopted in general English. In his novel *Ivanhoe* (1819) an outlaw was 'taken *red-handed* and in the fact.' Scott was here adapting the older Scots *red-hand*, recorded since the 15th century, to his purpose. *Red-hand* originally signified that a murderer had been captured with the blood of his victim still on his hands. It was later extended to mean taken with evidence of his crime still to be found on his person. Thus in 1700 a man who had stolen a pig was 'taken *redd hand* therewith.'

rift Belch; noun or verb. General Scots, and also in north English dialect. At one time *rift* also meant fart. Allan Ramsay is quite explicit when he relates how someone has 'to *rift* at the rumple' (1736), whereas 'he gied (gave) a muckle *rift*' is ambiguous (see MUCKLE, XV). *Rift* was first recorded in Scots in 1420: it is from Middle English *rift*, of Old Norse origin.

sapsy Sloppy, effeminate, 'soppy.' Localised Scots. Maria, a girl of Polish descent, was quite happy to be called Marushka till in 1987 she went to secondary school. Then she began to feel it was *sapsy*. *Sapsy* is from *saps*, bits of bread soaked in hot milk as a dish for children: *saps* is the plural of *sap*, a Scots equivalent of English *sop*.

sculduddery *Skulduggery* developed the sense of underhand malpractice in America, and is now regarded as general English. But it was in the form *sculduddery* that the word first appeared, in Scotland in the middle of the 17th century. In 1663 a member of a noble house noted that a relative was in trouble 'not for *sculdudry*, the old fault of the house, but for a less gentlemanny crime, theft.' A less permissive attitude is seen in a 1730 account of how someone was 'brought before a Presbytery to be questioned for *sculduddery*, i.e. fornication or adultery.' In a weakened sense *sculduddery* came to be used of obscene language or conversation: in 1931 it was admitted that a story was 'maybe garnished with *sculdudry* a wee bit.' The origin of the word is unknown. It is now used only in learned or literary Scots.

scunner The idea underlying *scunner*, whether used as a noun or a verb, is that of revulsion, a strong impulse to reject a person, thing or action. General Scots, and in familiar use on every level on which Scots is spoken. It is frequently used to express dislike or disapproval of a person. 'I'm really *scunnered* with Albert.' The same sentiment could have been expressed more forcefully as 'That Albert is a right *scunner*,' or more crudely as 'You're a rotten wee *scunner*.' Just as commonly a thing may be the object of a *scunner*. Circumstances may be so bad that they are 'a fair *scunner*.' In 1986 in a Radio Scotland chat show a supposed social injustice was described as 'one of the great *scunners* of all time.' *Scunner* may refer less to its object than to the feeling of aversion aroused in the speaker. To feel a sudden strong dislike is to *tak* (take) *a scunner*. 'We took a *scunner* at Scott because we had to read his novels at school.' One may take a *scunner* to baked beans. The intensity of the feeling depends on the context, or on the passion of the speaker. Differently, perhaps more gently, conveyed, is: 'The way thae students go on fair gies (gives) ye the *scunner*.'

As a verb, *scunner* is common in the phrase *to be scunnered with*. A girl ended a tale of woe with 'That's why I'm *scunnered with* where I'm working' (1986). The earliest recorded example of *scunner* in the 14th century tells us that an English force was '*skownrand* (scunnering, showing reluctance) *to*' advance too far into hostile Scottish territory: this usage survived into the present century. But *scunner* more commonly conveys disgust or revulsion: 'The smell doon the road *scunnered* them,' or (in 1917) 'He canna stand [members of a particular political party] . . . they fair *scunner* him.'

Scunner has spawned adjectives, such as *scunnerfu* and *scunnersome*, but they are not often heard. The origin of *scunner* is uncertain. It may be connected with a rare and obsolete northern English word *skurn* (flinch, take flight) of Scandinavian origin. Since the 17th century *scunner* has been found in the northern counties of England.

skeerie Flighty, skittish, silly. Localised Scots, and used mostly of girls who are liable to outbursts of hare-brained activity: many girls are never *skeerie*. Sheep are 'such *skeerie* creatures' that they are easily panicked by a dog (*Scotsman*, 1988). Formed from *skeer*, the Scots form of English scare.

slaister To mess about in liquid, semi-liquid, slime or mud. General Scots, though more common in colloquial usage. A child doing the washing-up may be accused of *slaistering* in the water instead of getting on with the job; and *slaistering* has, perhaps for similar reasons, developed a secondary meaning of working ineffectively or clumsily. It can also mean making a mess by failing to control one's materials – for instance, when making sandwiches by allowing the ingredients to soil a whole area: 'The cloth was *slaistered* wi lumps o butter an' jeelie.' A *slaister* is a person who seems capable of creating a mess when performing any activity of the kind described above, but more particularly it refers to a messy eater. A baby is expected to be a *slaister*, but 'You're a right wee *slaister*' is a sharp rebuke to an older child. And the resultant mess may be summed up as 'What a *slaister*!' The origin of *slaister* is not known.

sleekit Ingratiating and untrustworthy. General Scots. 'There's something *sleekit* about him (or her)' is quite commonly heard. Burns referred to the field mouse as a 'wee *sleekit* ... beastie.' This was no reflection on its moral character. *Sleekit* is from the verb *sleek*, to make smooth, and any creature with a smooth or glossy skin could be described as *sleekit* – a usage now found only in dialect.

smeddum Spirit, mettle. General Scots. In 1987 a writer in the *Scotsman* argued that 'a bit of *smeddum* in the community council' could do much for local interests. The first recorded user in this sense was Burns, who talked of putting 'some *smeddum* in a person' (1787). The original meaning of *smeddum* was strikingly different: in the late 17th century it meant ground malt put through a sieve to give a very fine powder used in baking, or as a medicinal powder. In these senses it corresponds to obsolete English *smitham*, and has the same origin – an Old English word for fine flour.

snifter To snuffle, as when one has a cold. General Scots. To have the *snifters* is to have a bad cold in the head, so that breathing through the nose is difficult or noisy. *Snifter* is also used of the snuffling brought on by weeping, as in the suppressed tears of an unhappy child. It is from Middle English *snyfter*, to snuffle, and is also found in northern English dialect. In colloquial English, *snifter* is a short drink, a 'quick one.'

stick 'I'm stuck' for 'I can't finish this sum' is common to Scots and English, but to be *stickit* is peculiar to Scots. It is best known in the colloquial Scots phrase 'a *stickit* minister', one who has failed to complete the course of study and training for the ministry, but in the past there have also been *stickit* doctors and teachers. To *stick in* is to persevere: children have to *stick in* with their lessons if they want to pass exams.

sweir Reluctant, unwilling. Colloquial Scots, and according to a writer in the *Scots Magazine* in 1985 'still in daily use.' One can be *sweir* to go back to a place where one has suffered. In this sense *sweir* was first recorded in the 14th century. An equally old meaning, now heard only in dialect, is lazy or indolent, as in 'a *sweir* man's aye bodin (is always waiting for) ill weather' (1929). *Sweir* is from an Old Northumbrian word for lazy, and is related to German *schwer*, difficult.

swither To be unable to make up one's mind. General Scots. Someone, unable to decide which turning to take, may stand *swithering* at a road junction. During the 1987 General Election someone described the 'don't knows' of the opinion polls as 'the *swithering* factor' in the election. The noun may name either the condition or a person suffering from it. To be in a *swither* means much the same as to *swither*. A door-keeper commented on a woman of high academic repute: 'She's an awfae (awful) *swither*, that woman.' First recorded in Scots in the form *swidder*, to hesitate, about 1500. Of uncertain, perhaps Scandinavian, origin.

thirled So bound to one way of thinking, feeling or behaving that one does not consider alternatives. It is only too easy to become so *thirled* to one's own way of doing something that one thinks there is no other way. General Scots. *Thirled* is from the verb *thirl*, which has a long and interesting past, but is now nearly obsolete. From the 16th to the 18th centuries the tenants of large estates were nearly always *thirled* to a certain mill – that is, they were bound willy-nilly to take their corn to that mill to be ground. When this custom died out, the obligation became a more personal one: a *thirled* labourer was a man hired to work for a particular master. From these earlier senses developed the present meaning of inability to escape from a custom or habit. The earliest recorded use of *thirl* was in the middle of the 14th century. It is the same word as older Scots *thrill* or *threll*, a thrall or bondman, and is another instance of a word in which *r* has changed its place in the course of time. *Thryll* goes back to an old English or Old Norse word which was the origin of English *thrall*.

thrang Scots form of English *throng*, but in Scots usage chiefly an adjective: now localised or dialect Scots. Pubs may be *thrang* (crowded) after a football match. A farmer may be *thrang* (busy) ploughing his land. People who are very friendly may be regarded as 'unco *thrang*' (very close; see UNCO, XIV), and the one will be spoken of as being '*thrang* wi (friendly with)' the other.

thrawn Used of a person, this means cross-grained, ready to take a contrary view for the sake of being in opposition. General Scots. The Scots are sometimes thought of as being 'dour and *thrawn*' by nature, but is also possible to be in a *thrawn* or perverse state of mind. '*Thrawn* Janet' is the title of a short story by R.L. Stevenson: in this instance *thrawn* refers to a physical characteristic. Janet was the victim of a *thrawn* or twisted craig (neck). When a person's face or mouth is twisted, as with pain, *thrawn* can be used: an old Scots proverb claimed that 'a toom (empty) purse makes a *thrawn* face' (1721). The novelist O. Douglas once noted that the trees were '*thrawn* with winter' (1920). *Thrawn* is the Scots form of English *thrown*; see THRAW (XV, to throw). It has been recorded in Scots since about 1500.

uptake Intelligence. General Scots; also found in northern English dialect. Virtually unknown outside such phrases as *quick* (or *slow*) *in the uptake*, sharp, quick (or slow) to understand. *Uptake* has been in Scots since the 15th century, and had and has other senses, but these are now obsolete or rare.

wabbit Tired out, exhausted. Colloquial and occasional Scots: pronounced to rhyme with *rabbit*. After his first outing in convalescence an invalid admitted, 'I'm fair *wabbit*.' A more extreme expression of the same condition is, 'I'm clean *wabbit oot*.' Known only since the end of the 19th century, and of uncertain origin.

waukrife Unable to sleep; wakeful, watchful. Colloquial Scots. A person may be *waukrife*, but so may the wind that keeps him awake (a *waukrife* wind). One man, after being bitten by an adder, spent 'a rotten *waukrife* night' (*Scotsman*, 1986). *Waukrife* is also found in northern English dialect. It has been recorded in Scots since the 15th century, and derives from *wauk*, the Scots form of English *wake*. The second syllable means liable to, and is the same as *rife*, plentiful, here reduced from a word to a suffix and pronounced *riff*. Another Scots word formed in the same way is **cauldrife**, cold or feeling the cold: it is now rare.

III

Health Appearance Dress

baffie see BAUCHLE (III).

balmoral The Balmoral bonnet, usually worn with a kilt, is a development of the traditional woollen Kilmarnock BUNNET (III). The *balmoral* has a round, flat, projecting top ornamented by a TOORIE (III, small pompom) on its crown; it is worn rather to one side, and the band is sometimes diced (see DICE, III). The *balmoral* still forms part of the uniform of some Scottish regiments. The name is from Balmoral Castle, the royal residence established in Aberdeenshire by Queen Victoria, and probably reflects her fondness for being surrounded by things she believed to be peculiarly Scottish.

bauchle A shoe or slipper that is worn down and so out of shape that the wearer has to shuffle along to keep it on his foot. Colloquial Scots. 'Pit yer *bauchles* on and answer the door.' A '*bauchled* shoe' is one worn out of shape. To *bauchle* is to walk with a shuffling or shambling gait. *Bauchle* is sometimes used of a person who is old, worn out or untidy: 'Get out, ye wee *bauchle*.' *Bauchle* was first recorded in Scots as a verb meaning to disgrace or discredit. It is of unknown origin – perhaps from the Scots adjective *bauch*, in poor condition, of Old Norse origin. In some parts of Scotland, notably in Fife, slippers are called *baffs*, which is perhaps a development from *bauchle*. The diminutive **baffie** has been known in Fife since at least the 1940s; one old lady from Kelty 'always says *baffies* when she means slippers' (1987).

beal To fester, as in 'a *beelin* finger.' Colloquial Scots. A *beelin* is a festering sore of any kind. A person boiling over with rage may be described as *beelin*. First recorded in Scots early in the 14th century, meaning to swell with moisture. The origin of *beal* is not certain: it may be related to *boil*.

boke, bock To belch, vomit. Colloquial Scots. The original sense in 15th century Scots was to belch, and in one dictionary the sense development is made clear by a second sense of 'to emit in or with belches.' A journey by sea, or too much to drink, may induce the second kind of *boking* or *bocking*. Can also be used figuratively. 'You make me sick' can be rendered as 'You gie (give) me the *boke(s)*.' *Boke* is probably sound-imitative: it is also found in English dialect.

bonnet see BUNNET (III).

bonny Pretty, beautiful. General Scots. A more emotive, subjective word than BRAW (III). A writer in the *Scots Magazine* in 1985 claimed that when he described someone as *bonny*, he expected them to be 'not only prepossessing but friendly.' In early use, from the 16th century, *bonny* could be used of a man or boy (one thinks of '*bonnie* Prince Charlie'), but now it is usually confined to women and children. Places or things too may be described as *bonny*. In the 16th century *bonny* was English as well as Scots, but it is now northern and midland dialect rather than standard English. The association with Scotland has probably been strengthened by the popularity of the song about 'the *bonny*, bonny banks of Loch Lomond.' The origin of *bonny* is uncertain.

braw Fine, splendid, excellent – a term of approval for practically anything. General Scots. On a '*braw* day' the weather is pleasant; a view may be *braw*; a performer may be, for example, a '*braw* singer' or a '*braw* fiddler.' A '*braw* lass' is good-looking, but 'You're lookin *braw* the day' is as likely to refer to her general appearance, including dress. *Braw* is from French *brave*, which has some of the same applications. In the 17th century Scots offered a choice between *braw* and *brave*, but only the former survived in the above senses.

breeks Trousers; underpants. General Scots; often used half-humorously. One man to save his good trousers from being soaked by snow pulled on 'a pair o' auld navy blue *breeks* ower (over) them' (*Tocher*, no. 36–37). A full Highland dress set may include *under breeks*. Recorded in Scots since 1494, when payment was made for a coat and *breeks*. Before that, ordinary usage was *breek*, which was (like *feet* and *teeth*) a plural. This fact was lost sight of, and a new plural with -s formed. The saying that it is difficult to 'take the *breeks* off a Highlandman' means much the same as 'you can't get blood out of a stone.' *Breek* came to Scots from northern Middle English.

brogue A heavy walking shoe. The modern English word derives partly from Gaelic, partly from Irish, the word being practically the same in both languages. The Gaelic *bròg* was originally a rough shoe of untanned hide, stitched with thongs of leather. In 1795 in Inverness 'the Highland *brogues*' were still the ordinary dress of the men. But by 1821 a poet could refer to the discarding of the '*brog* for Lowland shoe'.

bunnet, bonnet General Scots for almost any kind of informal headwear, usually male. A cap qualifies as a bonnet, but a hat does not. In Ayr in 1951 there were 'four small firms with about fifty persons all engaged in producing *bonnets* – glengarries, balmorals, tam o' shanters, balaclavas and berets.' In earlier times a bonnet must have been more formal wear, for in a 1375 poem a noble carried 'a rede (red) *bonnet*' on a spear to reveal his high rank. But in the 19th century a *bonnet laird* was a small landowner, an upstart whose headgear betrayed his humble status. *Bonnet* is from the Old French *chapel de bonet*, a hat or cap of *bonet* (some kind of unidentified material). The word did not gain currency in England till the 17th century and then thanks to

Scottish influence. General English use is very different from the Scots: it usually applies to female headgear. See also BALMORAL (III), GLENGARRY (III), TAM O' SHANTER (III).

cairngorm A semi-precious stone of a brown or yellow colour. The stone is named from the Cairngorm mountains, where the crystals were first quarried from quartz veins, and the name, like the stone, became known outside Scotland about 1800. 'That most beautiful of all the Scottish gems, the Topaz or Cairngorm, is found among the Grampians' (1809). *Cairngorm* is from the Gaelic for the blue 'cairn' or mountain.

claes Clothes. *Claes* is a contracted form of *claithis*, the Scots form of English *clothes* (itself often contracted to *close*). It has been in colloquial Scots since the 15th century. People still put their *claes* out to dry on a *claes-rope*, and prop the line up with a *claes-pole* or '*stretcher.*'

cloot A piece of cloth (as in English), or a cloth put to some use about the house, as a dish–cloth or duster. Colloquial Scots. Hence *clootie*, wrapped in a cloth (as in *clootie* DUMPLING, IV), or made of pieces of cloth, as is a *clootie rug* (1928). *Cloot* can also be a patch – of any kind, for in 1922 it was discovered that the 'thackit riggin (thatched roof) needs a *cloot*'. It can be used of garments, as in the *House of Cloots*, advertising its wares in late 1986, or it can be a baby's nappy, also known as a *baby-clout* or a *hippin* (from *hip*). *Cloot* goes back to an Old English word for a cloth, and has been in use in Scots since the 14th century.

corrie-fisted Left-handed. Colloquial and occasional Scots. A 20th century development from the older *car-handit*, now rare, from an older Scots word, *car*, left (hand or side). This in turn came from Gaelic *cearr*, wrong, left-handed.

dice To ornament with a chequered pattern. In 1668 in English some snakes were noted as being 'regularly diced or chequered.' In Scots the idea was extended, so that in 1704 one man wore 'short hose of red and green set *dyce.*' A *diced* band round the edges is a common feature of such Highland headgear as the GLENGARRY (III) or BALMORAL (III); the *dicing* usually consists of a red and white chequered pattern.

dirk A short dagger. The true Scots form, recorded from the 16th century, is *durk*, but in his dictionary Dr Johnson preferred *dirk*, and this is now the generally accepted spelling. Properly, a *dirk* is a weapon borne by a Highlander and carried in his belt: it still forms part of Highlan dress.   The origin of *dirk* is unknown.

dwam A fit of abstraction which leaves the person affected unaware of, or indifferent to, what is going on around him. General Scots; also known in northern English dialect. Someone may 'fall into a *dwam*' as he is walking down the road with you, and may for a short time seem to be deep in a daydream. In earliest use, about 1500, *dwam* (or *dwalm*) referred to a more physical ailment – a fainting fit or a sudden attack of illness. In W.L. Lorimer's *New Testament in Scots* (1983) Peter 'fell in a *dwaum* and saw a vision' (*Acts* xi). It was claimed in 1924 that *dwams* of this kind may be cured by a DRAM (IV), though presumably not in the case of the pig which in 1925 was observed to be 'in a *dwalm*.' This sense remains, though in less common use than the other. Probably from an Old English word for confusion.

flannen Flannel. Once general, now (when used) colloquial, Scots. 'If I'm spared, I'll need new *flannen* petticoats next winter' (1925). The *-en* is not necessarily a Scots deviation. The word may be from Welsh *gwlanen*, flannel; if so, it is the *-el* that is out of step.

galluses A pair of braces for trousers. Colloquial Scots, but often used jocularly in general Scots. The word is a double plural, since it is *gallows* (itself plural) with an extra plural ending. One man ran out of his house half-dressed: he 'didnae have his *galluses* or his belt on yet' (*Tocher*, no. 32). A well-known Glasgow shopkeeper still advertised braces as '*gallowses*' in 1953. See also GALLOUS (II).

gansey A jersey, especially of the kind worn by fishermen. Localised Scots. First recorded in Shetland in 1886. In Banff in 1923 fishermen were 'sheathed in a *gansey*, always blue.' *Gansey* is an altered form of Guernsey in the Channel Islands. It probably came into Scots from the English dialect pronunciation *Garnsey*, the -r- being silent.

glengarry A cap of a dark, thick, woollen material, with at its rear a couple of short black ribbons hanging down over the neck of the wearer. The crown folds inwards, and comes to a point at the front, which is straight. The *glengarry* was frequently worn as a part of Highland dress. It also forms part of the uniform of some Scottish regiments, and then it may have red and white dicing (see DICE, III) along the lower edges. The name is from Colonel Alasdair Macdonell of Glengarry, who in 1822 sat in this form of bonnet for the portrait by Sir Henry Raeburn, which may be seen in the Scottish National Portrait Gallery.

gley A cast in the eye, a squint. Colloquial Scots. *Gley-eed* (or *-eyed*) is squint-eyed. From the verb *gley*, to squint or look sideways, first recorded in Scots in the 16th century; also in northern English dialect. Of unknown origin. The related word *agley* is well-known from the lines by Burns: 'The best-laid schemes o' mice an' men Gang aft *agley* (often go wrong).' **Skellie** too means squinting. Sometimes used as a nickname. One man was called '*skelly* Thomson' because he was '*gley-eed.*' Localised Scots; also northern English dialect. Of Scandinavian origin. **Pie-eyed**, cross-eyed, also means drunk. Originally a Scots formation, though perhaps from English *spy*. Now colloquial English.

gravat Scots form of *cravat*. Colloquial Scots for a scarf or muffler – nothing as fancy as the cravat worn by a real gent. But at least it is more comfortable wear than a *hemp(en) gravat*, which was until early in the 20th century a name given to the hangman's noose.

hen-toed, *Sc* **hen-taed** Pigeon-toed. It is quickly and maliciously pointed out, when someone walks with the points of the feet turned inwards, that he is 'hen-toed.' A poem quoted in the *Scottish National Dictionary* remarks wittily, 'They're learnin' hoo tae (how to) walk *hen-taed* And dance the Tango' (1929). General Scots.

hoast A cough. Colloquial and occasional Scots. 'That's an awfae *hoast* you have.' It has been in Scots since the 15th century; in 1549 it was claimed that coriander is good for a troublesome '*hoste*'. Also used as a verb for to cough. *Hoast* was also common, as *host*, in the Middle English period in the north and the east Midlands, areas occupied by earlier Scandinavian invaders. It is of Old Norse origin.

hoggar see HOSHEN (III).

hoshen Stocking with the foot cut off, used as a leg-warmer or a cover for the arm. Localised Scots. Also, old stocking made into a slipper by doubling it down or by adding a sole. First recorded in Scots in the 18th century: probably derived from *hose*. **Hoggar**, or *hugger*, has almost exactly the same meanings. Also localised Scots. First recorded in Scots in 1666; its origin is unknown.

kilt The kilt as a garment did not appear till the 18th century, but its nature was foreshadowed by the use of *kilt* as a verb. To *kilt* a garment was to tuck or gird it up. In the first notable play in Scots, *The Satire of the Three Estates* (1541), a woman running an errand is advised to '*kilt* up' her clothes above her waist. From late in the 18th century *heich*- (or *high-*) *kilted* meant having the skirts tucked well up, and hence immodest, even indecent. '*Heich-kilted* was she,' wrote Burns in 1792. It is not till the middle of the 18th century that we find to *kilt* in a more Highland context: in a poem describing the mustering of clans for battle there is a reference to the '*kilted* plaid.' This was the belted plaid (see PLAID, III), the ancestor of the kilt. The plaid was half-cloak, half-blanket; early in the 18th century the skirt-like portion of the plaid from the waist downwards was separated from the rest and worn as a garment in its own right. This was for a time known as the *philabeg*, from Gaelic for a small blanket, but it soon came to be known as the *kilt*. After the Jacobite rising of 1745 the wearing of 'The Plaid, Philabeg or little *Kilt*' was banned by Parliament. When its use was again permitted after 1782, it became (and has remained) the recognised dress of the Highland regiments serving in the British army. After George IV's visit to Edinburgh in 1822, when it was worn not only by many Highland chiefs and their followers, but also by the King himself, it came to be accepted as the national dress of Scotland. Since then it has been worn on occasion by Scotsmen of all ages and from both Highlands and Lowlands, despite R.L. Stevenson's warning: 'it is unwarrantable ... to imagine Scotch extraction a sufficient guarantee that you will look well in a *kilt.*' The modern *kilt* is the main part of Highland dress. It is made in the form of a skirt from a 7–8 yard length of TARTAN (III) cloth, and is heavily pleated at the back, though plain in front. Properly worn, it should 'cut' the knee-cap. *Kilt* as a verb, meaning to gird, was used in north-midland areas of England in the 14th century. It is connected with an Old Norse word *kelta*, the fold of a garment.

luckenbooth brooch A brooch, usually made of silver, engraved and sometimes decorated with small stones. Frequently made in the form of a heart, or of two hearts intertwined, and therefore a suitable gift to a sweetheart or one's betrothed. *Luckenbooths* (first recorded in 1456) were stalls, or booths, that could be locked up when not in use: *lucken*, or *locken*, was an old form of *locked*. In the 18th century the part of Edinburgh where MERCHANTS (XII) had their shops was called Luckenbooths. Some of these merchants were silversmiths or jewellers, and it is from the Edinburgh *luckenbooths* that the brooch took its name.

oo Scots dialect form of wool; also sometimes *woo*. The form is worth recording as a reminder of the famous, **but** imagined, conversation in which only vowel sounds are used. *Oo? Ay* (yes), *oo. A* (all) *oo? Ay, a oo. A ae* (one) *oo? Ay,* *a ae oo*. The plural *oos* may mean woollen or other fluff. An Aberdeen poet has described how a housewife 'wages war 'gainst *oose* and stoor (dust)' from dawn to dusk. *Oosey* means covered with fluff.

Paisley Designed or woven after a design specially associated with the town of Paisley in Renfrewshire. It occurs most commonly in *Paisley shawl* and *Paisley pattern*, but in 1961 the *Sunday Times* mentioned a 'dress patterned in *Paisley*'. The thread and textile industry of Paisley became distinguished in the early and mid-19th century for the manufacture of shawls with an ornamental pattern based on an artistic representation of foliage. These *Paisley shawls* were made in imitation of Indian shawls from Kashmir, and the pattern came to be known as *Paisley* pattern. The Paisley shawl first appeared about 1800, and was highly successful commercially. The shawl is said to have gone out of fashion about 1870, but is still much in demand from antique shops. In 1955 the *Buchan Observer* noted that at one function 'all the older women wore . . . flamboyant *Paisley shawls.*' The pattern is known 'everywhere in the textile trade as the *Paisley* pattern' (1925). Yet it is claimed that in 1777, some twenty years before the pattern went into production, a series of designs made in Edinburgh were in the Paisley pattern. The original designs were discovered in the Edinburgh College of Art. If so, an opportunity was missed, for 'Paisley had gained a near monopoly in the 1840s' (*Scotsman*, 1925).

peelie-wally Sickly, thin and ill-looking. From an earlier Scots *peelie* (thin, emaciated), reinforced by a second element that supplies echo and contrast. Common both in colloquial and in occasional Scots, and still vigorous enough to be used figuratively: 'The last game between these two clubs was a rather *peelie-wally* affair' (T.V. commentator, 1986).

peenie Child's word for a pinafore. Recorded since 1850, when some child was presented with 'a braw (fine) new *peenie*.' In children's speech, also used to mean the 'tummy.'

You can have 'a pain in the *peenie*', or be told to '*pit* (put) that in your *peenie*' if you are not eating up your food.

pie-eyed see GLEY (III).

plaid A long rectangular piece of TARTAN (III) cloth worn over one shoulder as a kind of cloak. Nowadays seen only when part of the full dress uniform of regimental pipers. In Scotland pronounced *played*, elsewhere often *plad*. Especially in American English often used as if synonymous with tartan. From 1500 on the *plaid* is regularly mentioned in Scottish records, and it was soon particularly associated with the Highlands. By 1600 English visitors to Scotland were describing the Highlander's use of 'short mantels or *playds* of divers colours' (1597), some of which blended so well with the heather as to camouflage the wearers. These *plaids*, which were 7–8 yards long, 'not only served them for cloaths by day . . . but were pallats or beds in the night' when they were on the move: 'they cover the whole body with 'em . . . excepting the right arm' (1689). The *plaid* in this form was not confined to the Highlands. The 1960 *Statistical Account of Scotland* tells us that 'within living memory' plaids were used by shepherds in Lanarkshire 'for protection against the weather'. The plaid was also worn by women, but as a shawl. In 1594 an observer, describing the appearance of some Highlanders who were fighting in Ireland, noted that 'their belts were over their loins outside their cloaks.' This is the first reference to the *belted plaid*, which led eventually to the development of the KILT (III). The origin of *plaid* is uncertain. It seems likely that it is connected with standard English *ply*, to fold, and that a *plaid* was so called because it was a folded cloth or blanket.

plook A spot, pimple or boil. General Scots. To have a single *plook* on one's face is bad enough; at a certain stage in life to be *plooky*, covered with spots, is a public humiliation. First recorded in Scots in the 16th century. From a Middle English word, of unknown origin.

pouch A pocket in a garment. Still in use in colloquial Scots, pronounced to rhyme with *hootch*. The first *pouch* recorded in Scots in 1539 was made of buckram, a coarse material, and was perhaps a kind of purse. The plural was sometimes used instead of the singular: in 1612 someone put his key 'in his *pouches*', a usage repeated in the modern folk-song, 'I've got siller (money) in my *pouches*' (see SILLER, XV). But the singular is usual. 'If we'd siller in oor *pooch*, we wisna feart (were not afraid) tae spen' (1920). The same word as English *pouch*.

sark A man's shirt. Colloquial Scots, but becoming rare, perhaps thanks to the big High Street stores. A sark also meant a woman's chemise, as in: 'They'd better keep their *sarks* weel down when John's . . . near them' (1964). Though nearly obsolete, the female *sark* is known to a wider public than the male one. The most famous *sark* was that worn by the youngest witch in Burns's *Tam o' Shanter*, who took part in the dance wearing a *cutty sark* (short chemise). The name *Cutty Sark* passed to the famous tea-clipper because its figurehead was similarly clad, and is kept alive to this day as the name of a brand of whisky. As a verb, to *sark* meant to provide someone with a shirt, but it developed a secondary meaning – to insulate the roof of a house. *Sarking*, originally shirting material, developed similarly, coming to mean roof boarding, and in more recent times even roofing felt. *Sark* has been in Scots since the 14th century, and was once also common in northern English dialect. It is of Scandinavian origin.

semmit An undervest, usually male, and generally made of wool or flannel. Colloquial and occasional Scots. In my early years I had to wear a woollen *semmit*; since then, though preferring less abrasive materials, I have continued to refer to my undervest as a *semmit*. The origin of *semmit* is doubtful. When it first appeared in Scots in the 15th century it meant a Roman tunic. It may be the same word as English *samite*, which meant first fine silk, then a garment made of silk.

shilpit Thin; skinny and starved-looking. In a poem written in 1945, someone was described as 'bow-leggit and *shilpit*.' General Scots, as there is no satisfactory English equivalent for 'a poor *shilpit* wee body.' Can also be applied to things – 'a *shilpit* sun' or '*shilpit* beer' were both weak. First recorded in Scots in the 17th century; its origin is not certain. It may be an altered form of *shirpit*, which means much the same as, and is perhaps derived from, the Scots equivalent of *sharp*.

skean-dhu A short dagger with a black hilt. The *skean-dhu* (pronounced *skée-en doo*) is an unobtrusive part of Highland dress: it is worn 'either inside or outside the garter on the outer part of the right leg' (1950). In earlier times it was used for both carving and fighting. *Skean dhu* is from Gaelic *sgian-dubh*, a black knife.

skellie see GLEY (III).

snod Smart, well turned out. Colloquial Scots, now becoming localised. 'Uncle Rab's aye that *snod*' (1988). Less often said of things, though as a verb *snod* is used for to tidy or tidy up: someone '*snoddin* the grass wi a spade' would be trimming the edges of the lawn. First recorded in Scots in the 15th century, meaning smooth or even. Of uncertain origin; perhaps from Old Norse.

sonsie Attractive, buxom, plump. Colloquial Scots, but now much less common than it used to be, and applied only to women – 'a *sonsie* lass' – or to a healthy child, a '*sonsy* baby.' It was once used to convey general praise or approval: Burns in his address to the HAGGIS (IV) talks of its 'honest *sonsie* face.' Before that it was used of things that were believed to bring good luck, and in this sense it was also used in northern English dialect. *Sonsie* was first recorded in Scots in the 16th century. It then meant lucky, and was from a noun *sonse*, derived from Gaelic *sonas*, good luck, prosperity, happiness.

sporran A purse or pocket, usually of leather, suspended from a loose belt and worn over the front of a kilt. A description of Highland dress from 1752 tells that a dagger 'hangs before in a scabbard, along with a knife and fork, and a purse for their money, which they term a *sparren*'. Originally the sporran was looped over the belt, and in time it became an important part of Highland dress. The modern *sporran* is generally ornamented in some way, sometimes only with leatherwork but in the case of a full-dress regimental kilt often with goat-hair, fur or brass. *Sporran* is from the Gaelic word for a purse, adopted for this particular use into Scots.

suit In general Scots usage, the person *suits* the thing – Mary may, or may not, *suit* red, or a new dress. This sounds strange to those who prefer to say that a hat suits the wearer – and nowadays their number will include many Scots.

tam o' shanter A man's woollen BUNNET (III), round in shape, with a broad flat top often ornamented by a TOORIE (III) or pompom in its centre. One wearer was the hero of Burns's poem, Tam o' Shanter, and it is from him that the modern name was taken. Nowadays, often in virulent tartans, *tam o' shanters* are much in evidence at football matches in which Scotland is playing. At other times, the tartan version helps the native to pick out at a glance the tourists in Scotland's cities. The word came to be applied to a variety of beret worn by women. A character in a 1921 novel said, 'I like ye wi' that reid (red) *tam o' shanter* on, Liz.' The shortened form *tammy* was early accepted into Standard English: it denotes both male and female versions, perhaps more commonly the latter.

tartan A woollen cloth woven from yards of several colours or shades so as to produce a criss-cross pattern of lines, bands and squares at right angles to each other. *Tartan* is first mentioned in Scottish records in 1474, and in 1533 a '*tartane galcoit* (coat)' was given to the King. But *tartan* was particularly associated with Highlanders, whose characteristic dress was the tartan PLAID (III), often accompanied by tartan hose (see TREWS, III). The early tartans were made from yarns dyed locally, and so the tartan of one area, or even glen, might differ from that of another, but there is no evidence that each clan assumed a different pattern as a distinguishing mark.

The first uniform tartan was the dark-coloured pattern worn by the 'Black Watch', as they were later called – military units raised in 1739 to help to keep the peace in the Highlands. In the aftermath of the 1745 Jacobite rising tartan was banned until 1782. When it was again legalised, the new Highland regiments raised towards the end of the 18th century were permitted to wear it. By then, modern dying methods had made it possible to devise a greater variety of tartan patterns, and it was possible to supply each regiment with a distinctive tartan of its own.

These patterns soon became popular with a wider public, and interest in tartan was further stimulated by the visit of George IV to Edinburgh in 1822 (see KILT, III). Thereafter makers of tartan strove to design a different tartan for every Scottish family, and the number of patterns multiplied from fewer than fifty in 1800 to more than 1000 today. Recently a new tartan was devised for the Commonwealth Games held in Edinburgh in 1986.

The origin of *tartan* is unknown.

toorie A small ornamental pompom, or knot of wool, on the crown of a bonnet or a TAM O' SHANTER (III). A song popular during the 1914–18 war was addressed to someone who wore a bonnet 'wi a red *toorie* on it.' An official description of the uniform of one of the Scottish regiments in 1956 defined the headgear as a 'Kilmarnock bonnet, blue, with diced border, red *tourie* and blackcock's tail'. *Toorie* is a diminutive of *toor*, the Scots form of English *tower*.

tousie Unkempt, dishevelled. 'Your hair's a' *tousie* again.' The Scots pronunciation is *toozy*, but *towzy* is also heard, perhaps because the word is related to *tousle*. Both *tousie* and *tousle* come from an earlier English *touse*, to knock about. *Tousie* is also found in northern English dialect.

trews Tartan trousers worn by certain Scottish regiments, or tartan underpants worn beneath the kilt. But, as a writer put it in 1950, 'the so-called trews worn in Highland regiments today ... are not *trews* at all, but merely tartan pantaloons or trousers.' On the other hand, a poet in 1917 called ordinary trousers 'Saxon *trews.*' Genuine *trews* as worn by Highlanders for centuries (they were first mentioned in Scots in 1563) were more like modern 'tights' than trousers. They were close-fitting, were intended to cover both legs and feet, and were usually of TARTAN (III). The English traveller Burt, who saw them about 1730, wrote: 'Few besides gentlemen wear the *trowze*, that is the breeches and stockings all of one piece, and drawn on together.' Some believed that *trews* rather than the KILT (III) should be regarded as the proper form of Highland dress, but they failed to compete with the kilt in popularity. *Trews* is the Scots form of a Gaelic word which now means trousers.

tweed is a woollen cloth, manufactured chiefly in the Border counties and in Harris in the Hebrides. It is woven in a twill, not a plain, pattern. The Scots for *twill* is *tweel*, and cloth so woven would be *tweeled*. This is the source of an extraordinary story long current in the Border towns. About 1830 an invoice accompanying a consignment of cloth to London was misread, and the word *tweeled*, or *tweeld*, was taken to be *tweed*. Since the river Tweed runs through several of the cloth-making towns, it was assumed that *tweed* was a local trade name for the cloth. The name stuck, and by 1949 someone was ready to claim that his great-uncle was 'the clerk who wrote the famous *tweel* letter.' What is certain is that since 1841 the cloth has always been referred to as *tweed*.

IV

Eating and Drinking

For a fuller account of traditional Scots cooking see F. Marion McNeill *The Scots Kitchen* (Blackie, 1929), a work referred to several times in the following entries.

Athole brose A drink consisting of a mixture of oatmeal, honey, whisky and water, sometimes with cream added. It is often served for specifically 'Scottish' occasions when it seems desirable to impress on visitors the unique nature of Scots hospitality. Special care is then taken in selecting and preparing the ingredients. Malt whisky, heather honey and double cream may be used, and some recipes insist that the mixture should be stirred with a silver spoon. According to legend, *Athole brose* is named after a 15th century Earl of Athole, who immobilised an enemy by lacing his favourite well with whisky and honey, and captured him when he was helpless. See also BROSE (IV).

bannock A round flattish cake, formerly baked exclusively on a GIRDLE (XII); 'a *bonnick* . . . is a big oatcake' (1975). The traditional bannock of oatmeal is now rare, but a friend tells me that her mother still (1986) says *bannock* for a thick scone. It is true that a 'bannock' may be bought any day in the market place of Selkirk. But this *Selkirk Bannock* is a different species: it is a rich fruit loaf made with a yeast dough and baked in an oven. It dates back to before 1819. *Bannock* is of Old English origin, and was once common in the north and east of England.

bap A soft bread roll baked in the oven. Marian McNeill insisted that '*baps* appear exclusively on the breakfast table, and should be eaten warm from the oven.' The word, common fifty years ago, is now usually replaced by morning roll or simply ROLL (IV), though *baps* may still be seen in Edinburgh shop windows. A 1973 *Good Housekeeping* cookery book contains a recipe for 'Floury Scotch *Baps* and Morning Rolls.' Perhaps baps are slipping out of Scots into standard English. The *bap* has a long history in Scotland: in 1575 it was possible to buy nine '*bappis*' for twelve pennies. The origin of the word is unknown.

barley bree see BREE (IV).

beer *Ale* and *beer* are common to Scots and English, but over the centuries there have been differences in brewing practices and in the names given to different kinds of beer. In general, Scots draught beer has had the reputation of being stronger than its English counterpart. On my first adult visit to England I was puzzled by the question 'Mild or bitter?' when I asked for a pint of beer. Scottish pubs may present visitors with a similar problem. If they want draught beer, they would be well advised to ask for *heavy, special, export* or *light*. The last corresponds to English *mild*. *Heavy* is a medium-strength beer, and *special* is much the same, not quite so strong but more carbonated. *Export* was originally, as the name implies, intended for markets abroad, and so is of a superior quality; it is stronger and slightly darker than *heavy*. As for bottled (now also canned) ales, *Pale Ale* and *India Pale Ale* were originally peculiarly Scottish brews intended for the consumer in hotter lands. There used also to be a particularly dark strong beer, sold in smaller bottles containing one third of a pint. These were popularly known as *wee heavies*, and could be eked out by being poured into a pint glass, and the glass filled up with draught beer. This mixture was known as a *Happy Days*. Another common order was for a *whisky chaser*. This was a double order, for a small whisky and a glass of beer (in Glasgow, known as *a hauf* (half) *an' a hauf-pint*). The whisky was drunk first, and then the beer – or *chaser* – was drunk off immediately afterwards. It was popular because it seemed a cheap way of getting drunk. Another method of ordering ale, peculiar to Scotland, is open to the customer. He may ask, for example, for a pint of the 80/–. This 'shilling system' is a survival of an earlier way of classifying beers in Scotland – by their invoice price per barrel in 1880. The lightest beer was 40/– ale; light and mild beers were 54/– or 60/–; stronger export beers were 70/–, 80/– or 90/–. At the very top of the scale were Twelve and Fifteen Guinea ales: these were of the quality sold in wee heavies.

black bun is a spicy fruit cake particularly associated with HOGMANAY (IX, New Year's Eve). The bun is made in two stages – a thick pastry casing, and a filling of a rich mixture of dried fruits, candied peel, almonds, a selection of spices, some brandy, milk and/or eggs, and flour. The cake is completely enclosed by the casing, the top of which is generously pricked with a fork. The bun is baked for 3–4 hours. *Black bun* is usually made well before the New Year, so that it can mature in good time for Hogmanay.

black-strippit ba A black-striped ball, a boiled sweet, the Scots equivalent of a 'bull's eye'.

bree A liquid in which something has been cooked, or only soaked, and which may then serve as a stock, soup or gravy. *Bree* has also been used for liquid of any kind (including water, a sense in which it was used by Burns). **Barley-bree** is whisky. *Bree* was first recorded in the 18th century; of French origin.

bridie A kind of pie, originally made in Forfar and so still known to many as a *Forfar bridie*, though it is now popular in most parts of Scotland. The filling of minced steak and onions, with quite sharp seasoning, is placed on a circle of pastry, which is then folded over to give the bridie its characteristic semi-circular shape. *Bridie* may be a development of the obsolete 18th century *bride's pie*, a pie made by the friends of the bride for distribution at her wedding.

brose A simple dish of oatmeal with boiling water stirred in and a little salt and sometimes butter added. Also made with peasemeal, pease *brose* and buttermilk being a favourite. Vegetables such as kale or turnips were sometimes used instead of meal, giving *kail brose* and *neep brose*. See also ATHOLE BROSE (IV). Until the 18th century Scottish soldiers on active service used to carry with them a bag of oatmeal until they had time to 'set on pans to make their *brose*' (1681). The origin of *brose* is unknown.

broth A thick soup, as opposed to the English sense of a clear or thin soup or stock. *Scotch broth*, also known as *barley broth*, is distinguished by the addition of meat and a variety of vegetables. Scots usage was the same as English in the early 18th century, but must surely have diverged before 1773, when Dr Samuel Johnson made his first visit to Scotland. As he supped *Scotch broth*, he was asked by Boswell if he had ever tasted it before. Johnson replied, 'No, Sir, but I don't care how soon I taste it again.' Such appreciation suggests something other than the clear broth he was used to. *Broth*, like PORRIDGE (IV), was once spoken of as if a plural: '*Broth* are very good' (1782) and 'a few *broth*' (1880). *Broth* is from an Old English word meaning soup or stock.

butterie see ROLL (IV).

carry out, *Sc* **cairry oot** General Scots for liquor bought on a licensed premises for consumption elsewhere; also, at a later date, food bought and taken home for consumption. The golden age of the *cairry-oot* was probably when public houses had to close at 10 p.m. As closing time drew near, the bar was beseiged by those who wanted cans of beer, or bottles of spirits, to drink later in the evening. But with the 'take-away' meal now such an institution, a *cairry-oot* is just as likely as likely to consist of a pizza, a Chinese meal, or whatever you fancy.

chitterin(g) bit (or **bite**, or **piece**), **chittery bit(e)** A piece of bread, a biscuit, or other small snack, eaten on one's return to the shore after a swim. It is reckoned to reduce the risk of a cold. A poem written in 1935 warns, 'But gin (if) ye'd keep clear o' the hoast (cough), Ye'll remember yer *chitterin'-bite*' (see HOAST, III). One of the snack-bars at the 1988 Glasgow Garden Festival was called 'The *Chitterin Bite.*' To *chitter*, now dialect Scots, is to chatter, or to shiver with cold.

cock-a-leekie, **cockie-leekie** A soup, now known far and wide outside Scotland, made from a cock or chicken boiled with leeks. Onions, and sometimes prunes, may be added. It is first mentioned by name in 1737 in some household jottings.

collop A thin slice of meat fried or stewed gently in a closed pan. *Minced collops*, or simply *collops*, is minced steak cooked with onion. *Collop* also occurs in northern English dialect, with the same meaning. Its origin is unknown.

cookie A semi-sweet yeast bun, rounded on top. It is not to be confused with an American cookie ('a small sweet cake, either flat or slightly raised'). The U.S. word is from a Dutch word for a little cake; the Scots one is more likely to be a development from 'to cook'. *Cookies* sometimes have additional ingredients, but these are always mentioned – a fruit cookie, an iced cookie, even a cream cookie.

cranachan A dessert. According to one writer in 1986, it is 'Scotland's greatest contribution to the dessert table of the world.' In his gourmet version, whipped cream is sweetened with sugar or heather honey, and CROWDIE (IV, soft cheese) is added. Into this is mixed toasted oatmeal and perhaps some soft fruit like raspberries. The whole may be flavoured with whisky or rum. *Cranachan* is from a Gaelic word which meant no more than beaten milk served as a Halloween treat, sometimes with a ring or other trinkets hidden in it. The stress is on *cran*.

crowdie A kind of soft cheese, originally according to Marian McNeill 'a rural breakfast article', but now in a refined form obtainable all over Scotland. When home-made, milk was warmed over a low fire until the curds could be separated from the whey. Salt, and sometimes cream, were added. *Crowdie* derives from *crud*, a Scots form of *curd* with the *u* and *r* transposed.

Cullen skink see SKINK (IV).

cuts of beef are in some cases differently named, and in others differently prepared, in Scotland. **Heukbone** (steak) in Scotland is in England rump steak for frying or grilling. It is also in some places called **pope's eye (steak)**, a name believed to have originated in Glasgow. In Scotland **rump steak** used to be the name given to topside and silverside, but because of possible confusion with English 'rump steak' this is now often known as **round steak**. English chuck steak is sold in Scotland as **shoulder steak**, and bladebone steak cut from the shoulder is known as **spalebone**. *Brisket* in England is sold on the bone, but in Scotland it is boned and rolled, so that while you pay more for the same weight, you get more meat in return.

See also HOCH (IV).

d(e)ochandorus A drink taken before departure – 'Won't you have a *dochandorus* before you go?' It was made widely known by Sir Harry Lauder's song 'Just a wee *Deoch-an-Doris*' (1910). It consists of three Gaelic words meaning a drink at the door – the 'stirrup cup' offered to a rider who could not or would not dismount. Outside the Highlands usually pronounced *dóchn-dóris*.

dram A drink of whisky. In the sense of a small measure of liquor, *dram* was borrowed from Scots (or English) into Gaelic. In Gaelic, a 'dram' is a glass of whisky – not a nip (a small measure), but an amount suited to the occasion. In general Scots 'Will you have a *dram*?' is therefore an invitation to drink whisky. This is the significance of the subtitle to a recent book (1973) on Scotland's whiskies: 'A *Dram* by *Dram* Guide.' The *wee dram* beloved of Scottish comedians and their imitators is genuine colloquial Scots, but one should not be misled by the use of *wee*, which is more a term of endearment than a suggestion that the quantity poured should be small.

drappit egg An egg poached in stock made from the liver of a fowl. In 1753 '*dropped eggs*' was included in a list of supper dishes, and *drappit egg* still appears on the menu as an accompaniment to HOWTOWDIE (IV, a chicken dish).

drop scone The *drop scone*, now usually known as a **pancake**, is a peculiarly Scottish phenomenon. It is made from a dough similar to that of the English pancake, but of a thicker consistency. This is dropped, a spoonful at a time, on to a hot lightly-greased frying-pan, hot-plate or GIRDLE (XII). It forms into little rounds, which should be cooked lightly and turned. Eaten cold with butter, jam, etc. See also SCONE (IV).

dumplin(g) In Scots, a rich boiled or steamed fruit pudding, not a savoury doughball. In one Border village on Shrove Tuesday 'every house [used to make] a big currant *dumplin* ... [with] flour an' treacle an currants an ... ginger' (*Tocher*, no. 39). When served as a birthday treat, as still sometimes happens, it may have charms or small coins hidden in it. A *clootie dumpling* is wrapped in a CLOOT (III, a piece of cloth) for boiling.

Edinburgh Rock A sweetmeat made from sugar, cream of tartar and water, and formed into brittle sticks in a range of flavours and pastel colours. Originally made in Edinburgh. 'The world famous rock,' Marian McNeill writes, 'is one of the triumphs of the Scottish confectioner's art.'

farl A triangular piece cut from a round of baked BANNOCK (IV). Two crosswise incisions were made on the dough, so that the finished article could be easily divided into four parts, or *farls*. *Farl* is a shortened form of an earlier word *fardel*, once common in English, which came from two Old English words for 'fourth' and 'part'.

Finnan haddie A smoke-cured haddock, prepared, whole and unsplit, after the method used in the village of Findon, south of Aberdeen. According to Scott, this involved drying the haddock over the smoke of burning sea-weed, and sprinkling it with salt water as it dried, but most accounts refer to smoke from greenwood, sawdust or peat. The true Finnan has to be cleaned and smoked on the day on which it is caught.

fish supper A portion of fish and chips bought in a fish-and-chip shop, and eaten off the premises. General Scots. The *supper* does not mean that the food is destined for a meal called supper: a *fish supper* can be asked for at any time of the day. So indeed may a PUDDIN (IV) *supper*, a *chicken supper*, a *pie supper*, and nowadays even a *pizza supper*.

flesh Meat. Apart from the meanings which it shares with English, *flesh* in Scots has clung to the sense of butcher meat, though it is very rarely used in that sense today. A meat-hook was formerly called a *flesh-crook*, and meat could be bought in the *flesh-market*. The latter still survives as a place name, as in Edinburgh's *Fleshmarket Close*. *Fleshing* may still be used for the butcher's trade. In 1988 a spokesman for the Incorporation of *Fleshers* of Edinburgh reminded listeners to Radio Scotland that '*fleshing* is a craft.'

gigot General Scots for a leg of mutton or lamb (also, more recently, of pork), or the meat to be obtained from it – 'a pound of *gigot*', or 'two *gigot* chops'. Also commonly used in England till about a century ago. From the French *gigot*, a leg of mutton or lamb prepared for cooking. The lower, thinly fleshed part of the *gigot* of lamb is known as the **shank end**.

haggis Scotland's national dish. Consists of the lungs, liver and heart of a sheep, minced and mixed with toasted oatmeal, suet and onion. The whole is then generously seasoned with salt and black pepper, and is boiled in the stomach bag of a sheep. Until the 18th century the dish was also popular in England, and in the north of England a local variety is still to be found. *Haggis* enjoys an honoured place at a BURNS SUPPER (IX), when it is addressed, in the words of the bard himself, as 'Great chieftain o' the puddin race' (see PUDDIN, IV). It is then served with, traditionally, turnips and mashed potatoes, and washed down with whisky or some lighter beverage. The earliest mention of *haggis* in Scots is in a poem written by William Dunbar in or about 1500. It was once believed that *haggis* was from French *hachis* (mince), but it is probably derived from a northern English verb *hagge* (to hack or chop).

hard stuff Whisky. First recorded in 1896, in 'a drap (drop) o' the *hard stuff*', the phrase has been welcomed into general English.

heukbone see CUTS OF BEEF (IV).

high tea An evening meal consisting of a single cooked course, followed by all the provisions for afternoon tea – bread and butter, scones, cakes, etc. 'Tea' usually means *high tea*, not afternoon tea, and is often applied to the evening meal, no matter what it consists of. Though regarded as a typically Scottish institution, it seems to exist in many other parts of the British Isles, especially in the North of England.

hoch A joint of beef, also of mutton or pork, cut from the flesh at the rear of the shin. In England it would be called 'a shin (of beef, etc).' Most butchers now advertise it as *hough*, though they still pronounce it to rhyme with *loch*. They may also sell it in the form of *potted hough*, hough prepared according to the recipe used for POTTED HEID (IV).

howtowdie A pullet. The word is apparently from an older French *hétoudeau*, a fat young chicken for the pot. It is also a method of cooking chicken which may owe something to

French influence. When the dish is first mentioned in a 1759 cookery book, the chicken was 'farced (stuffed) with oysters.' One Edinburgh restaurant not only gives currency to the name by calling itself The Howtowdie, but also offers *howtowdie* on its menu. In this instance the chicken is stuffed with haggis, pot-roasted, and served on a bed of spinach. The final addition is DRAPPIT EGG (IV), eggs poached in the gravy and placed on the spinach surrounding the chicken.

jeelie The Scots form of English *jelly*. As a preserve made from the juice of apples, brambles, etc, *jeelie* at one time graced most tea tables, so that *jeelie* came also to mean jam in general. In colloquial Scots bread and jam is *a piece and jeelie* or, now more usually, a *jeelie piece*.

malt whisky see WHISKY (IV).

mask To make or infuse tea. Localised Scots. Someone asked to *mask* the tea will in parts of Scotland use a *maskin pot* (teapot). There will then be a pause to let the tea *mask*. Before tea became popular it was ale that was *masked*. *Mask* is the Scots form of standard English *mash*, a term still used in both brewing and tea-making. The Scots form may have been influenced by Old Norse.

meal Oatmeal. So important has oatmeal been as a food in Scotland that *meal* has since about 1500 been taken to refer to oatmeal unless some other kind – *barley-meal, bere-meal, pease-meal* and so on – is specified. *Meal Monday* in the middle of the Candlemas term is still a recognised holiday for the students of the University of St Andrews, though it has relatively recently been abandoned by the Universities of Glasgow and Edinburgh. It was widely believed to be a survival from a time when students from country districts were allowed the opportunity to go home and replenish the store of *meal* that to them was the staff of life. The adjective *mealie* means made with, or containing, oatmeal. A *mealie-puddin* is a kind of sausage with a predominantly oatmeal filling (see PUDDIN, IV). A *mealie-dumpling* is a fuller, rounder version of the same thing: fat and seasoning are added to the oatmeal, and the DUMPLING (IV) is boiled or steamed.

meat Food. As in earlier English and in English dialect, *meat* in Scots (in which it is often spelt *mate* and so pronounced) means food in general, as well as flesh meat. In 1944, it was written of someone that 'as lang as he gets his bed and his *mate*, he disna (does not) bother.' It used to be said of a well-fed person that he (or she) 'looked *like his meat.*'

The *Selkirk Grace*, written by Robert Burns and still often recited at functions, runs:

Some hae (have) *meat* and canna eat,
And some wad eat that want it;
But we hae *meat* and we can eat,
And sae the Lord be thankit.

oatcake The Scots for *oat* is *ait*, and an *oatcake* was originally an *aitcake*. We find *otecake* in English in 1599, and the first Scots *aitcaikis* recorded were provided for James VI in 1588. *Cake* often meant *oatcake*, as in references to Scotland as 'the land o' cakes'; it almost certainly refers to *oatcakes* when John Knox states that 'the French men ... learned to eatt caikis, which at thare entrie thei skorned' (1560). Oatcakes have remained a staple of Scottish diet for centuries. See also BANNOCK (IV).

pancake see DROP SCONE (IV).

pan drop A circular sweet, rounded on top and bottom, with a hard white peppermint-flavoured coating; first mentioned in the *Encyclopaedia Britannica* for 1877, and once described in a court of law as 'a classical line of traditional Scottish sweet.' The same as an 'imperial', or 'mint imperial'. *Pan drops* were often smuggled 'into the kirk to suck during the sermon' (*Scots Magazine*, 1987).

pan loaf The *pan loaf* proper, or *square pan*, is baked in an individual pan or tin, and has a smooth crust all round. There was also a *high pan*, more commonly known as a 'plain loaf.'

This was a 'batch loaf' and had a black slightly curving crust on top, and a floury crust underneath. The plain loaf cost less than the *pan loaf.* From this difference in price arose a series of class-conscious idioms. To *speak pan loafy* or to *talk pan loaf* is to speak with a pretentious, English-sounding accent. A Glasgow writer has accused people from certain areas of speaking in 'genteel or *pan-loaf* accents' (1980). The loaf itself is general Scots, the idioms colloquial Scots. First recorded in 1887.

parkin, perkin A round ginger-flavoured biscuit made from oatmeal, flour and treacle, and topped with a single almond. First recorded in the 19th century. Of unknown origin – perhaps from the surname Parkin. Also found in the north of England.

petticoat tails Triangular shortbread biscuits cut from a round, sometimes after the centre has been removed, so that the ends of the biscuits are flat rather than pointed. The dough is sometimes flavoured with caraway seeds. There is some dispute over the origin of the name. One explanation offered is that the outer edge of the dough, when rolled, is scalloped, so that it looks like the ornamental hem of a petticoat. The other is that the biscuits were originally called *petites gatelles*, little cakes, and were of French origin. In support of the second theory is a legend that *petticoat tails* were introduced to Scotland from France by Mary Queen of Scots.

piece While retaining the usual senses of *piece* in standard English, in Scots *piece* has developed one particular sense – a piece of bread and butter, sometimes with jam, or a light snack (as an oatcake or sandwich) that can be carried until it is needed. The child or workman takes his piece with him to school or work in a POKE (XV, paper bag) or in a *piece box*, and it sustains him till he gets home for tea. In 1937 a writer to the *Border Magazine* recalled that 'all carried lunches were *pieces* then.' He added, 'I hope you have not begun to call them lunches.' As early as the 17th century we may read of a 'bairn greeting (child crying) for a *piece* or drink', and children still enjoy *jeelie pieces* (bread and jam) between meals (see JEELIE, IV).

pokey-hat An ice-cream cone. Colloquial Scots. The first element is said to be from colloquial English *hokey-pokey*, ice cream. The whole word suggests the tall pointed hat once worn by pierrots. An ice-cream wafer is a **slider**, though what with prepackaged choc-ices, etc., a genuine *slider* is now in some places hard to come by.

pope's eye steak see CUTS OF BEEF (IV).

porridge, *Sc* **parritch** Oatmeal porridge is now known and eaten throughout the British Isles, but as a specifically oatmeal dish it originated in Scotland, as a reference to 'Scotch porridge' in 1705 acknowledges. It has been of particular importance in the Scottish diet, and the Scottish contribution to the legends surrounding the dish has been large. In 1795, a few years after Burns had written of 'the halesome *parritch*, chief o' Scotia's food', the *Statistical Account of Scotland* confirmed that 'the diet of the labouring people [at breakfast] . . . is porridge, made of oatmeal, with milk and beer.' Properly the milk should be served in a separate bowl, and each spoonful of porridge should be dipped in it on its way to the mouth. Marian McNeill tells of a friend who was slapped by her Highland nurse for not eating her porridge standing – a custom also observed in the upper-class English home portrayed by L.P. Hartley in *The Go Between*, though there ladies were allowed to sit. There may be minor differences between Scottish and other ways of preparing porridge. In Scotland medium or coarse oatmeal is often preferred to porridge oats, and the addition of sugar tends to be frowned on. Porridge when being cooked is stirred with a stick called a SPURTLE (XII) or *theevil*.

The word *porridge*, which is an altered form of *pottage*, appeared in English in the middle of the 16th century, but in the more general sense of pottage or stew. It is interesting to note that in the past *pottage* was often used in Scots in the

sense of oatmeal porridge. Grammatically *porridge*, like
BROTH (IV), was treated as a plural. One of R.L. Stevenson's
characters says, 'They're grand food, *parritch*,' and in 1923 an
Ulster speaker varies between singular and plural: 'The
porridge is hot, and I need some milk in them.'

pottit heid (potted head) is a dish of the meat from the
head of a cow or pig, boiled, chopped, and embedded in jelly
made from the stock. First recorded in 1861, it is still
popular.

puddin A type of sausage made from the stomach or entrails
of a pig, sheep or other animal stuffed with a mixture of
minced meat and/or other ingredients. This meaning was
once common to Scotland and England, and survives
alongside the dessert variety in Scotland and in some English
dialects. In Scotland the other ingredients may include
oatmeal, flour, onions, blood and seasoning. An obvious
example of a pudding is the HAGGIS (IV), but almost as
popular is *black pudding*. A *white puddin*, or *mealie puddin* (see
MEAL, IV), is an oatmeal sausage. Most fish-and-chip shops
offer a *pudding-supper* as an alternative to a FISH SUPPER (IV).

red biddy A mixture of cheap red wine with methylated
spirits or other alcohol – an 'alcoholic concoction' as *The
Times* called it in 1930. It was the refuge of some of the
Glasgow poor in the 20's and 30's when gin and other spirits
were priced beyond their means. *Biddy*, a pet form of the
Irish name Bridget, seems to associate the drink with Irish
immigrants. At present *red biddy* may mean only the cheap
red wind drunk by 'winos' or down-and-outs.

roll As in England, a bread roll, but more particularly a
morning roll or BAP (IV), one to be eaten at breakfast, and once
obligingly delivered with the morning milk by many dairies.
The true Scots form would be *row*, pronounced to rhyme
with *cow*. This form is preserved in the north-eastern **rowie**,
also known as a *butterie rowie*, or more simply a **butterie**,
now popular all over Scotland. *Butteries* differ from ordinary

rolls by having a high proportion of butter to flour, which gives them a flaky consistency rather like that of a croissant. In north-east Scotland, a 'buttery morning' (1986) apparently sometimes replaces a coffee morning. The *morning roll* enjoys a very special place in Scotland. In 1962 it was claimed that 'the honour of being the universal breakfast in Scotland goes not to porridge, but to a *rou an'* a cuppa tea, the *rolls* being eaten hot from the bakehouse.' One may still see in the street after midnight, especially on a Sunday morning, a queue waiting to buy newly baked *rolls* from the bakery. These may be floury, soft or WELL-FIRED (IV).

round steak, rump steak see CUTS OF BEEF (IV).

rowie see ROLL (IV).

scone As pronounced in Scotland, *scone* rhymes with *gone*, but in general English into which it was adopted in the 19th century it is frequently made to rhyme with *bone*. Traditionally, a *scone* was a large, flat, round cake or BANNOCK (IV) baked on a GIRDLE (XII). The basic ingredients were flour and milk or buttermilk. The cake was usually scored several times crosswise, so that the finished article was easily divided into triangular pieces, themselves called *scones*. Nowadays oven scones, which are usually baked as small separate rounds, are more popular. *Scones* are first mentioned, as '*flowr sconnys* in an early 16th century Scots poem. The name is evidence of continental influence on the early Scots kitchen, since it probably comes from a Dutch *schoonbrot*, fine bread (a kind of loaf). There is also an early German *schönbrot* for wheaten, as opposed to rye, bread.

shank end see GIGOT (IV).

shoulder steak see CUTS OF BEEF (IV).

skink, a shin of beef, came from a Dutch word for the shin or ham of the leg, and is connected with *shank*, as in a shank of beef, or a ham shank. But as early as the 16th century *skink* came to be used for soup made from boiled shin of beef. **Cullen skink** however, though a soup, has nothing to do with shin of beef, or indeed any other kind of meat. Cullen is a fishing village on the Moray Firth, and the people of Cullen preferred their '*skink*' to be based on smoked fish. So *Cullen skink* is made from smoked haddock, potatoes, onions and milk.

skirlie Oatmeal fried with chopped onions in suet, dripping or other fat. This dish is much the same as the filling for a *mealie-puddin* (oatmeal sausage; see MEAL, IV). It is sometimes eaten as an accompaniment to a meat dish, or with potatoes. It may derive from SKIRL (V) in the sense of to sizzle.

slider see POKEY-HAT (IV).

smokie A fish cured by being smoked over a fire. *Arbroath smokies*, the best known of the class, are small haddocks, which are first cleaned and salted, but not split open until they are 'highly smoked'. Before being served they are warmed, cut open for removal of the backbone, buttered and then rewarmed. This method of preparation originated, not in Arbroath, but in Auchmithie, a small fishing-village a few miles further north.

soor dook see DOOK (XV).

soor plooms 'Sour plums', bright green boiled sweets with a very tart flavour, said to be originally a product of Galashiels. *Soor plooms* is also the motto on the arms of Galashiels. It commemorates an occasion in the 14th century when English raiders were surprised when gathering wild plums and put to flight.

spalebone see CUTS OF BEEF (IV).

stovies are sliced potatoes, cooked with fat, onions, seasoning and water in a manner that has features of stewing, braising and steaming. In the spring of 1986 the *Buchan Observer* announced a fund-raising event, the cost of admission to which included a '*stovie* supper and tea.' The dish is also known as (*Scotch*) *stoved potatoes* or *stovie tatties*, and allows of some additions (nowadays, often sausages). In 1953 the *People's Journal* distinguished between 'the *barfit* (barefoot) *stovies*' and the 'high-heelers' – the latter were accompanied by plenty of left-over meat. *Stovie* is from the verb *stove* (to stew), first found in Scots in 1631. It appeared in English in the 18th century, but is now limited to Scotland and the north of England. It is the same word as *stove*, a heater.

sup to take soft or liquid food by small mouthfuls, usually with a spoon: it is normal to *sup* porridge. General Scots: in English in this sense it is now chiefly dialect. An early Scots proverb, as quoted by James VI, runs: 'They that *sup* kail with the Devill have need of long spoones' (1597). This was recently adapted by a Scots M.P., who said in the House of Commons, 'If I were you, I would take a long spoon in *supping* with Downing Street' (*The Guardian*, 16.2.1987). A *sup* is a mouthful, or a quick drink: a caller may be offered 'a *sup* tea' or, on special occasions a *sup* (of whisky).

sweetie Colloquial Scots for a sweet or sweetmeat. When it originated in Scotland, *sweetie* may have come from the adjective *sweet*; surprisingly, *sweet* as a noun is later than *sweetie*, which remains chiefly Scots, though it is occasionally used in England. The first known use is in an account book for 1705, which notes that eight shillings were spent on '*sweities*' for a child. 'The wee *sweetie-shop*' was earlier in this century very much part of the local scene, though today the specialised *sweetie-shop* has become something of a rarity. A *sweetie-wife* was originally a woman who retailed *sweeties*, and then by a natural extension of meaning a person of either sex who retailed at length the local gossip. Thus it was noted in 1963 that 'a man who chatters is contemptuously called a *sweetie-wife* by both sexes'. *To work for sweeties* is to work for contemptibly low pay.

tablet, *Sc* **taiblet** A sweetmeat made from sugar, butter and flavouring. The consistency varies: it is sometimes brittle, sometimes crumbly, and if condensed milk is used in the making it may resemble fudge. The flavouring may be of cinammon, coconut, ginger, lemon, vanilla or walnut. One comment on the result, from Glasgow, was '*taiblet's* awfu' guid (very good).' The name presumably describes the oblongs or small squares in which tablet is usually presented.

tattie scone Potato scone. Mashed potatoes are mixed with fat and just enough flour to make a manageable dough. This is rolled out thinly into rounds with triangular incisions. They are baked on a GIRDLE (XII), then eaten with butter.

usquebaugh see WHISKY (IV).

well-fired describes bread, rolls, etc. that are baked till very brown, even blackened, and have a firm crust. Nowadays many prefer to ask for *crispy* rolls or bread.

whisky Until just over a hundred years ago *whisky* was a local drink little known outside Scotland, and so strong that you had to be brought up on it to stomach it. When it was liked, this was partly because, as a poet put it in 1715, '*whiskie* shall put our brains in a rege (rage).' Even in 1849 many Scots preferred what was often called 'Highland *whisky*' to other forms of spirits, and this was because it was made entirely from malted barley. Yet the '*gude maut whisky*' (1828) did not capture a wider market, probably because the old malt whiskies 'were, on the whole, too powerful and heavy for sedentary town–dwellers' (1930).

In the nineteenth century new and improved methods of distilling allowed the production, in greater quantity and at a lower cost, of whisky made from a mixture of malted barley, unmalted barley and grain (often maize). Grain whisky could then be mixed with some malt whisky, matured, and sold as a blend that was not too robust for the refined palate. There had already been blends of malt whisky, but it was this new *blended whisky* that made whisky an international drink; if you ask for *Scotch whisky*, or *Scotch*, today, it is almost certainly this kind of blended whisky that you will be given. These whiskies are usually known by the name of the distillers, or by a brand name.

Malt whisky, now more refined by long maturing, is still popular today. Most brands are *single malts*; that is, they are the product of one distillery, and the only water used in their preparation is the water of the glen in which they have been distilled. A *single malt whisky* is named after the glen in which it was made, and connoisseurs will tell you that there is as much difference between the flavours of the different malt whiskies (or *malts*, as they are often called) as there is between the products of different vineyards. There is therefore a certain mystique about the selection and consumption of *malt whisky* that is pleasing to its devotees. *Whisky* in the older Scottish records (1497 on) was called *aquavit(a)e*, the Latin for the water of life. This is also the name given to spirits by French *eau de vie* and Gaelic *uisgebeatha*. The Gaelic was adopted into Scots as *usquebae, iskie-bae* (1584) or **usquebaugh** (pronounced   ). *Whisky* is an adaptation of *usque–* (Gaelic *uisge*, water).

willie-waught (*gh* is pronounced like *ch* in loch) A good hearty swig at some drink, as beer. This 'word' would not exist at all if it were not for a misunderstanding of what Burns wrote in *Auld Lang Syne*. What Burns wrote was, 'We'll tak a richt *gude-willie waught* For auld lang syne'. *Gude-willie* meant cordial or friendly, and *waucht* was Scots for a good long drink: in 1925 you could still drink '*waucht* o' watter (water).' But in the singing of *Auld Lang Syne* the words came to be wrongly divided, and as early as 1826 we find someone boasting, 'That was a *willie-waught*, I *haena* (have not) left a dribble in the jug.'

V

Communication   Speech   Sound

ask for In general Scots to *ask for* a person means to enquire about his health or general well-being. 'Tell your parents I was *asking for* them' is a common parting remark after a friendly exchange.

blether To talk foolishly or lengthily. 'Stop *blethering*' is a common way of trying to stem a torrent of words. The noun is even more common. A *blether* is someone who has much to say, but nothing that is worth listening to. It can also refer to what is said, often in the plural. 'Awa wi yer *blethers*!' means 'Don't talk nonsense!' But in more kindly vein one person parting from an other may say: 'We must meet some time and have a good *blether*', a long chat. In all these uses *blether* is general Scots. It was first recorded in Scots in the 15th century, and comes from an Old Norse word meaning to speak indistinctly. Until the 19th century, it was used in Scots for to stammer. Of the same origin is **bladderskite** (or **bletherskate**), an occasional Scots term for a foolish or empty talker. The second element is from either SKITE (VI, to splash) or *skate*, the fish (often in the past used as an insult).

bum To make a buzzing or humming noise. Colloquial Scots. An insect (a *bumbee* is Scots for a bumblebee), or a spinning top, may *bum*. A picturesque example tells how someone heard stones '*bummin* past his head.' The word was first recorded in Scots, in this sense, in the 16th century. It came from Middle English, but in modern English it is obsolete except in dialect. In localised Scots to *bum* is also to brag or boast. This has given rise to the phrase *heid bummer*, 'boss', manager, still heard in the Glasgow area.

cheep in the sense of chirp (noun and verb) is perhaps earlier and more common in Scots than in English. It has also one special Scots usage: in warnings to keep quiet about a matter, the phrases '*nae a cheep* (or *never a cheep*) aboot it' are commonly used, with *cheep* here meaning a hint or whisper. This negative use is general Scots, and is also sometimes heard in north English dialect. A *cheeper* is a quick kiss – a peck on the cheek of the kind given by small boys to elderly aunts. Localised Scots.

clishmaclaver Idle talk, gossip. First recorded early in the 18th century, and now chiefly literary or occasional Scots. In 1985 a speaker on Radio Three, talking about the richness of Scots language, commented on the 'onomatopoeic quality of the word *clishmaclaver*. There is in the actual structure of the word ... a feeling of tongues wagging endlessly' (*The Listener*). The word has also, though rarely, been used as a verb for to chatter. *Clishmaclaver* is made up of two other words tacked together: *clish*, to retail gossip, and *claver*, gossip, idle talk.

clype A telltale: to *clype* is to tell tales. At school someone who *clypes on* his fellows will soon become unpopular, and find himself shunned as a *clype*. General Scots. In some parts of Scotland *clype* is used to mean the tale itself, and also a lie or falsehood. *Clype* is related to a Middle English verb meaning to call or name somebody: students of Chaucer will remember that one of his pilgrims was '*cleped* madame Eglentyne.' In this sense *clype* was recorded in Older Scots; then developed the secondary meaning of to accuse, from which came the main modern sense.

coronach A dirge. One of Scott's short poems in *The Lady of the Lake* (1810) is called *Coronach*, and it has been included in

several anthologies under this title, so introducing the word
to English readers. Scott explains that 'the *coronach* of the
Highlanders . . . was a wild expression of lamentation over
the body of a departed friend', and his poem expresses in
words the feelings of the mourners. In his book *Scottish
Pageantry*, Albert Mackie described the Scottish National
War Memorial as 'a *coronach* in stone' (1967). *Coronach* was
originally a Gaelic word.

crack A chat or conversation. Colloquial Scots. 'Come ben
(in) and hae a *crack*.' In the late 1920's a book with a certain
vogue in Scotland was called 'More *cracks* with We Twa': it
was by Lord and Lady Aberdeen, and contained much
PAWKIE (II) humour. As a verb, *crack* in the sense of to talk or
gossip was well established in Scots by the 16th century.
More recently when 'travelling folk' came together they
would 'swap stories round the fire . . . and they would *crack*
away there to one anither' (*Tocher*, no. 31). The phrase *gie's
yer crack* means tell me your news. The same word as *crack*, a
sharp noise.

cry in Scotland has much the same range of meanings as it
has in standard English, but some senses are now peculiar to
Scots. In 'Whit (what) dae ye *cry* that kin' o hammer?' and
'They *cried* the bairn efter its granny', *cry* means to name. *Cry*
(a shout) developed the additional sense of the distance that a
shout can carry. From this came the phrase *a far cry*, first used
in Scots in the 18th century, and now commonly used in
standard English for a very long distance. The common
English sense of to announce or proclaim (as in town *crier*) is
in Scotland particularly associated with the proclamation of
banns for a marriage – a wedding could be '*cried up*' (1912), or
the banns may be *cried* in the church. '*The cries*' could mean
the banns. This usage was also found in Cumberland, and is
known in American English. To *cry in on* (someone) is to pay
a short visit: 'I havenae *cried in on* her for a while.'

deave To pester with talk or noise. Colloquial and occasional
Scots. In 1988 a teacher complained that his pupils had been

deaving him all day with questions about their exam marks. The original sense of to deafen is now heard only in dialect. In older Scots a very noisy or talkative person was sometimes accused of '*deaving* the devil.' First recorded in Scots early in the 15th century. It came through Middle English from the Old English for to deafen.

Doric has in the past, in standard English and indeed in Scottish English, been applied to any 'rustic dialect' that seemed to the urban ear uncouth in sound and expression. *The Doric* sometimes meant SCOTS (V) itself, but in Scotland today it refers particularly to the dialect of north-east Scotland (Aberdeenshire, Banff, Moray and Nairn). Hence a criticism (*Scotsman*, 1988) that the aim of a radio programme called *North East Neuk* was apparently 'to promote the *Doric* and North-east culture' at the expense of other Scottish regional dialects.

flyte To scold, rail at. Localised Scots. To *flyte wi* someone is to quarrel noisily with him or her; to *flyte at* (or *on*) a person is to abuse him. On the literary level the *flyting* is the name given to a special kind of poetic exercise in which two poets may in turn abuse each other in verse in the most insulting terms they can think up. The most famous example is probably *The Flyting of Dunbar and Kennedie*, written about 1500. It is tasteless, but interesting linguistically. Some claim that in Scotland 'the art of *flyting* has never died' (*Scots Magazine*, 1983). *Flyte* was first recorded in Scots in the 15th century: it is from an Old English word for to contend or argue.

Gaelic The native language of the Celtic people of the Scottish Highlands and Western Isles. It has been spoken there since about 200 A. D., when the 'Scots' from Ireland started to expand northwards, bringing their language with them. The number of native Gaelic speakers is now sadly reduced. *Gaelic* is pronounced in one of several ways: by most Scots, like *Gallic*; by Highlanders, like the standard English pronunciation of *garlic*; and by some Scots and many

English people, as *gay-lik*. Highlanders speaking English use several expressions unfamiliar to most English speakers because the wording is based on Gaelic rather than English idiom. One example is 'Have you the *Gaelic*?' a polite inquiry made to find out if a stranger can speak Gaelic. The Gaelic spelling is *Gaidhlig*.

haiver To talk in a foolish or nonsensical manner; to chatter. General Scots. 'Stop *haiverin* and get on wi the job.' This can also be expressed as 'Stop yer *haiverin*.' In 1921 someone was described as 'a *haivering*, garrulous BLETHERSKATE' (see BLETHER, V). A person talking nonsense can be classed as a *haiver*, but this noun more usually refers to what is said, and it is then plural: 'Awa wi yer *haivers!*' or, more simply, '*Haivers!*' *Haiver* is not recorded in Scots till the end of the 18th century. It is of unknown origin – perhaps the sound of the word suggested its sense to the first users.

heckle The modern sense of heckling a public speaker originated in Scotland in the 19th century, and it quickly spread all over the English-speaking world. *Heckle* originally meant to dress flax by combing out its fibres: in 1609 someone was in trouble because he had dared to '*hekill* lint on the Sabath.' In the 17th century it developed the figurative meaning of to scold or reprove someone: it was no doubt from this that the political sense came. A *heckle* in older Scots was a flax-comb, and also the long feathers on the neck of a cock. From the second of these meanings came the use of *heckle* (nowadays in this sense written *hackle*) for the cockade of coloured feathers worn on the BUNNET (III) of certain Highland regiments, and for the feathers used in making fishing flies. *Heckle* was first recorded in Scots in the 15th century: it was also found in Middle English, and was a borrowing from the Low Countries. The form *hackle* is southern English.

hooch (the final *–ch* is pronounced as in *loch*) is frequently heard when an eightsome reel is in progress. It represents the cry uttered by the dancers to spur each other on to greater effort. In 1987 it was noted with relief by neighbours that after midnight the '*hooching* and heeching' at a Dundee party had ceased.

Kailyard school A group of Scottish writers who aimed to present in their works a realistic picture of rural domestic life in Scotland at the end of the 19th century. The *kailyard* (cabbage patch, see KAIL, XII) was reckoned to be a suitable symbol of their aspirations. They made considerable use of Scots dialect in their works, which were however marred by false sentimentality. The best-known of these writers was J.M. Barrie. According to a writer in the *Scotsman* early in 1989, *kailyardism* is not yet dead in Scotland.

Kelvinside accent Kelvinside is a residential part of Glasgow, and its residents, many of them well-heeled, are suspected by the less fortunate of being snobs and giving themselves airs. To 'speak posh,' to affect an Anglicised manner of speech, is to 'speak *Kelvinside*', or to have a *Kelvinside accent*. In Edinburgh the equivalent is a **Morningside accent**. In both cities the *–side* is often pronounced *–sade* by mockers, in supposed imitation of refined speech.

Lallans is another name for Scots. It is an altered form of *law* (low)–*lands*, which in the 18th century came to mean the speech of Lowland Scotland. No longer in common use in this sense. More recently, since about 1940, it has been applied to the literary form of Scots used by members of the *Lallans* movement. This movement started in the 1920s: its supporters tried to enrich Lowland Scots by using words from different Scots dialects, and also from Scotland's literary past. Its best known representative is Hugh MacDiarmid (1892–1978). A magazine devoted to the revival and encouragement of Lowland Scots speech and writing is called *Lallans*.

leed A speech or language. Now chiefly literary, and commonly used by revivalists: 'the lallan (lowland) *leid*' (1936), or 'Scots is a *leid* wi its ain history' (*Scotsman* letter,

1987). First recorded in Scots in 1375 in the sense of a national tongue; from Middle English, and ultimately from Old English.

leet A list of the applicants selected as the most likely candidates for an appointment. General Scots. A preliminary interview may be needed to reduce the numbers before the final interview, but one way or another the initial *long leet* is reduced to a *short leet* of the serious contenders. To be *on the short leet* for an important post is helpful even to unsuccessful candidates. *Leet* was first recorded in Scots in the late 16th century. It is a shortened form of *eleit*, which came to Scots from Old French *élite*, chosen, selected.

lichtlie To scorn, belittle. Localised or literary Scots. The poet Robert Garioch in 1962 challenged his readers to *lichtly* one of the actions of Robert Burns, and earlier someone protested that he was not trying to *lichtlie* the local landowner. Recorded in Scots from the middle of the 15th century: from an adjective *lichtly*, scornful.

line Any short writing, often one needed for some official purpose. General Scots. A man who has been off work for a few days is expected to produce a doctor's *line* to explain why he was absent. Children who have been off school, or want permission to be off, have to bring a *line* to the teacher from their parents. A *line* can also be an account with a shop, and to *pit* (put) something *on the line* is to have it charged to one's account.

makar (pronounced *macker*) A 'maker' or poet. Literary or learned Scots. A *makar* was once, in both Scots and English, one who made or composed a work of art, but that sense is obsolete in English. One modern Scots poet, William Soutar, has been particularly praised for his work as 'a *makar* of bairn (child) rhymes.' About 1500 William Dunbar wrote a poem now called 'Lament for the *Makars*', mourning the deaths of many of the poets, or '*makkaris*', who had been his contemporaries. Perhaps because of this 'the *makars*' is sometimes used to refer specifically to the poets of that period, something of a golden age for Scottish poetry. The older spelling with –*ar* has been retained.

misca, miscall To speak ill of, or to speak abusively to, someone. General Scots. In the first of these senses Scott wrote, in almost proverbial manner, 'Dinna *misca* him . . . that never *misca'd* you' (1818). In the second sense, one may respond to an insult with 'You've nae right tae *misca* me like that.' In England *miscall* is used in the sense of to slander, but only in dialect.

Morningside accent see KELVINSIDE ACCENT (V)

Norn A variety of Norwegian, and the old native language of Orkney and Shetland. A 17th century antiquary wrote that many of the inhabitants 'are descended from the Norwegians and speak a Norse tongue, corrupted, [which] they call *Norn*, amongst themselves.' Since the 17th century it has been increasingly displaced by Scots, and now survives in the local dialects chiefly in individual words, many of them preserving allusions to an older way of life. First recorded in Scots in the 15th century: from the Old Norse word for the Norwegian language.

plunk is imitative, of a dull and heavy sound. General Scots. If someone 'falls *plunk* into the river', *plunk* reflects the weight of the falling body, and also the suddenness of the event. Various other things cause a *plunk* – a fall of any kind, something being set down heavily. Can also be used as a verb – 'He *plunked* the shopping down on the table.' In some parts of western Scotland to '*plunk* the school' is to play truant.

Scots The language of Lowland Scotland; also known as *braid*, or *broad, Scots*. See also LALLANS (V). Originally a development from the north Anglian dialect of Old English, it became progressively differentiated from northern Middle English, and by the 16th century was the official language of Scotland. Since the Union of the Crowns of Scotland and

England in 1603 it has, for a variety of reasons, become increasingly anglicised. It survives as a group of dialects, as a literary language, and as a powerful influence on the speech of nearly all Scots. Even today some of the best Scottish poets prefer to write largely or wholly in Scots. *Scots* is also used as an adjective alongside *Scottish* and *Scotch*. Many modern Scots have developed a profound antipathy to the form *Scotch*, for no good historical or linguistic reason, and except in set phrases (e.g. Scotch whisky, Scotch bun) prefer *Scottish*.

scrieve To write. A writer is sometimes called a *scriever*. These words survive, but precariously. Formerly, both were used dismissively. To *scrieve* suggested ability to write at length rather than well, and *scriever* was used of a scribbler rather than of an author. But both words have been adopted and given new status by those who seek to revive Scots as a spoken and written language. Thus in *Lallans*, a periodical devoted to this end, we find in 1984 a reference to some leading Scots writers of this century as modern 'Scots *screivers*; McDiarmid, Goodsir Smith' and others. There was an older Scots *scrive* as early as 1500, and in the 17th–18th centuries English *scriver* meant a scrivener. These, like English *scribe*, probably derive from Latin *scribere*, to write.

sherrakin, shirrakin A public dressing-down, a verbal attack intended to make someone the object of popular indignation. 'He gave him a real *sherrakin* before starting in on him.' Chiefly Glasgow and the Glasgow area. The slightly earlier *sherrack*, a noisy row, a brawl, dates from the 19th century: its origin is unknown.

skirl To make, or utter, a shrill sound. General Scots. In the past this could be said of someone shrieking, screaming or even singing. In modern times it is used most frequently of the sound of the bagpipes: 'the *skirl* of the pipes' is common in standard English as well as in Scots. Another meaning of *skirl* is to sizzle or spatter when being fried. From this sense comes *skirl-in-the-pan*, the sound of fat frying, and also an alternative name for the dish SKIRLIE (IV). *Skirl* was first recorded in Scots at the beginning of the 16th century. It is from Middle English *skyrle*, of Scandinavian origin, and is related to English *shrill*.

slogan is one of the numerous words that passed into standard English because they were used by Sir Walter Scott. A *slogan* was originally a war-cry, but a meaningful one – perhaps the name of the chief of a CLAN (I), or of a place known to his followers. It was used as a rallying-cry, or as a password, by both Highlanders and Borderers. Hence in *Marmion* (1808), a narrative poem set in the BORDERS (XI), Scott tells how 'The Border *slogan* rent the sky, A Home! a Gordon! was the cry.' First recorded in Scots in 1513 in the form *slogorne*, no doubt influenced by the Gaelic words from which it derived, *sluagh ghairm*, the cry of the army. Before 1600 it had already taken the form *slogane*.

snash Abusive or insulting language, insolence. Colloquial Scots. An early example is from Burns, who wrote of 'a factor's *snash*.' Someone may still be told, 'Keep yer *snash* tae yersel.' First recorded in the 18th century: probably onomatopoeic in origin.

souch A sighing or rushing sound, as (frequently) that made by the wind. General Scots. The English equivalent is spelt *sough* and pronounced *soo*; the Scot pronounces the final –*ch*. Also used as a verb: 'Last night a cold wind was *souching* over the hills.' The phrase to *keep a calm souch*, to keep quiet or calm, must be less used than it once was. Quite recently a broadcaster advised his listeners to 'keep a calm *sow*.' There had been a break in oral transmission somewhere.

speir To ask. Colloquial Scots. *Speir* will usually serve the Scots speaker where the speaker of English will use *ask*. 'I'm gaun tae *speir* whaur ye a (all) were last nicht.' It is possible to ask too many questions: a hospital worker complained to one of the nurses, 'You're *speirin* the guts oot o me' (1986). *Speir* can also mean to ask for: a vivid if sexist example from 1921 is, 'Ye dinna *speir* a kiss frae a lassie: ye just tak it.' To *speir for* a person means to inquire after their well-being, to send them kind regards. 'Tell yer mither I was *speirin* for her.' A specific *speiring* was asking for a girl's hand in marriage. One man had remained a bachelor into middle age because he lacked the courage to *speir*: eventually in desperation he sent a friend 'to *speir* her' on his behalf. First recorded in Scots in the 14th century: it came from Middle English, and is a distant relation of the word *spoor*.

whinge Whine; complain in a whimpering manner. General Scots, and applied to the behaviour of dogs and children (in Australia of 'poms'). In 1725 Allan Ramsay complained of '*whindging* getts (brats).' First recorded in Scots about 1500. Also found in northern English dialect, but now used in all parts of the British Isles. From an Old English derivative of *whine*, which if it had survived in English would have given *whinse*.

yammer To make a loud noise, chatter. Said of human beings or large birds. A noisy talker may keep '*yammerin* awa;' one may be annoyed by the '*yammerin* o gulls' when a catch of fish is being landed. Also used as a noun: 'Stop that *yammer*, boys!' First recorded in Scots in the 16th century. From Middle English *yamer*, now obsolete except in dialect.

yatter To talk on endlessly, often in a meaningless way. General Scots. A class of children left teacherless will seem to a neutral listener to be *yatterin*: so will a group speaking rapidly in an unknown language. *Yatter* is of onomatopoeic origin – the sound of the word helps to convey the idea of someone rattling, or chattering, on.

VI

Movement Commotion Violence

argie-bargie A dispute or quarrel. Also used as a verb. General Scots. In 1987 a football commentator noticed that there was some '*argie-bargieing* on the terraces' after a controversial decision by the referee: the situation was more than a mere verbal disagreement. Now also in standard English use. *Argie-bargie* is a 20th century term which follows upon several earlier and similar attempts to describe a situation in which argument begins to develop into conflict. *Argle-bargle, argue-bargue* and, even earlier, *argle-bargain* all tried – from the 18th century on – to express the same idea. In older Scots *bargain* meant a conflict or struggle.

belt in Scots has been coloured by the use of *belt* as a synonym for TAWSE (VI). To 'get the *belt*' was to be punished by being struck on the hand with a *tawse*, and to *belt* someone was to punish them in this way. This legitimate use may have given *belt* enough respectability in Scotland to allow 'a *belt* (blow) on the jaw' to be acceptable usage: *belt* in this sense is not given in the *Oxford English Dictionary*.

birl To whirl round (and round). General Scots. Children in the playground like to *birl* each other round, or to give each other a wee *birl*. Someone, especially a dancer, can '*birl* roon' on his own – an action that can be performed even better by a top. *Birl* also means to make a whirring noise: this too can be done by a top. But it is cheaper to use a 'windmill' – a paper or plastic star at the end of a stick, free to *birl* round in the wind. In Fife this was, till recently, known as a *birler*.

A *birl* is a quick twist or turn. If a boy gives a *birl*, he can wriggle out of another's grasp. It may also refer to the quick twist given to the bow at the beginning of certain strokes by many traditional Scottish fiddlers. A delightful television programme some ten years ago showed Sir Yehudi Menuhin trying to perfect this style of fiddling, but his instructor was not satisfied: 'Verra guid, Mr Menuhin; but you haena quite got the *birl*.' A *birl* is also, surely not by coincidence, a particular grace-note played in piping. *Birl* is probably onomatopoeic in origin. It was first recorded in 1612 in the compound *birl-quheill*, a spinning wheel.

blooter To kick (a ball) with force rather than skill. General Scots. 'He *blootered* the ball over the bar.' A ball may also be *blootered* past a goalkeeper. Perhaps connected with Scots *bluiter*, to work in a blundering way, current until earlier this century.

breenge To rush forward in an uncontrolled manner. Colloquial Scots. *Breenge* has been recorded in Scots only since the 19th century. When someone *breenges* into a drawing-room it is wise to move anything fragile to a safer place. A *breenge* is a forceful, rather clumsy dash forward: a footballer may be noted for his *breenges* into the penalty area rather than his skill. In 1987 a Scottish political leader complained of another party, 'They are making a *breenge* at us.' Of unknown origin.

carfuffle A fuss or outcry. When in 1986 there was speculation that the phones of some important personages had been 'bugged', a speaker on Radio Scotland said, 'There'll be a fair *carfuffle* over that.' The word has now spread outside Scotland, where it originated: the English version is *curfuffle*. Earlier, *carfuffle* could mean a state of excitement; one could get into a *carfuffle* about something. It could also mean disorder: knitting could be in a *carfuffle*. Even before that, it was used as a verb for to be in a disordered state: in 1583 a poet described how someone's ruff *'curfuffled'* about his neck. In the 16th century Scots *fuffiling* meant moving about roughly: this word is the origin of the *–fuffle* part of *carfuffle*.

chum has in Scots developed the special sense of to accompany someone in a friendly way. 'I'll *chum* you down the road.' A natural extension of the use of the standard English noun. General Scots.

claymore Originally, the large two-edged sword once carried by Highlanders. Later came to mean also the basket-hilted sword with a single edge, which in modern times has served as a dress sword for the officers of some Lowland Scottish regiments. From the Gaelic for a great sword.

collieshangie A noisy quarrel, an uproar. Colloquial Scots. 'They got into a *collieshangie*.' Also used until recently for a lively conversation: 'I had a *collieshangie* with her.' The origin of *collieshangie*, first recorded in Scots in 1737, is unknown. The fact that in 1913 it was used in the sense of a dog-fight has prompted some to suggest a connection with COLLIE (XII).

coorie To snuggle; to stoop. A mother may tell a small child to '*coorie in* here,' come close to me. Colloquial Scots. The two main senses are both found in Matt McGinn's *Miner's Lullaby* (1962). While the miner '*coories doon* . . . in a three-fit seam' in the mine, his wife sings '*Coorie doon*, ma daurlin' to the baby in its cot. *Coorie* comes from *coor*, the Scots form of *cower*. First recorded in the 18th century.

dauner, dander To stroll, walk in a leisurely manner. General Scots. In 1986 an Edinburgh man was glad to be able to '*dauner* through the Meadows [a public park]' on his way to work. Also used figuratively: a path can *dauner* quietly along the bank of a river. Used as a noun in 'he went oot for a wee *dauner* roon aboot.' *Dander* is also common in English dialect, especially in the north. It has been recorded in Scots

since about 1600, and may be connected with Scots *dandill*, to
move uncertainly (English *dandle*).

dinger To *go one's dinger* is to do something, or to react, with
all the energy one has. The action taken is not specified. 'The
foreman *went his dinger*' when he found the job left
unfinished; in this case, he was angry, and gave full vent to
his anger. Colloquial and occasional Scots; pronounced to
rhyme with *singer*. *Dinger* is from *ding*, which was very
common in Scots from the 14th to the 19th century: its basic
sense was to strike or beat, and it may still occasionally be
heard in this sense. *Dinger* has been recorded only in the last
hundred years.

dump A heavy blow, a thump. This word has been
preserved by the curious custom of giving a child 'his *dumps*'
on his birthday – a custom that has made some children
reluctant to attend school on that day. A *dump* on the back is
administered to the birthday boy or girl for every completed
year by all who can get near enough to contribute.

dunt A dull or heavy blow. General Scots. The emphasis can
be on the sound of the blow, but is more usually on its
heaviness. A player 'got a *dunt* on the head as he went down'
(rugby commentator, 1986); spectators clearly heard the *dunt*
of the impact. As a verb, *dunt* means to thump, or to give a
heavy blow. A special instance, heard only in the north-east
of Scotland, is to *dunt* (stamp) down the herrings packed into
a barrel; the finishing touch is *dunting* down the circular top
that seals the barrel. 'That's the very *dunt*!' is a modern, but
localised, idiom for that's the very thing. *Dunt* was first
recorded in Scots early in the 16th century: it is probably, like
English *thump*, imitative in origin.

fecht Scots form of English *fight*. Colloquial Scots. One who
fights is a *fechter*, and a daring or good fighter may be
recognised as a *bonnie fechter*. In this sense the phrase may
have originated with Alan Breck in R.L. Stevenson's
Kidnapped (1886), who claimed to be a '*bonnie fechter*.' It is

also used of a person ready to espouse causes that may not be popular. Of an English M.P. who visited Scotland in 1987 to speak in favour of a Scottish Assembly, one delegate said, 'If there's one thing the Scots admire, it's a *bonny fechter*.' See also *sair fecht* (SAIR, XV).

flit General Scots for to move, bag and baggage, from one dwelling to another. A *flitter* may be either a person moving house, or one of the men doing the hard work of removal. My mother was concerned to hear that *flitters* should be supplied with beer when on the job. Her grocer, asked for advice on beer, replied, 'It all depends on the class of *flitter*, madam' (1923). The act of *flitting* can also be called a *flit*. In 1987 a newspaper headline announced, 'Glasgow Transport Museum begins flit.' *Flitting* is also used in the north of England. *Flit* has been in Scots since the 14th century. It is from an Old Norse word for to transport or migrate.

gae Scots form of English *go*. Colloquial Scots. The form *going* is most commonly represented by *gaun*: 'Are ye *gaun* tae (sometimes shortened into *gaunae*) the fitba (football match)?' The past is *gaed*, which perhaps explains the child's error in saying 'goed'. His mother corrected him: 'Dinna say, I wish I hadnae goed; say, I wish tae Goed (God) I hadnae went.' *Gane* would have been better Scots.

gang To go. An alternative to GAE (or *go*), and of equal antiquity, since both existed in Old English. Has survived longer in Scots than in English, though still heard in northern English dialect. Now used only in the *gang* and *gangin* forms: 'I'm *gangin* hame.' For past tenses it relies on *gaed* and *gane*, which properly belong to *gae*. Colloquial Scots: less common than GAE (VI). Both words occur in 'Are ye *gaun* tae *gang* doun (down) wi him?'

hirple To walk with a limp, to hobble. A Glasgow hospital gets 'an average of 21 soccer and rugby players *hirpling* through' the doors of its casualty department every week (*Scotsman*, 1987). This expressive word has been in Scots since the 15th century. Its origin is unknown, but it has been suggested that it derives from a Middle English word *hippe*, to hop. *Hirple* is also found in northern English dialect.

hurl A ride in a car, cart or anything on wheels. General Scots. Can refer to either a joy-ride – 'We got a *hurl* from the milkman' – or a lift – 'a *hurl* the LENTH (XIV) of the toon (as far as the farm).' From the 17th century, long before it was used as a noun, *hurl* was a verb meaning to move (something) on wheels. In a popular radio programme of the 1950's a borrowed piano was '*hurled* outside' for an open-air concert. Someone has recalled that in his childhood he 'had *hurled* four-wheeled cairties on the pavement' (*Scots Mag.*, 1982).

The 'cairtie' just mentioned could also have been called a *hurlie-cairt*, a home-made vehicle consisting of a box mounted on any wheels that came to hand. A wheel-barrow, or a hand-cart, can be known as a *hurl-cart*, and at one time a bed with wheels was known as a *hurlie-bed* (also sometimes a *hurl-bed*). The same word as *hurl*, to throw vigorously.

jink To elude by evasive running, to dodge. The original sense of to move quickly, suddenly or jerkily is vividly illustrated by a line from an early 18th century poem, 'Raithie on his fiddle *jinks*', which describes how the fiddler (Raithie) sways, or moves, to his music. It is probably to represent in sound just such a movement that the word came into being, but it is in the sense of dodge that it entered standard English, perhaps because of its appropriateness in football or rugby contexts. A Glasgow Celtic footballer, much admired in the 1970s for his elusive or *jinkie* dribbling, was popularly known as *Jinkie* Jimmy, *Jinkie* Johnstone, or even plain *Jinky*. By an extension of the idea of evasion, in some parts of Scotland to play truant from school is to *jink the school* (or *class*). As a noun, also refers to elusive movement or dodging. In early use it was common in the sense of a playful trick or frolic, and then chiefly in the plural, as in *high jinks*, originally a Scottish drinking game.

jouk, jook To dodge or duck. Colloquial Scots. If someone tries to hit you, you can *jouk* out of the way, or you can '*jook yer heid*,' so that the blow does not land. You may then decide to remove yourself from the danger zone by *jouking* into a side-street, so managing to *jouk* (escape) the person threatening you. Children up to mischief may *jouk* (slip quietly) out of sight on the approach of authority. A special form of evasion is to '*jouk* the schule (school),' or to '*jouk* from' the school – to play truant. But when a fish is said to be *jouking aboot* in the water, this refers simply to its rapid darts, twists and turns. *Jouk* is probably a variant of *dook* (to duck): the *d*– has been modified to *dj*–, as it has in the popular pronunciation of standard English *duke*.

laldie Vigorous punishment. Colloquial and occasional Scots; now usually figurative. The presenter of a jazz programme on Radio Scotland in 1987 suggested that 'the *laldie* of the 1920s' had given way to the sweeter sounds of the 1930s. Earlier in the century, more literally, someone remembered getting '*laldie* owre the bum' (1912). Very common is the phrase *to gie* (give) *laldie*. Samson of Old Testament fame has been credited with giving 'the Philistines *laldie* wi the jaw-bane o a cuddie (ass)' (1935). Football supporters call on their team to 'gie it *laldie*' – give it everything you've got! First recorded in the 19th century, and uniquely Scots. Of unknown origin – perhaps sound-imitative.

lowp To jump, leap, as when one talks of fish *lowpin* in the river; also, to jump over – a man recalled how he '*loupit* the dyke on his way to school' (*Scots Mag.*, 1987). Colloquial and occasional Scots, and variously pronounced in different parts of Scotland. Can also be used of somone dancing energetically to lively music: the dancing witches in Burns's *Tam o'Shanter* were described as '*loupin* and flingin' (1791). In some parts of Scotland leap-frog is known as *loup the* CUDDIE (XII). *Loup* can be used to describe a loping, springy manner of walking; and long-distance walkers may develop 'a long *louping* step.' Also used as a noun for a jump or start. A '*loup* into the air' may be from excess of energy or in response to a shock. First recorded in Scots in the

14th century. From Middle English *lope*, of Old Norse origin.

raid, the Scots form of English *road*, developed the special sense of a foray made on horseback. This was the sense in which Scott used it when in 1802 he wrote of 'a *raid* into England' made in an earlier century. Scott's use of the word was taken up and its meaning extended by English writers and speakers.

rammy A violent scuffle, a 'free-for-all.' There is sometimes a *rammy* after a football match, and on occasion there may be 'a dance hall *rammy*.' General Scots.

rax To stretch or extend. Colloquial Scots, with quite a wide range of meaning. To *rax oneself* is to stretch oneself, as after rising from bed. Alternatively, some like a morning jog to help them to '*rax* their legs.' You can *rax oot* your hand to take something. *Raxing* can stretch a person to the limits, as when a piper *raxes* his cheeks as he pipes, or even beyond the limits, so that if you aren't careful you may *rax* yourself, or *rax* (sprain) your wrist or ankle. A woman remembered that her father had been *raxed* by continual coughing – overstrained, even tortured. The stretching need not be stressful. In 1935 a man was said to eat 'a' (all) that he could *rax* (reach).' What he could not reach, he could ask for: '*Rax* me yon (that) bottle.' *Rax* has been recorded in Scots since the 14th century. It came from northern Middle English, and before that from Old English, perhaps influenced by Old Norse.

rummle To handle roughly, beat. Colloquial Scots. Years ago I remember hearing some rugby supporters inciting their team to '*rummle* 'em *up*.' Apparently *rummeling up* has now spread to football, where normally it has to be done more subtly, but with no less vigour. *Rummle* is the Scots form of *rumble*.

scart To scratch or scrape with nails or claws, or with any instrument that may serve. As early as the 14th century we read of someone *scarting* her face with her hands, and of people disfigured by *scarts* and sores. In modern times a hungry hen '*scarts* the ground,' and in 1927 men sometimes *scartit* matches on their BREEKS (III, trousers) to strike them. Colloquial Scots. *Scart* is an altered form of an English *scrat*, of which *scratch* was a later development.

shauchle To walk in a shambling manner, to shuffle. The comment that someone was '*shauchling* doon the road' is almost self-explanatory. A rowing-boat making little headway on roughish water may be described as *shauchling*; so may a rickety cart or barrow. The legs, feet or even the shoes of someone who shuffles along may be *shauchled* – rather less than serviceable through age or poor condition. At one time a worn-out shoe was called a *shauchle*. *Shauchle* is probably imitative in origin, like similar words (e.g. *shaffle, shockle*) in English dialect. It was first recorded in Scots in the 18th century.

shog see SHOOGLIE (VI).

shooglie Unsteady, shaky. Colloquial and occasional Scots. 'This chair is awfae *shooglie*' (1987). As a hill-walker vaulted over a DRYSTANE DYKE (both VIII), he became aware that it was 'somewhat *shoogly*' (*Scots Mag.*, 1983). Back in 1925 a visitor to Italy, fearful of earthquakes, was relieved to find that Italy was 'no near so *shoogly* as what folks try to make out.' *Shooglie* is from the verb *shoogle* or *shoggle*, to shake, first recorded in the 18th century and still widely used in Scots. This in turn derives from an earlier verb **shog** with much the same senses, first recorded in the 16th century. From it came the names of such things as the *shoggin-boat* or *shoogie-boat*, a swing boat at a fair, and the *shoggy-shoo*, a seesaw or a swing: these are now heard, if at all, only in localised Scots. *Shog*, still known in the sense of to shake or jog, came from Middle English.

skail To scatter or disperse. Localised Scots. When those attending a school, meeting or church service disperse at the end of the gathering, they are said to *skail* (or the church, etc., *skails*). Another sense is to scatter things here and there, to spread them about: asked what he was doing, a boy replied that he was '*skailing* the peats in rows' to let them dry. *Skail* may also mean to spill. A man slipped on the road and *skailed* the groceries that were in his box. First recorded in the 14th century. From northern Middle English; perhaps originally from Old Norse.

skelp To hit (often with something flat), smack, slap. General Scots. Parents used to '*skelp* [children] on the bottom' with the hand or a slipper, whereas teachers had to be armed with a TAWSE (VI) with which to *skelp* pupils. Both forms of punishment are now frowned on. A *skelp* is a smack, or a hard well-administered blow. 'Gie him a *skelp* on the lug (ear).' A goal-kicker in rugby may 'give the ball a good *skelp*' (1987). In golf, two good *skelps* with your woods may leave you on the green. First recorded in the 16th century. From a northern Middle English word, probably of Scandinavian origin.

skite To fly though the air, often at an angle as the result of a slip, a rebound or unexpected momentum. Colloquial and occasional Scots. A well-directed stone at curling may suddenly gather speed and *skite* past the TEE (X). A shot at golf may *skite* off a tree, sometimes to the danger of one's partner, even of oneself. Hail is notable for '*skiting* aff the ground', and has been described by a poet as '*skiting* hail.' In winter, especially where children have been making slides, there is danger of *skiting* and ending up on your back. A push may send you '*skiting* into the ditch', and you may comment ruefully that the road was 'gey *skitie* (very slippery).' *Skite* is less common as a noun. It can mean a glancing blow at someone: a good '*skite* on the heid (head)', for example. To 'go on the *skite*' is to embark on a good evening's (or night's) entertainment. *Skite* was first recorded in Scots in the 18th century. It is perhaps from an Old Norse word connected with standard English *shoot*.

stramash A noisy row, an uproar, a 'free-for-all.' General Scots. A *stramash* is the sort of commotion that breaks out when several people at once lose their tempers, and voices and soon fists are raised. A *stramash* often precedes a 'sending off' at a football match. The first moves to drop Latin from the school curriculum apparently 'caused a *stramash*' (1988). First recorded in Yorkshire dialect in the late 18th century as a noun meaning a smash. Of doubtful origin. The *Scottish National Dictionary* suggests a possible connection with French *escarmouche*, or with a variant of its English derivative *skirmish*.

stravaig To wander about from place to place. Colloquial and occasional Scots. Someone has recalled spending part of his youth *stravaiging* all over the Highlands on a motor-bike. A *stravaig* is a stroll or ramble, usually with no particular destination; but in 1937 someone was described as a great *stravaiger* to horse-races and country fairs. *Stravaig*, which has been recorded since the 18th century, is from an obsolete Scots word *extravage*, to wander about, also to stray from the point in conversation. *Extravage* was from Latin *extravagare*, to wander, and so is related to standard English *extravagant*.

stushie, stashie A row, uproar; widespread and loudly voiced criticism. A recent book about Imelda Marcos caused a '*stushie*' in the Phillipines (*Scotsman*, 1987). To *raise* (or *create*) *a stushie* about something means to raise a fuss, try to stir up trouble. In 1987 a number of people and organisations were trying to *create a stushie* in Scotland about the apparently imminent 'community charge' or 'poll tax'. First recorded in the 19th century. It has been suggested that *stushie* is an altered form of English *ecstasy*.

tawse A leather strap devised to inflict 'condign and salutary punishment' on classroom offenders. The supreme exemplar was known as a *Lochgelly special*, after the town where it was manufactured. The *tawse* is now banned in Scottish schools, a fact that calls forth frequent protests from ageing masochists who claim that in their schooldays it did them nothing but good. The plural of *taw*, a throng: a good *tawse* had two or more tongues. See also BELT (VI).

toddle, now general English, was originally Scots in the form *todle*. The sense of walking unsteadily was applied not only to children but also to old or infirm people. The figurative sense of to walk in an easy, leisurely manner was also known in Scots. In the song 'Tail *Toddle*', sometimes attributed to Burns, the title is a reference to sexual intercourse, and in the line 'Tammy gars (makes) my tail *toddle*', toddle means to move irregularly. *Toddle* was first recorded in Scots early in the 16th century in the sense of to toy with. Its origin is unknown.

trauchle To walk, or work, slowly and wearily; to exhaust. Colloquial Scots. A word 'depicting struggle and difficulty in performing a task is *trauchle*' (*Scots Mag.*, 1982). In 1986 the leader of a party of ramblers complained, 'Some of them are *trauchled* (worn out) already.' In 1952 a tired walker was compared to an itinerant hawker '*trauchling* frae door to door.' Work that is tiring and unsatisfying can be called a *trauchle*. Preparing to move house can be a *trauchle*; but it is better than having a job which you regard as 'a daily *trauchle*.' Someone who is overburdened with chores may be '*trauchled* wi a that work.' *Trauchle*, when first recorded in Scots in the 16th century, meant to spoil (something) by ill-treatment, but it soon developed the meaning of to exhaust or tire out. It is apparently of Dutch origin.

wheech, wheek To move quickly, to whisk (something) away. 'He grabbed my cap and *wheekit* awa.' In 1987 a diner complained that a waitress had '*wheeched* away' his plate before he had finished eating. In 1955 the *Scotsman* sympathised with shopkeepers whose customers had suddenly been '*wheeched* away' to distant housing estates. A quick whirring movement through the air can be described as a *wheech*. Some still remember the *wheech* of the BELT (VI) as it descended on their out-stretched palm. In its origin, *wheech* was an attempt to imitate such a sound. It was first recorded in Scots in the 19th century.

VII

Law Administration

Scots Law developed separately from English Law and since the Act of Union in 1707 has maintained its own identity. Its institutions differ from the English ones and the terms used – even when commonly employed in English Law – often have a very different application.

advocate One qualified to plead in a court of law – the Scottish equivalent of English *barrister*. Only an advocate can plead in one of the supreme courts, and in the HIGH COURT (VII) prosecution is by an *advocate-depute*, so called because he is representing the *Lord Advocate* (see LORD, VII), the chief law officer for the Crown in Scotland. The collective name given to the members of the Scottish bar is the *Faculty of Advocates*. Recorded in Scots since the 14th century: from Middle English *advocate*, one who speaks for another.

arbiter Someone chosen to settle a dispute. The Scots equivalent of *arbitrator* in English law. *Arbiter* is also used in English, but not in legal contexts, whereas in Scots law it is the usual term. A deed drawn up in 1987 provided for the referral of disputes to 'an *Arbiter* to be mutually agreed upon.' Recorded in Scots since the 15th century: from Latin.

assoilzie To find in favour of the defender in an action, and so to absolve him from guilt. In one case heard in 1987, the defenders argued that 'since they had acted without malice, they should be *assoilzied*' (*Sc. Law Times*, 1987). In the second syllable the *z* is either pronounced like a γ or is not pronounced at all. *Assoilze*, which was first recorded in Scots in the 15th century, is from a French word which is itself derived from Latin *absolvere*, to absolve.

bailie is now rarely heard, though it has been retained in some areas as a courtesy title. But until 1975 a *bailie* was a person of considerable importance in the local administration of towns. A *bailie* was an elected member of a town council who had been appointed a magistrate by the vote of his fellow councillors. The office was similar to that of an alderman in England. First recorded in Scots in the 14th century; has the same Old French origin as *bailiff*.

blackmail, now general English, originated in the border areas between Scotland and England. It was first recorded in Scots in 1530, when someone was convicted of taking *blak maill* from a landowner. *Mail* was a Scots word for rent, and *black* rent was money extorted illegally, an early instance of protection money; it was paid to freebooters to induce them not to damage the payer's land and stock. *Blackmail* was recorded in the north of England about 1600. *Black* is here used figuratively, in the sense of evil or shameful. *Mail* came from northern Middle English, and earlier from Old Norse.

broo, buroo Scots forms of English *bureau*, thanks to the Scottish tendency to pronounce *eau* as *oo*. Colloquial Scots. From 1920 on the *buroo* was the Labour Exchange from which dole money had to be claimed. The name *buroo* has now been transferred to the Unemployment Benefit Office. *Buroo* may also mean the money so paid, and to be in receipt of such money was, and sometimes is, to be *on the broo*.

burgh is in Scotland the preferred form corresponding to English *borough*. A *burgh* is a town originally established under a charter which conferred on it certain privileges, such as the right to hold a fair and the right to set up its own municipal corporation. Certain Scottish burghs were distinguished as *Royal Burghs* because their charters were granted to them by a king: one of their special privileges was the right to maintain a COMMON GOOD (VII) fund.

From the 16th century on, commissioners from the Scottish burghs met annually to consider common problems and to act in concert where possible. The Convention of *Burghs*, later of *Royal Burghs*, played an important part in Scottish life until in 1975 it became part of the more widely representative Convention of Scottish Local Authorities (acronymically, COSLA).

caution Bail, security. Still in common use in legal contexts, in which the first syllable is pronounced *cay*, not *caw*. If you are asked to 'find *caution*', the next step is to look for someone who is willing to stand surety, or to be a *caution* (or *cautioner*) for you. On occasion, an Insurance company is willing to issue a *bond of caution*, as when for example someone dies without making a will. Used in these senses since the late 15th century.

children's hearings were introduced in Scotland in 1971. They are an attempt to deal helpfully with children who are in difficulty, either because they have committed offences or because their family background is disturbed. Such children are brought before a *children's panel* of three members, all of whom are specially trained volunteers. A panel treats children brought before it with as much understanding of their circumstances as possible. Evidence is heard from anyone with knowledge of the child's background, including the parents. Where necessary, the panel will recommend compulsory supervision of the child, sometimes at home, sometimes away from home. The long-term interest of the child is the deciding factor.

common good Revenues derived by a former Royal Burgh (see BURGH, VII) from lands granted under its original charter. For example, in St Andrews the *common good* is funded in part by the letting of STANCES (XV) for stalls during the annual fair. The *common good* may be used only on projects which benefit the whole community. Such funds are now administered by the appropriate District council (see REGIONALISATION, VII). In this phrase *good* does not mean benefit, as in standard English *common good*; it means property or possessions. The nearest English equivalent is *goods*.

Court of Session The supreme court in Scotland for civil matters: established in 1532. There is right of appeal from its decisions to the House of Lords in London. The *Court of Session* is divided into an Inner House and an Outer House. The Inner House deals mainly with appeals and sits in two divisions, each of four judges. The Outer House deals with cases of the first instance: in it the judge sits singly. See also LORD (VII).

culpable homicide The act of wrongfully killing another person, but without the premeditation or malice considered as requiring a charge of murder. Much the same as the English verdict of manslaughter. The term was first used in the 18th century.

decree as a legal term is pronounced with the stress on the first syllable (*dee–*). In Scotland it is the usual term for a final judgment, and has been so since the late 18th century: thus in 1981 a document referred to '*decree* granted against [the defender] in an action of divorce.'

defamation in Scots law corresponds to both *libel* and *slander* in English law (cf. LIBEL, VII); in Scotland 'both written and spoken *defamation* are treated as slander.' In 1987 a well-known public figure agreed to settle 'a *defamation* action . . . out of court' (*Glasgow Herald*). Used in this sense since the late 17th century.

defender see PURSUER (VII).

dispone, disposition see MISSIVES (VII).

feu A holding of land which continued as long as the holder of the land, or *feuar*, paid rent to the landowner and implemented 'all *feuing* conditions' (1987). The rent, or *feu duty*, was a fixed annual payment: since 1974 land-holders, usually proprietors of houses, have been allowed to redeem the *feu* by a single payment. *Feu duties* are now rare, though mutual repair bills for a tenement may have to be shared in proportion to the amount of *feu duty* once payable by each householder. When first recorded in Scots in the 15th century, *feu* was paid in goods or money in place of the military service then owed by a vassal to his overlord. It is from Old French *feu*, a feudal holding, and is related to the English words *feudal, fee* and *fief.*

In the same feudal terminology, the landowner who has made the grant of land is often referred to as the **superior**, and the *feuar* is still sometimes known as the *vassal*. A **servitude** is a right over property allowed to the owner of another property: my neighbour may have 'a *servitude* for a drain' through my garden. It corresponds to English *easement*.

fire-raising is the Scottish legal term for arson, the crime of maliciously setting fire to property. In 1988 some inmates of a Scottish prison were charged with *fire-raising* during an outbreak of violence.

holograph has the same meaning as in English, but *holograph* documents are regarded differently in Scots law. A *holograph* deed does not require witnesses: it is in itself legally effective. A *holograph will* must be written and signed by the person concerned: if any part of it is not in his handwriting it is not a valid *holograph will*. A Covenant Form concluded: 'Please write these words, *Adopted as holograph*, in your own handwriting in the space below. No witnesses will then be required' (1986).

heritable in Scots legal use means connected with houses, lands and any rights pertaining to them. Thus *heritable property* means much the same as English *real property*. This meaning developed because under Scots law this form of property formerly passed to the heir when its owner died. All other property (e.g. personal belongings) is classed as **moveable** property: hence in a will drawn up in 1981 there is a reference to 'my whole means and estate, *heritable* and *moveable*.'

High Court see JUSTICIARY (VII).

indictment (*–dict–* is pronounced *dite*), a formal written charge against someone accused of a crime, is somewhat differently used in Scotland. It applies only in more serious cases in which the formal charge is brought in the name of the Lord ADVOCATE (VII), and which are to be tried before a jury in the High Court of JUSTICIARY (VII) or a SHERIFF (VII) Court. In 1988 one accused 'went to trial in the High Court on an *indictment* containing four charges.'

interdict corresponds to *injunction* in English legal use. It is a decree of court forbidding the performance of some intended act as being illegal or wrongful. An *interdict* ensures that the act cannot be proceeded with until the matter has been tried in court. In an emergency an *interim* (or provisional) *interdict* may be obtained at short notice; the onus is then on the party complained of to satisfy the legal authorities that his action is lawful. Early in 1988 'the Government obtained an *interim interdict* to prevent the *Scotsman* from publishing certain information contained in the private memoirs' of a former intelligence officer. The *interdict* banned the paper 'from publishing any fresh stories on the matter' (*Scotsman*). *Interdict* was first recorded in Scots as a noun in the 18th century. It is from a Latin word for to forbid.

Justiciary, (High Court of) The supreme criminal court of Scotland, now usually referred to as the **High Court**. *Justiciary* once meant the office of a *justiciar*, one of the supreme judges of Scotland in the 16th century. The president of the *Court of Justiciary* is now known as the *Lord Justice General*. *Justiciary* was first recorded in Scots in the 14th century. It came from medieval Latin.

law lords see LORD (VII)

lesion in Scots legal use means damage done to someone's interests. First recorded in Scots in this sense in the 16th century; from Middle English, and ultimately from a Latin verb for to hurt. In 16th century Scots *lesion* was also used for physical injury, and its modern use in general English for a morbid change in an organ of the body apparently developed from this Scots usage.

libel is often used by Scots in the general English sense of slander (cf. DEFAMATION, VII), but not so in Scots Law. In legal use a *libel* means an INDICTMENT (VII), a carefully drawn-up statement of the grounds on which a civil or criminal charge is based. A libel must set forth 'the particular facts inferring the guilt, and the particular place where these facts were done' (Gloag & Henderson *Introduction to the Law of Scotland 8th ed., 1980*). First recorded in this sense in the 15th century. Its legal use preserves in part the sense of Latin *libellus*, a little book, from which *libel* ultimately derives. It meant this too in 15th century Scots, and in the 16th and 17th centuries *libel* could mean a publication attacking the character of another person.

lockfast Shut and locked; fastened by a lock. To steal from a *lockfast* place is to aggravate the offence in the eyes of the law, and to let yourself in for severer punishment if caught. This was the fate of the man caught 'stealing hens from *lockfast* henhouses.' The *–fast* means fastened, secured.

lord is as in English a rank or title, but it appears in certain contexts or combinations, several of them legal, that are peculiar to Scotland.

Until 1707 a **Lord High Commissioner** represented the sovereign in the Scottish parliament. Now one is appointed annually to represent the Crown at the GENERAL ASSEMBLY (VIII) of the Church of Scotland.

The **Lord Advocate** (see ADVOCATE, VII) is the principal law officer of the Crown in Scotland. He is appointed by the government of the day, and acts as public prosecutor or pleads on behalf of the Crown.

A judge of the COURT OF SESSION (VII) is given the courtesy title of *lord* during his lifetime, and collectively these lords are known as the **law lords**. When sitting on a case in the Outer House of that court, a judge is known as the *Lord Ordinary*. The President of the Court of Session, the head of the Scottish judicature, is known as the *Lord President*.

Lord Lyon King of Arms is the title of the chief officer of arms, or herald, in Scotland: it is often shortened to *Lord Lyon*. Any person or organisation wanting to bear arms must first seek the approval of the *Lord Lyon* and the *Lyon Court* (of heralds). If he does not do so, he may be summoned before the Lyon Court and punished. The *Lord Lyon* has the responsibility for organising state pageantry in Scotland, and when a public proclamation has to be made on a state matter the *Lord Lyon* does so from the MERCAT CROSS (XIII) in Edinburgh. The first mention of the office in the Scottish records was in 1377. *Lyon* is the same word as *lion*, and the title of *Lord Lyon* probably came into being because of the use of the heraldic lion by the Scottish king in his coat of arms.

Lord Provost is the courtesy title given to the chairman of certain Scottish district councils, those of Edinburgh, Glasgow, Aberdeen, Dundee and Perth. Until 1975 a **provost** was the chief magistrate of a Scottish burgh and the chairman of its town council, but the reorganisation of Scottish local government in that year (see REGIONALISATION, VII) abolished the office except in the cases of the *Lord Provosts* mentioned above. The office of *provost* of a burgh was first mentioned in Scottish records in 1387. The attendant *lord* was first prefixed to the name of a *provost* of Edinburgh in 1487 because he happened to be already a nobleman. Later *provosts* there and elsewhere apparently assumed lordship for the duration of their provostship.

march see RIDING OF THE MARCHES (IX).

minor As in England, someone under the age of 18 (formerly 21), but in Scots law a lower age limit is also set – a male minor must be over 14, a female one over 12. Below these ages, a child is regarded as a **pupil**, one under the age of legal puberty. In everyday use a *pupil* is, as in English, a schoolchild.

missives Letters exchanged between parties to a proposed contract to agree upon its terms. Missives are binding, but may be followed by a formal legal document. In purchasing a house from its builders, the first step is for *missives* to be exchanged by the sellers and the purchaser's solicitors.

After the sale of a house the seller is required to sign a **disposition** – the deed by which a transfer of property is finalised. The Scots legal term for to convey property to another person is to **dispone**.

moveable see HERITABLE (VII).

not proven In a criminal trial in Scotland, this is a third verdict that may be returned by a jury. If they find that the prosecution has failed to prove the accused guilty beyond reasonable doubt, yet still suspect that he is not innocent, jurors may find the charge *not proven*. If they do so, the accused is then unconditionally discharged. This verdict has been acceptable under Scots law since the 18th century.

pertinent Any accessory or additional item joined to HERITABLE (VII) property (i.e. land or a house). *Pertinents* may be, for example, outhouses or other additions to the original property. Usually found in the plural, and nearly always linked with *parts* in *parts and pertinents*. In 1987 a flat was sold with 'the whole parts, privileges and *pertinents* effeiring (belonging) thereto.'

poind, pind   (both pronounced like *pinned*) To take possession of goods belonging to a debtor with a view to selling them if the debt is not settled. *Poinding* is carried out by Sheriff Officers after a SHERIFF (VII) has granted the creditor a warrant to sell. Until recently the warrant sale was held in the street outside the debtor's house, but it may now take place in an auction room. *Poind* has been in Scots since the 15th century. It is from an Old English word for to enclose, and is closely related to the *–pound* in *impound*.

precognition An examination of possible witnesses before a trial to discover what evidence they are likely to give. This may be conducted by both prosecution and defence when preparing their cases: defence lawyers may *take precognitions* (statements of intended evidence) from Crown witnesses. In a criminal case, a *precognition* is conducted by the PROCURATOR FISCAL (VII), who will then decide whether there is sufficient ground for a trial. When necessary, witnesses may be cited for *precognition* by a magistrate.

procurator fiscal A local offical (often called simply the *fiscal*) who acts in a Sheriff Court as prosecutor for the crown. He is appointed by the Lord Advocate, and it is his office to carry out the preliminary examination into suspected crimes and to decide whether to prosecute or not. In Scottish news bulletins there is almost daily mention of the fact that after a crime 'a report has been sent to the *procurator fiscal*' of the sheriffdom concerned. In the Middle Ages in several European countries a procurator was an important official with power to conduct financial, legal or other business. When the *procurator fiscal* first appeared in Scottish records in the 16th century he exercised all these powers. It was however his legal responsibility that proved most lasting, despite the fact that *fiscal* seemed to stress the financial aspects of his duties.

See also ADVOCATE (VII) and SHERIFF (VII).

provost see LORD (VII).

pupil see MINOR (VII).

pursuer The prosecutor in a civil action, the plaintiff. To prosecute is to *pursue*. If the Scots usage seems surprising, note that the *−sue* is from Old French *suir* (*suivre*, to follow), and that this in turn comes from the Latin verb for to follow which gives the *−secute* in *prosecute*. In Scotland the defendant in a civil action is known as the **defender**.

regionalisation Local government in Scotland was reorganised in 1975. Under *regionalisation*, as it was called, the old system based on BURGH (VII) and county was swept away, and Scotland was redivided for purposes of local government into 9 *regions* and three island areas. The *regions* were further subdivided into 53 *districts*. Each *region*, island area and *district* has its own elected council and each council had until 1988 the right to levy its own rates.

Register House in Edinburgh is so called because it houses what was once known as the *Register*. This was the name given from the 15th to the 19th centuries to the Scottish records – State papers and various classes of official documents. The official in charge of the records was in the 15th century also called the *Register*, and later the *Lord Clerk Register*. The latter title still exists, but the bearer is no longer in charge of the records. That duty now falls to the Keeper of the Records.

relevant, when said of a charge or claim, means that if the facts brought forward by the PURSUER (VII) or claimant can be proved, then the accusation made or the DECREE (VII) sought will be granted. If it is argued by the defence at the beginning of a trial that the indictment is *not relevant* (or *irrelevant*), the trial can not proceed until the 'defender's attack on the *relevancy* of the pursuer's case' (1988) has been rejected. This sense, first recorded in the early 16th century and still current in Scots law, introduced the word *relevant* to standard English. It was probably first made known in England by Scots in Parliament, then adopted and extended in use to its present meaning.

reset To receive goods knowing them to be stolen, usually with the intention of reselling them. Also, the act of receiving stolen goods. An unusual instance was reported in the *Scotsman* in 1986. Certain persons were accused of '*resetting* [tropical] fish in their home.' When police appeared at the front door, the *resetters* flushed the fish down the lavatory, a piece of quick thinking that did not save them from a £600 fine for *reset*. One can also *reset* a criminal or fugitive by giving him shelter and protecting him from pursuit – a meaning now rarely heard. *Reset* is from Old French: it was first recorded in Scots in the 14th century.

roup (pronounced *rowp*) To put up for public auction; a sale or let by public auction. In the past, when the usual method of providing public services was to invite contractors to undertake to perform them for profit, the right to do so was *rouped*, leased for a time to the highest bidder. Nowadays a *roup* is more commonly a sale of property, frequently that of a bankrupt whose belongings have been taken over, and are being sold, by the authorities. Other modern instances are the *rouping* of a catch of fish at the pier to the highest bidder, and (in 1986) 'A grand *roup* in aid of [the funds of a bowling club].' *Roup* has been recorded in this sense since the 16th century. Earlier than that it was used in Scots for to shout or to make known by shouting. Since auctions were announced by proclaiming them abroad, *roup* developed the special sense of a public auction. It is from an Old Norse word for to boast.

sasine , pronounced *sáy-zin*, is the act of giving possession of property held in FEU (VII) by recording the deed conveying the property in the General Register of Sasines in Edinburgh. In the past the act of *giving* and *taking sasine* was symbolic: for example, earth and stone from the land might be handed over by the seller to the person taking possession. A record was made of the ceremony and of the details of the transaction: this was then registered. *Sasine* was first recorded in Scots in the 14th century. It is from a Latin or Old French word from which the word *seize* also derives: one of the earlier meanings of *seize* was to give or take possession. The English legal term *seisin* has the same origin.

servitude see FEU (VII).

sheriff A legal officer whose chief duty is to act as a judge in one of the *sheriff courts* that exist in many of the larger Scottish towns. These courts deal with the bulk of legal business in Scotland. A *sheriff* may also perform certain administrative functions, and in some respects has replaced what used to be

known until 1971 as a *sheriff-subsititute*. In the Scottish records
of the 14th century a *sheriff* was the chief officer of a shire or
county, administering it on behalf of the king. Until the 18th
century the office was hereditary, and was held by a member
of a landed family. The *sheriff* was responsible for law and
order in his district. In legal matters he was assisted by a
lawyer called the *sheriff-depute*, who was the real ancestor of
the modern *sheriff*. For legal purposes Scotland is divided into
sheriffdoms. Each of these is under the jurisdiction of a
Sheriff Principal, who is its senior judge. In Scots the word
sheriff has often, into the present century, been given the
shortened form *sherra* or *shirra*.

solicitor has been used informally in Scotland since the 18th
century, but it is only in the 20th century that it has been
officially adopted throughout Scotland (though in Aberdeen
'solicitors' are called 'advocates'). The older name for a
solicitor was *writer*. The term is now obsolete, but is
preserved in the name *Writers to the Signet*, a society of
solicitors practising in Edinburgh. The letters W.S. after the
name of a solicitor or of a legal firm indicate membership of
that society. The *signet*, once one of the crown seals of
Scotland, became the official seal of the COURT OF SESSION
(VII), and at one time *writers to the signet* had the exclusive
right of preparing writs for that Court. All solicitors now
belong to the Law Society of Scotland. The *Solicitor General*
for Scotland is the next-ranking law officer to the Lord
Advocate (see LORD, VII), and is his deputy. The Solicitor
General and the Lord Advocate represent the Scottish legal
system in the government of the day.

superior see FEU (VII).

term, or **term-day**, in Scots is the same as *quarter-day* in
English. In England *term* is applied to a period of time. The
Scottish *terms* are the four days in the year on which such
payments as rents or settlements of accounts are due, and on
which certain contracts begin or conclude. The *term-days* are
Candlemas (2 February), Whitsunday (15 May), Lammas
(1 August) and Martinmas (11 November).

VIII
Education   Religion
The Supernatural

bejant A first year student at the University of St Andrews (where it was pronounced *bee–*), also until recently at the University of Aberdeen, where the form used was *bejan* or *bajan* (pronounced *bay–*). Now very rare: chiefly learned Scots. A female 'fresher' was known at St Andrews as a *bejantine*, at Aberdeen as a *bejanella*. *Bejan* is from French *bejaune* or *bec jaune*, a fledgling bird, a term used in some of the medieval universities on the continent for new and supposedly 'green' students.

bursary A scholarship. In 1988 a Scottish girl was awarded a bursary to enable her to study violin in Moscow or Leningrad for six months (Radio Scotland). Until the 1970s the nearest Scottish equivalent to English 'A' level exams was provided by the *Bursary Competition* (popularly known as the *Bursary Comp*). This was a competitive examination, and a separate 'competition' was run by each of the older Scottish Universities. A high place in the *Bursary Comp* was eagerly sought after: it brought a bursary at the University concerned to the successful pupil, and credit to the school he or she attended. First recorded in Scots in 1670 as *bussary*, though a century earlier there are references to the 'sustenatation of *bursars* within the University [of Glasgow]' (1569). Ultimately from the Latin word for a purse.

cantrip was originally a charm or spell, and was associated with magic, black or white. A witch was able to 'cast *cantraips*', and Burns described corpses enabled to hold up lighted candles 'by some devilish *cantraip* sleight (magic trick).' In 1901 a writer noted that *cantraips* were once used to cure minor troubles or illnesses. The word has survived, chiefly in literary Scots, in the weakened sense of a trick or antic. In 1987 a rugby correspondent wrote approvingly of 'the attractive *cantrips* of the Kelso midfield [players].' *Cantrip* was first recorded in Scots about 1600, in the sense of a harmful spell. It is of unknown origin.

college Long the usual Scots word for a university. The University of Edinburgh used to be known as 'the Toun's (town's) *College*'. One of the 'Scotticisms' proscribed in the 18th century was 'the Oxford *College*' for 'the University of Oxford'. Scots colloquial usage may still prefer 'going to the *College*' to 'attending the University'.

dean The *Dean* of a Faculty in one of the Scottish Universities is the head of that faculty. The *Dean of Faculty* is the president of the Faculty of Advocates (see ADVOCATE, VII) in Scotland.

deil Scots form of *devil*, also heard in northern English dialect. As in English, used for both people and fallen angels. 'The *deil*' plays a prominent part in Scots folklore, whether presiding over gatherings of witches, as in *Tam o' Shanter*, or making off with the wicked, as in 'The *Deil*'s awa wi the exciseman' – both products of the imagination of Robert Burns.

disruption The Disruption is the name given to the division caused in the established Church of Scotland in 1843, when more than one third of the ministers, followed by a like proportion of lay members, left the Church in protest against its submission to what they considered civil interference. A particular bone of contention was the right of certain lay patrons to appoint ministers to parishes. The dissidents set up the Free Church of Scotland (see WEE FREE, VIII). The breach was partially healed in 1900 when the majority of members of what was then known as the United Free Church formed a union with the Church of Scotland. As the name '*Disruption*' suggests, the split was a painful ordeal for those involved. It is nevertheless 'one of the great facts of the modern history of Scotland' (G.M. Trevelyan *English Social History* 1942).

dominie A schoolmaster. Occasional Scots. The word *dominie* looks back to a golden age when the school teacher was respected for his learning and devoted to his task. It is in common nostalgic use by those who write with feeling about the present state of Scottish education: 'The *dominie* has ceased to be the man of stature in his community that he once was' (quoted view of a politician, 1987). Scott's portrait of Dominie Sampson in *Guy Mannering* (1815) may give a truer picture of the past. First recorded in Scots in the 18th century. From the Latin word for a lord or master.

dux The pupil or student holding top place in a class or school. In St Andrews University in 1937 prizes were awarded to the *Dux* in Greek, the *Dux* in French, and so on. The *dux* of a school is the pupil whose record in the top class is judged to be outstanding. A uniquely Scots usage since the 18th century: from Latin *dux*, a leader.

eerie began as northern Middle English. It is now accepted as standard English, though the *Oxford English Dictionary* regarded it as 'properly Scots.' When first recorded in Scots in the 14th century it meant afraid or fearful: people could be '*hery*' of others, or could have *eerie* hearts. It was in the later sense of weird or uncanny that the word passed to English in the late 18th century.

elder in the sense of an *elder* of the kirk, a church *elder*, has had a special place in Scottish culture since a Catholic apologist, just after the Scottish Reformation, asked indignantly: 'Why invent ye in your kirk a new order of *elders*?' (1563). There are two kinds of elder in the Presbyterian Church, both ordained: one is a member of the ministry, or a *teaching elder*; the other is elected to take part in the government of the church, and is a *ruling elder* (it is to the latter that the word *elder* usually refers). Since 1966, both offices have been open to women.

eldritch Weird, uncanny. Now only literary Scots. Applied to certain classes of people ('*eldritch* hags') or to things (an '*eldritch* chant' or an '*eldritch* wind'). The witches in *Tam o' Shanter* when roused uttered 'mony an *eldritch* skreich and hollow' (1791). *Eldritch* may originally have been a compound word, made up of *elf* and *–rich*, a kingdom (cf. German *reich*). Of Old English origin.

fey Fated to die. Now virtually restricted to literary Scots. When it was first recorded in Scots in 1375 *fey* men were those who fell in battle. At a later date *fey* came to be used of those who by their behaviour – often, what seemed abnormally high spirits – suggested to observers that they were destined to an early death. *Fey* was also used of someone who had apparently some kind of contact with the supernatural world – a '*fey* body' was on the verge of being regarded as a witch. And perhaps because the foolish were sometimes thought to have more than ordinary human perception, a 'fool' was sometimes called *fey* as well as GLAIKIT (II). *Fey* was also known in Middle and Old English, and in modern times it is sometimes used by English speakers of someone who is thought of as unworldly, even fairy-like. It is of Old Norse origin.

General Assembly The highest court of the Church of Scotland (see also KIRK SESSION, PRESBYTERY and SYNOD, all VIII). The first *General Assembly* met soon after the Reformation of 1560. It now meets annually in Edinburgh in May. It is presided over by a MODERATOR (VIII), and the reigning sovereign is represented by a Lord High Commissioner (see LORD, VII), who is appointed for one particular Assembly. The *General Assembly* is attended by ministers and elders chosen as delegates from all over Scotland. Debates range over a wide variety of issues, many of them of social and national interest, as well as matters of church government.

General Council Each of the four older Scottish Universities has a *General Council*, which serves as a link between the academic staff of the University and its graduates, most of whom are corresponding members. It meets twice a year, and discusses matters of common interest. The Chancellor of a University is elected by its *General Council*.

glamour 'An elusive, mysteriously exciting and often illusory attraction that stirs the imagination and appeals to a taste for . . . the exotic.' Since this is the sense that has made *glamour* a favourite with publicists in the film industry, it is apt that the definition quoted comes from an American dictionary. But as first recorded in Scots *glamour* was a magic spell, and *glamorous* meant magic, supernatural.

It was the early popularity of Sir Walter Scott's narrative verse, in England as well as in Scotland, that introduced the word to standard English, probably through these words in *The Lay of the Last Minstrel* (1805): 'One short spell . . . had so much of *glamour*-might [that it] Could make a nutshell seem a golden barge.' In a note, Scott explained that *glamour* 'in the legends of Scots superstition, means the magic power of imposing on the eyesight of the spectators, so that the appearance of an object shall be totally different from the reality.' This power, Scott noted elsewhere, was 'a special attribute of the race of Gipsies'. Today few Scots are aware of the word's Scottish origin: it belongs now to general English.

Glamour has also been used in Scots as a verb, though rarely, and then only in learned or literary contexts. In April 1986 a letter-writer to *The Scotsman* complained that 'Mr Reagan has got our Prime Minister so *glamoured* and bewitched that she loses her common sense when she is dealing with him.' Since the words *glamour* and *grammar* now differ widely in sense, it may seem surprising that in its origins *glamour* was an altered form of *grammar*. *Grammar* is from the Old French *grammaire*, which meant not only grammar in its usual modern sense, but also learning in general, and more particularly knowledge of occult matters or magic. At one time English *grammar* had the same meanings, but in time it shed its associations with magic. *Glamour*, on the other hand, was restricted to senses relating to occult learning.

glebe The piece of land provided for the use of a parish MINISTER (VIII), usually along with a MANSE (VIII) to live in and a stipend to live on. See also TEIND (VIII).

Guid Book The Bible. First recorded in the 19th century: now in pious or occasional use. In 1955 it was noted that '*the Good Book*' had become a best seller.

Highers Common parlance for the Scottish Certificate of Education examinations, held annually in April and May at the end of the five-year secondary school course. Subjects on which papers are set are known as Higher English, Higher Maths, etc. Until 1961 it was possible to take subjects on the Lower Grade, but since then an alternative to the *Highers* has been the Ordinary Grade Certificate examinations, held at the same time of year, but at the end of the fourth year of secondary education. These are known as the *O Grades*. Earlier in the fifth year, schools hold **prelims** or tests in all subjects. Prospective *Highers* candidates must sit these, and unless they pass they may not be allowed to sit their *Highers*. It they 'get their *Highers*' they may be able to go on to some form of further education. *Highers* is short for Higher Leaving Certificate, a name often given to these examinations until 1961. In 1988 it was claimed that 'in contrast to its Southern rival, the A-level, the breadth of the *Highers* system with its five subjects had avoided the gap between the arts and sciences' (*Scotsman*).

high school The name given to, and in many cases retained by, the 'grammar' school in many towns in Scotland. The first Scottish *high school* was that of Edinburgh, founded in 1519, and described some years later as the 'Grammer scole of this burgh' (1579). Often shortened to the '*High*', as for example Kircaldy High or in Edinburgh the Royal High. Normally a *high school* offers a five-year course of secondary education, and a sixth year for further studies. Some schools have preferred the name *academy*, eg. Fraserburgh *Academy*. This does not indicate any difference in the kind of curriculum offered. Perth rejoices in a High School, an Academy and a Grammar School – all apparently of equal status.

kirk A church. General Scots, but unevenly used: it is heard more often in Presbyterian circles, perhaps because *the Kirk* is taken to refer only to the Church of Scotland, whereas *the Church* admits of a more ecumenical interpretation. *Kirking* is a ceremonial visit to a church by an official body – for example, by a newly elected local council. *Kirk* is the northern English and Scots form of southern English *church*.

kirk session The lowest of the four courts in a Presbyterian Church: see also PRESBYTERY, SYNOD and GENERAL ASSEMBLY (all VIII). As a court, it is responsible for the discipline of the congregation of the single church over which it has authority: it consists of the minister and ruling elders of that church (see ELDER, VIII). In the late 16th, 17th and 18th centuries the *kirk session* ruled with a rod of iron, 'fornicators' in particular being severely dealt with, but nowadays it wields its authority more gently. At one time the session was also largely responsible for education and for administering poor law relief in its parish. *Kirk sessions* were, a historian has written, 'in a very wide sense of the word, the local authority in their respective parishes' (1885).

learn Still heard in the sense of to teach, which is nowadays unacceptable in standard English. A boy, asked what the teacher of Speech and Drama did with his class, answered: 'She *learns* us to speak right.'

licence see PROBATIONER (VIII).

manse The house provided for a MINISTER (VIII), particularly a minister of the Church of Scotland, to live in with his family. Hence the frequently heard title *son* (or *daughter*) *of the manse* given to the child of a Presbyterian minister, and unfailingly mentioned in the press when one achieves any kind of eminence. One of the most famous Scots of the 20th century, John Buchan, was a *son of the manse.*

minister A clergyman, most commonly one of the parish ministers of the Church of Scotland: the *ministry* is the collective term for all its ministers, and also refers to the office of *minister.* It still sounds faintly odd to Scottish ears to hear a member of any government addressed deferentially as '*minister*' by an interviewer: the natural assumption is that a person so addressed is a member of the clergy.

Moderator Every year a MINISTER (VIII) is chosen to preside over the GENERAL ASSEMBLY (VIII) of the Church of Scotland as its *Moderator.* He holds that office for one year, at the end of which a successor is chosen. During that year the *Moderator* carries out certain official duties, and recently has even been known to visit the Vatican. His statements on matters of pubic interest are given some prominence, but he is not authorised to be an official spokesman. For the duration of his office, he is first among equals. From time to time there are meetings of local church courts of lesser status than the General Assembly. Each of these too is presided over by a chosen *moderator*: 'Even a parish minister is addressed as *Moderator*' when presiding at a meeting of his KIRK SESSION (VIII). In any of these circumstances to act as chairman is to *moderate.* First recorded in 1563. From the French *modérateur,* the president of a 'reformed' assembly.

ordinary In the older Scottish Universities in the 19th century a distinction was drawn between *ordinary* and honours courses in the faculties of Arts and Science. An *ordinary* course lasted for one year, and dealt with the subject of study in general terms; it provided a complete review of that subject. It could be supplemented by a *Second Ordinary* course, which examined certain aspects of the subject in some detail. At one time it was accepted that the *First Ordinary* class was taught by the professor of the subject – a custom that is no longer observed. Those who completed the *ordinary* courses in a subject with merit might seek admission to the honours courses, and might later graduate with honours. Those who did not gain such merits, or who preferred a general degree with passes in a wider range of subjects, spent one further year in other *ordinary* classes. If they had then obtained a sufficient number of passes, they were awarded an *ordinary degree*. In one, or both, of these applications, *ordinary* is still in use at the older Scottish universities; of the more recent ones, only Dundee awards an *ordinary* degree.

For *Ordinary Grade* see HIGHERS (VIII).

pape Scots form of *pope*. Also, a shortened form of *papist*, and as such often applied to members of the Roman Catholic church, usually in a less than friendly manner. Old antagonisms between Catholic and Protestant are less sharp than they were, but they die hard. One may find comfort from the story of the man who had offended a Catholic friend by insulting 'the *pape*.' He explained, 'I didnae ken (didn't know) the *pape* was a Catholic.'

paraphrase took on a special sense in Scotland from a book published in 1781 and entitled 'Translations and *Paraphrases* in verse, of several passages of Sacred Scripture.' In the Presbyterian churches, a *paraphrase* is a verse rendering of any passage from the Bible other than the psalms. *Paraphrases* are still sung at church services.

piskie A member of the Scottish Episcopal Church. This shortened form of *episcopalian* has been recorded since the end of the 19th century, and is often used by Episcopalians when speaking of themselves.

precentor An official appointed by a KIRK SESSION (VIII) to lead the singing of the congregation at Presbyterian church services. At the 1988 General Assembly of the Church of Scotland one hymn was sung 'unaccompanied and beautifully *precented.*' The provision of accompanying music has in most churches made the office obsolete, but in some parts of Scotland, particularly the remoter Highlands and Islands where some churches frown on instrumental music in church, *precentors* may still be heard. The precentor's office is to let the congregation know what psalm it is to sing next, to indicate the melody to be sung by singing it himself, and to keep the congregation together as a unit while they are singing. The resultant music is quite unfamiliar to Lowland ears, but it has a strange beauty of its own. First recorded in 1586. From Latin *praecentor*, a person who leads singing.

prelims see HIGHERS (VIII).

presbytery A church court, ranking in a Presbyterian Church above a KIRK SESSION and below a SYNOD (both VIII). For its membership a *presbytery* draws upon several churches, each of which contributes its minister and one ruling elder. The area in which these churches lie is also known as a *presbytery*, in this sense referring to the group of parishes in the designated area. The right of appeal from kirk session to *presbytery* forms part of the theme of Burns's *Holy Willie's Prayer*. The decision went against Holy Willie, who expresses his displeasure with the '*Presbyt'ry* of Ayr.'

Principal The title traditionally given to the academic head of a Scottish University. A Principal is appointed for life, or until he retires. While in office he is president of the **Senatus**, an academic body responsible for the curricula and discipline of the University. He also acts as Vice-Chancellor of the University.

probationer In the Scottish Presbyterian churches, a student MINISTER (VIII) who has, after examination, been granted licence (*Sc leeschence*) to preach by a PRESBYTERY (VIII), but has not yet been called (see CA, XV) to a charge as minister.

public school A school run by a local Education Authority – a sense now never heard and seen only on the walls of old school buildings. In *Who's Who* in the early 1980s the entry on a well-known Scot gave as his first school *Earlston Public School*. It is worth noting that, according to a writer in the *Third Statistical Account of Scotland*, 'to the Scots [a public school] is not (as quaintly it is south of the border) a private school' (1958).

rector has in Scotland two uses quite unconnected with the church. The first is rector of a university. The four older Scottish Universities – St Andrews, Glasgow, Aberdeen and Edinburgh – have had rectors since medieval times, when a rector was the elected head of a university. Since the 19th century, however, the rector has in these universities been elected by the students as their representative on the University Court, the governing body of the University. This he does by presiding over meetings of the Court, and putting to them the views of the student body. The *rector* must not be a member of the academic staff, and generally the students choose a prominent public figure as their representative. Some of these have seemed to outsiders unsuitable candidates, but in the event those chosen have usually worked hard to make a success of their three year term as rector. *Rector* is also the title enjoyed by the headmasters of some Scottish high schools or academies. When in 1960 Ellon Secondary School changed its name to Ellon Academy, it was agreed that in future its headmaster should be known as *Rector*.

Senatus see PRINCIPAL (VIII).

synod A Presbyterian Church court, ranking between a PRESBYTERY and a GENERAL ASSEMBLY (both VIII). A *synod* exercises power over a 'province', which includes a number of presbyteries. Membership consists of ministers and ruling elders from these presbyteries, and also representatives from neighbouring *synods*.

teind A standard levy on landowners, payable to the Church of Scotland, and used to help pay the stipend of the

MINISTER (VIII) of the parish in which the owner's lands are situated. In the *Third Statistical Account of Scotland* it is recorded that in 1962 the stipend of one minister amounted to £600, plus a GLEBE (VIII) rent of £16. Of this, £548 were raised by *teind*. Nowadays 'the Church is almost totally supported by voluntary contributions' (J.G. Kellas *The Scottish Political System* Cambridge University Press 1975). *Teind* is the older Scots word for a tenth part, and corresponds to English *tithe*. *Teind*, like *tithe*, once meant the tenth part of the produce of the land which was levied for the support of religion.

uncanny see CANNY (II).

unco guid, the Those who are over-conscious of their own virtue, and correspondingly disdainful of the shortcomings of others. Occasional Scots. Certain modern developments, such as Sunday golf, may cause 'vexation to the *unco guid*.' One of the first to use the phrase was Robert Burns, who in 1787 wrote a satirical 'Address to *the Unco Guid*.' See also UNCO (XIV).

warlock Though occasionally used of a witch, *warlock* is generally taken to mean the male equivalent of a witch, a man who has entered into some kind of compact with the Devil. The 'hellish legion' stumbled upon by Tam o'Shanter included both '*warlocks* and witches' (1791). At present, *warlocks* seem to be rather thin on the ground.

Wee Free After the DISRUPTION (VIII) in 1843, the Free Church of Scotland split from the established Church of Scotland. A partial reunion came about in 1900, but a minority of members of the Free Church rejected the union, and continued to call themselves the Free Church of Scotland. This church, which has remained particularly strong in the Highlands and in most of the Western Isles, is known to outsiders as the '*Wee Frees*'. The name reflects not only the comparatively small number of its adherents, but also the suspicion held by many that 'this church tends to be narrow, doctrinaire and puritanical in its view' (*Scottish National Dictionary*, in 1965). A '*Wee Free*' is a member or adherent of this church.

weird Fate, destiny. Not often heard nowadays, though you may still be told that you have to 'dree your *weird*', put up with your lot (see DREE, XV). The word has however won a place in the standard English vocabulary in rather curious circumstances. The Fates, the three classical goddesses who presided over men's destinies, were known in older Scots as the *weirds*, or *weird sisters*. From the 15th century on Scots writers repeated a legend that the Fates, or *weird sisters*, had appeared to Macbeth to lure him to his fate. The story was taken over by Holinshed, the English chronicler to whom Shakespeare went for the plot of *Macbeth*. Later, people came to believe that the *weird* in the *weird sisters* in *Macbeth* meant supernatural or uncanny. This misunderstanding gave *weird* its main modern meaning in English. *Weird* was first recorded in Scots in 1375. It is from the Old English word for fate.

Riding of the Marches (IX)

scoor-oot (IX)

Uphellya (IX)

IX
Festivals   Local Customs
Music and Dance

Beltane The 1st or 3rd of May; once a Celtic fire-festival. The second of these dates seems to have been the choice of the pre-Reformation Church; *Beltane* could then be identified with a Christian feast-day instead of a pagan one. In Druid times *Beltane* was celebrated by lighting fires on hill-tops; and in Ayr in 1792 it was still the custom to kindle fires on the high grounds in honour of *Beltoun*.' Young people who go out early to see the sun rise on the first of May are carrying on another ancient custom in honour of *Beltane*, especially if the girls in the party wash in the May dew. But belief in its efficacy is dead, and Beltane survives only as a relic of the past. Thus in Peebles the RIDING OF THE MARCHES (IX), though it takes place in June, is also the *Beltane Festival*; a *Beltane Queen* is elected, and a Beltane Festal Song is sung. *Beltane* is fom the Gaelic word for May-day.

Burns night 25th January, the anniversary of the birth of Robert Burns (1759–96), Scotland's national poet and her lay patron saint. Scots honour Shakespeare, but they love Burns. Hundreds of *Burns Suppers*, many of them organised by *Burns Clubs*, are held annually in honour of Burns in every country in which Scots can congregate in force.

Burns suppers follow a fairly set pattern. When the guests have assembled, a HAGGIS (IV) is 'played in' by a piper and placed on the top table. It is there apostrophised in the words of Burns's 'Address to the Haggis', at the end of which the reciter is offered a glass of whisky. Supper follows, the main course traditionally being haggis. After the meal the **Immortal Memory** of Robert Burns is proposed, usually by a specially invited speaker. Most speakers try to bring out one aspect of the life or work of Burns; humour is encouraged, but not levity. There may then be other toasts, of which the commonest is 'To the lasses'. Thereafter there are recitations of poems and renderings of songs from the works of Burns. At the end of the evening 'Auld Lang Syne' is sung before the guests disperse.

In its annual publication, *The Burns Chronicle*, for 1986, The Burns Federation (formed in Kilmarnock in 1885) lists 1057 Burns Clubs or Scottish Associations affiliated to the Federation. Many other organisations, including schools, hold Burns Suppers. And one should not forget the respect accorded to Burns in the USSR. At least one Burns Supper is held every year in the Soviet Union, and the Soviets issued a stamp to commemorate the bicentenary of the poet's birth.

ceilidh (pronounced *kayly*) A combination of a friendly gathering and a semi-informal concert. A Gaelic word, it originally meant a meeting of neighbours in someone's home for mutual entertainment through conversation, music (especially singing) and story-telling. To some extent this meaning survives in Scots: after a folk concert both performers and audience may proceed to someone's house to hold a *ceilidh* there before dispersing. *Ceilidh* is also applied to a concert in which the appearance of informality is retained as far as possible. Some performers are there by invitation but others from the 'audience' may be given an opportunity to perform. Drinks may be available, and those present sit around in a relaxed manner. There is also the *ceilidh-dance* at which the music is interspersed with, or concluded by, dancing; the dance music may be provided by a *ceilidh band*, consisting usually of stringed instruments, especially fiddles, and perhaps an accordion. One reason for the present popularity of *ceilidh* is the increased interest taken by Scots Lowlanders in Gaelic culture and language in the last thirty years. Another is the prominence given to *'ceilidhs'* in folk song gatherings in Scotland.

chanter The part of the bagpipe on which the melody is played. It is a small straight pipe with holes for fingering, a wood instrument supplied with a double reed. There is also a practice chanter, a separate instrument with a weaker reed, for practising fingering, and for beginners to learn to play a melody before progressing to the bagpipe proper, perhaps by way of the GOOSE (IX), or practice bagpipe.

clarsach The old Celtic or Highland harp, strung with wire. In 1941 the *Scottish National Dictionary* wrote a premature obituary of the *clarsach*: 'now rare, with the disappearance of the instrument from ordinary use.' Since then there has been a revival, encouraged by the Clarsach Society, and one modern folk group included in its repertoire a duet between a bagpipe and a *clarsach* (the latter assisted by amplification). *Clarsach* is from the Gaelic word for a harp, and it occurs frequently in old Scots records.

Common Riding SEE RIDING OF THE MARCHES (IX).

diddle To sing, usually in rather a low key, and with sounds rather than words. Consequently *diddling* has a more positive rhythm than humming. In 1917 it was claimed that 'a mother's *diddlin'* till (to) her bairn (child)' can bring it sleep. *Diddling* is probably best known as mouth-music to accompany dancers, and someone who specialises in diddling is a *diddler*. Perhaps thanks to the folk song revival *diddling* has come to be held in renewed esteem, and *diddling* contests have a place in many local festivals. This may also have brought *diddle* back into English usage, from which it had apparently been lost early in the 18th century. In origin, *diddle* is probably from one sound commonly made by a *diddler*, as in 'Hey diddle diddle'.

eightsome Performed by an organised group of eight people, as in *Eightsome Reel*, the dance so performed – 'Are

you going to do *the eightsome?*' (general Scots, 1986). The
word is otherwise almost unused, even in Scots. *Eightsome* is
first found in a dancing context in 1745, when the *Atholl and
Tullibardine Family Chronicle* recorded the performance of an
'*eightsome* minuet'. This does not sound like the vigorous
dance that has achieved such popularity in the present
century. See also REEL and FOURSOME (both IX).

Fair, the The right to hold a fair every July was granted to
Glasgow by King William the Lion in the 12th century. But
in modern times *the Fair*, or **Glasgow Fair**, or *Fair Fortnight*
is the name given to the last fortnight of July viewed as the
annual holiday period for the working people of Glasgow.
The first Monday of the fortnight is known as *Fair Monday*,
and is a public holiday in Glasgow. In the heyday of *the Fair*,
Glaswegians in their thousands spread over the resorts of
Scotland, east and north Ireland, north England and the Isle
of Man with one aim – to enjoy themselves. Fife too has a
Fair Fortnight, in the same weeks as Glasgow. In Edinburgh
the annual fortnight's holiday is known, and perhaps
celebrated, more soberly as the **Trades Holiday(s)** – the
singular form is a reminder that this holiday was once the
single day off work allowed to the craftsmen of the town.

first-foot, Sc first-fit Your *first-foot* (or *first-footer*) is the first
person to cross your threshold on the first of January to wish
you a happy New Year. An intending first-foot should be
able to hand over some small gift, and ideally should be a
man with dark hair if he is to be a good omen for the coming
year. A century ago a 'fair-haired, flat-fitted (flat-footed)'
man was described as an '*unlucky first-fit*'. In 1986 a hospitable
schoolboy essayist wrote, 'When New Year came around, I
would like *first-footers* to come to my house, and let them
have as much food and drink as they wanted.' *To first-fit*
someone is either to fulfil the role just described or, more
loosely, to visit a friend for the first time early in the New
Year. *To go first-footing* is to set out on a round of such visits,
expecting a warm welcome from your hosts whether you are
their *first-foot* or not. Much or all of the night may be spent

on such visits, and will involve an exchange of greetings and drinks between host and visitor. The latter will produce a 'bottle' carried specially for the occasion, offer his host a drink from it, then regain the bottle to take it on to the next port of call. In its earliest use, a *first-fit* was the first person met on any outing, but more particularly the first person met by a group on their way to the church for a wedding or christening. See also FIT (I).

fling A dance; in modern use heard only in **Highland fling**. This is a solo dance, though often performed by several dancers simultaneously, and it is a favourite exhibition piece with both very young learners and regimental dancers at tattoos. It is danced in STRATHSPEY (IX) rhythm, that is rather more slowly than a reel, and the dancer remains on the one spot throughout. In the earliest reference to 'a fling' in 1715, it was danced by a group, and probably meant no more than a lively dance, perhaps done in the Highland manner. In 1868 an alarmed observer of Highland dancing confessed, 'The worst thing to me was the kicking and *flinging* at Highland reels.' And indeed an earlier and obsolete meaning of to *fling*, in both Scots and English, was to kick sharply backwards, like a horse or other animal. Only in Scots was the meaning extended to dancing: in other respects *fling* has much the same meanings in Scotland and England.

foursome A party of four people organised for some particular activity. A *foursome reel* is a dance, more difficult to perform and therefore less widely popular than an EIGHTSOME (IX; see also REEL, IX). We find a reference to 'foursome reels' as early as 1792, in Burns. The dance may also be called *a foursome*. If the word is better known than *eightsome*, this is because it is also a golfing term, and so has achieved international status. In golf a *foursome* is a match involving four players, two on either side, each player playing his own ball to try to win the hole for his team. In 1921 there is mention of a 'Scotch foursome', in which 'two players have one ball against the other two players, and strike it in turn.' It can also be used more generally, as when in 1952 a plea was sent to a friend, 'Wad ye come roun (round) . . . and mak up a *fowersome* at whist?' At one time the word *–some* could be added to any number in English to give the same sense of 'a group of –'; but in modern times it has been rarely done except in Scots.

gathering A call to assemble. In 1785 a notice announced that '*the Camerons' Gathering*, to be played by John McGregor' would be one of the items at a concert. In this sense, *gathering* is a translation of the Gaelic word for a signal, sounded by drums or PIPES (IX), to assemble a clan for war. A *gathering* is a recognised form of PIBROCH (IX), the classical music of the pipes. A gathering is also an assembly devoted to games or other contests. A *Highland Gathering* is much the same as *Highland Games* (see GAMES, X), and presents the same diet of athletic, dancing and piping contests. The first recorded was the 'Athole Gathering or Highland meeting' of 1828, but the most famous is the Braemar Gathering. In 1850 Queen Victoria noted that 'We . . . went to the *Gathering* at the Castle of Braemar'. But Marian McNeill in *The Silver Bough* does well to remind us of the numerous 'smaller gatherings in the villages, glens and islands . . . [which] preserve . . . a close community spirit' somehow lost at the larger events.

Glasgow Fair see FAIR, THE (IX).

goose A practice bagpipe, consisting of a small sheepskin bag to which a CHANTER (IX), but no 'drones', is fitted. It allows the learner to progress without undue expenditure of breath by squeezing air out of the *goose* with his upper arm. The name was chosen because the instrument was seen to resemble a goose in flight, and was even humorously portrayed as such in Glen's *Bagpipe Tutor* (about 1860).

guiser A masquerader. The term is very much alive in Shetland, when for the festival of UPHELLYA (IX) large numbers of the population of Lerwick dress up to take part in the torchlight procession. This '*guizing*' is so important a part of the proceedings that the master of ceremonies, once known as the Worthy Chief *Guiser*, is now known as the *Guiser Jarl* (leader). At Comrie in Perthshire on Hogmanay *guisers*, both old and young, dress up in fanciful costumes and there is a torchlight parade at midnight.

But these are special cases: nowadays '*the guisers*' are usually children who dress up and go from door to door, chiefly at HALLOWEEN (IX), offering brief entertainment in return for some money or a gift. One appeal is 'Please to help the *guisers*', but the verses beginning, 'Please put a penny in the old man's hat' were often sung, usually with more speed than melody. The '*guizin* tyme of year' (1884) used also to include Christmas and Hogmanay. *Guisers* must have been known in the north of England, for *guizard* or *guiser* appears in a glossary of Northumberland words published in 1893. The word is derived from French *guise*, a way or manner.

Halloween Short for Allhallow Even, the eve of the feast of All Saints, or the 31st October. But the traditions connected with the occasion have little to do with Christian beliefs. They rather have their origin in the belief that on this day, in the old Celtic calendar the last day of the year, witches and the powers of evil came out into the open at night and held celebrations of their own. In ancient times an attempt was made to counter these manifestations of evil by lighting bonfires on the tops of hills. This custom has with modifications been maintained till the present, though its origin has been forgotten. Yet Marian McNeill recalls in *The Silver Bough* that 'in Aberdeenshire up to our own time the formula used by the lads who went about collecting fuel for their Halloween bonfire was, 'Gie's a peat to burn the witches.'

Halloween has long been an occasion for entertainment of and by children. In 1808 it was 'young people' who kindled fires, and in 1898 a writer noted that in Ayr 'the wee callans (fellows) were ... rinnin' aboot (running about) wi' their fause-faces (masks) on and their bits of turnip lanthrons (lanterns) in their haun (hand).' The masks were part of the disguise adopted by the GUISERS (IX), who went about performing for money or gifts. Children dressed up as guisers still go out, though nowadays perhaps more in hope than expectation. Halloween, like other festivals, is not what it was. In pre-Christian times *Halloween*, looking forward as it did to a new year, was a favourite occasion for trying to foresee the future, sometimes making use of products of the last harvest, especially hazelnuts and apples. These attempts involved rituals, some of which survived well into the Christian era. Traces of a superstitious belief in the virtue of the apple as a clue to the future are to be found in certain games still played at Halloween parties. Trying to pick an apple out of a tub of water with one's teeth, or *dooking for aipples* (see DOOK, XV), and trying to bite a piece out of an apple suspended from a string, are genuine if seemingly unlikely relics of rites once fearfully performed at Halloween.

Highland fling see FLING (IX).

Highland schottishe A kind of polka done in imitation of the Scottish manner of dancing, and so called in German *der schottische Tanz* (the Scottish dance). In the 19th century it was brought to Scotland, and when danced to modified STRATHSPREY (IX) music it became, and remained, very popular. In 1875 Queen Victoria remarked that it was 'much liked' at a ball. The German *schottische* has been retained, but the ordinary Scottish dancer pronounces it 'scoteesh'.

Hogmanay New Year's Eve, traditionally an occasion of celebration and hospitality in both family and the wider community, and spilling over into the festivities marking the arrival of the New Year and the rituals of first-footing (visiting friends on New Year's Day: see FIRST-FOOT, IX). Also, in earlier days, a New Year gift itself, and a New Year song or cry.

In its first recorded appearance in Scots, in 1604, *hagmonay* was a plea for a gift, and the idea of giving has remained central to Hogmanay. Until recently, older people in St Andrews could recall children going around the town on Hogmanay singing, 'My feet's cauld, my shune's thin, Gie's (give me) my cakes and let me rin.' Similarly remembered elsewhere are the verses, 'Rise up goodwife and shake your feathers, Dinna think that we are beggars, We're only children come to play, Rise up and gie's our Hogmanay' (1950). On the adult level, a Hogmanay visitor might be offered a drink, and very likely shortbread, cake or BLACK BUN (IV). After the New Year had been 'brought in', either at home or at some recognised place of outdoor assembly (in Edinburgh, outside the Tron Church in the High Street), the more dedicated revellers would set out to first-foot friends.

The word *Hogmanay* is almost certainly a product of the auld alliance (see AULD, XV) between Scotland and France – perhaps a popular borrowing from the French in Scotland during the 16th century. Difficulty in recognizing and writing down French sounds may in part account for the fact that there are twenty-two different recorded spellings of *Hogmanay* in Scots. The word was also well-known in some northern counties of England, probably through Scots influence. One nineteenth century folklorist claimed that 'Hagmena songs were formerly sung throughout England, Scotland and France'. In 1790 a correspondent to *The Gentleman's Magazine* sought further information about the cry of 'Hagman heigh' raised at the end of some 'balderdash verses sung on New Year's Eve' in Yorkshire, and the custom of giving a New Year's Eve present 'called an Hagmenay'. One reply told how in Scotland the last night of the old year was 'peculiarly called Hagmenai': people would gather in one house until 'the clock struck twelve, when they rose and, mutually kissing each other, wished each other a happy new year'. But it was Scots emigration that gave the word its wider modern currency; thus in 1897 there appeared an advertisement for 'a grand *Hogmanay* concert for the special benefit of patriotic Scots in London', and in 1986 British Rail urged patrons to spend '*Hogmanay* North of the Border'.

In Scotland the last few decades have seen a steady erosion of the traditional customs. In 1953 a contributor to the *Third Statistical Account of Scotland* commented that 'Hogmanay is much quieter than heretofore, and first-footing is more honoured in the breach than the observance. On the other hand', he adds significantly, 'Christmas Day is now observed by all.' Seasonal visitors to Scotland nowadays may well find that households prefer to gather round a television set, watching a Hogmanay party organised in a fashionable hotel or remote studio. *Hogmanay* is ultimately connected with an Old French word *aguilanleu*, in etymologies more often quoted in the later form *aguillanneuf*, perhaps because the latter apparently contains identifiable elements in *an neuf* (new year). The Scots form may derive from a north French dialect form *hoganine*.

Immortal Memory see BURNS NIGHT (IX).

jiggin *The jiggin*, or *the jigging*, is an evening's dancing or (in Scots, more correctly) 'the dancin(g).' Both are colloquial Scots, and THE (XIV) is all-important. 'To go out dancing' is English: 'to go to *the dancin*' is Scots, and so is to go to *the jiggin*.

kirn A 'harvest home', a celebration to mark the end of the harvest. The same name, *kirn*, was given to the last sheaf of corn to be cut in the harvest: this was often done in a ceremonial way, and the sheaf was then ornamented with ribbons and prominently displayed in the farm till the next harvest. Frequently it was twisted into a human shape and clothes were put on it; in some places it was then called a *kirn-dolly*. In Marian McNeill's *Silver Bough* there is a photograph taken in East Lothian of 'a *kirn-dolly* astride a corn-rick' (1956). Changes in country life have made the traditional *kirn*, with spontaneous feasting and dancing, a thing of the past. In 1960 the *kirn-supper* was still held in Ulster, but a notice from south-west Scotland in 1956 advertising a 'Harvest *Kirn* with the Solway Band' seems more in key with the times. In some shops in December 1986 *corn-dollies* were on display in the windows. *Kirn* is in fact related to *corn* and also to *kernel*, and was also found in the north of England.

lament A piece of music for the Highland bagpipes, to

commemorate someone deceased. At first, it meant a sung elegy. In 1698 when mourning a death the inhabitants of St Kilda were observed to make 'doleful songs which they call *laments*'. These songs contained a panegyric of the person being buried. In time *lament* came to be applied to the music only, this being played on the pipes. Now at a military funeral or at a public commemoration of the dead, a piper or pipe band will play a *lament*, frequently *The Flowers of the Forest*.

Lammas is 1st August, one of the Scottish TERMS (VII). This is why the name has survived in Scotland, whereas in England where it was once common it is preserved only as a fossil. *Lammas* was sometimes wrongly spelt *lambmas*, due to a not unnatural assumption that the first element was derived from *lamb*. In fact, it is from the old English word *hlaf*, which means a loaf, and *lammas* was *hlaf-maesse* (loaf mass), a harvest festival. On *Lammas* a loaf, as a symbol of the whole harvest, was blessed in church. There is still an annual *Lammas Fair* held in St Andrews. It draws large numbers of visitors, but few of them are aware that they are attending a festival intended to celebrate the harvest.

mod An annual festival of Gaelic culture. The first *National Mod* was organised in Oban in 1892 by An Comunn Gaidhealach (The Highland Society), on the model of the Welsh Eisteddfod. Its aim was to encourage Gaelic language, literature and music. It has now not only become an annual event, but has also led to the holding of provincial *mods*, organised locally in various centres.

The National Mod is held in a different centre each year, and not only in the Highlands. It lasts for several days, and the most important events are competitions in singing, music and dancing. Prizes are given to the best performers in different events, and the Gold Medal for adult solo singing is a coveted award. Much of the singing is choral, and choirs travel to the Mod, not only from all parts of Scotland, but also from Scots communities overseas, and sometimes even from south of the border. In 1988 the first Gaelic *Mod* in the

United States was held in Alexandria, Virginia. *Mod* is from the Gaelic word *mod*, meaning originally a court or assembly.

moothie A mouth organ. Early in 1987 a programme on Radio Scotland dealt with music played on the accordeon, the squeeze-box (concertina) and the '*mouthie* or harmonica'. From *mooth*, the Scots form of *mouth*.

Ne'er day or **Neer's day** A Scots form of New Year's day. Much used in the papers around the turn of the year, especially in references to the *Neer's day* football matches, the Scots equivalent of the English Boxing Day matches. To give someone his *Ne'erday* is to give him a New Year drink or present. Similarly, 'What are ye gettin fur yer Christmas?' refers to your Christmas present or presents.

pibroch Classical music of the Highland bagpipe. A *pibroch* consists of a musical theme (known as a *ground*) proposed at the outset, followed by a number of variations; the piece closes with a restatement of the theme. *Pibroch* is best known from music of the GATHERING (IX) or of the LAMENT (IX) types. Scott's poem, *Pibroch of Donuil Dhu*, sets words to a traditional 'gathering', which is said to have been first played at the battle of Inverlochy (about 1430). The word *pipe* was borrowed into Gaelic as *piob*, and *piobaireachd* is the Gaelic for piping. *Pibroch* (prounced *pea–*; the second syllable rhymes with *loch*) is Scott's attempt to make this somewhat forbidding-looking Gaelic word appear easier to English speakers.

pipes The Scottish bagpipe. Used in the singular only in compound words. General Scots. The Scottish, or Highland, bagpipe consists of a bag, a CHANTER (IX), three drones (Northumberland pipes have only two) and a blow-pipe. The third drone was added about three hundred years ago, and it gives the Highland pipes a much fuller sound. The addition was probably made because the *pipes* were essentially an outdoor instrument, and were carried into battle with a clan when at feud or war. The most typical music of the *pipes* (see PIBROCH, IX) grew out of battle situations, and it was this association that led to the banning of the pipes after the battle of Culloden in 1746.

Pipe for an instrument appeared very early in Scots, but it is not until 1592 that we find a reference to the 'great pipe', presumably the Highland pipes; in Elgin a piper was in trouble for playing his 'great pipe' at night. It is difficult to say precisely when the plural form became normal. In 1657 a letter-writter spoke of being ready 'to tune up [his] pipes.' Examples are often ambiguous, as in 'the pipes of the Prince's army' (1746).

Pipes and drums refers to a *pipe-band*, in which pipers and drummers, under the direction of a *pipe-major*, but led by a drum-major, play together. Pipe-bands, and so *pipe-music*, have been taken to every part of the world visited by Scottish regiments or settled in by Scottish emigrants. In 1955 one of the features of the celebrations of Pakistan's Independence Day in a small hill-town was the playing of 'Bonny Dundee' by a Pakistan Army Pipe Band. It sounded very well in the appropriate mountain setting.

rant A lively tune or song, especially one suitable for dancing; consequently, *rant* is common in the names of dance tunes (the Cameronian *Rant*; Struan Robertson's *Rant*, etc.). A *rant* is also a lively party with music and dancing, a sense that is now preserved only in the north-east. The same word as standard English *rant*, to talk in a noisy, disconnected, often complaining manner.

reel A lively traditional Scottish dance, or the music to which it is danced. A *reel* is a dance involving several dancers who follow interlacing patterns as they pass back and forward between or around the other dancers. In an early 16th century poem dancers are described as doing exactly this in the words 'athir (each) thro other *reland* (reeling).' At one time apparently a reel usually involved three dancers, but the *threesome reel* is no longer danced, though some of its features may still be seen in the popular *Dashing White Sergeant*. The classic, and most intricate, reel is the *Foursome Reel*, also once known as the *Scotch* or *Highland Reel*. It combines both fast and slow steps. *Reel* may be the same word as a *reel* of cotton; perhaps the whirling movement of the reel when winding yarn suggested the movements of those dancing a reel.

See also EIGHTSOME, FOURSOME (both IX).

Riding of the Marches, Common Riding Alternative names for the ceremonial inspection of the traditional boundaries of the common lands of a community – an ancient custom revived in the 19th century, and still observed annually in a number of Scottish towns, most of them in the BORDERS (XI). Originally, such an inspection was a necessity, to ensure that all boundary marks were intact, and that there had been no encroachments on the common land. Each 'riding' is now the occasion of a local festival, and is carried out by a cavalcade led by a 'cornet' or standard-bearer – whichever title is observed locally – chosen from among the young men of the town. These 'ridings' are weekly events in the Borders from June to August, and the accompanying festivals continue for much or all of the following week, dominating the life of the town for that period. The season begins with the Hawick *Common Riding*, and then moves on from one town to another. Lauder among other places prefers the title *Riding of the Marches*: so does Linlithgow, the most northerly venue.

March is an older Scots and English word for a border or frontier. At one stage it referred specifically to the Scottish-English border: a 16th century English chronicler mentions 'the lord warden of the east marches, and governor of Berwike' (1577). The word came from Middle English, and goes back to a Latin original. It is still often used for a boundary in Scottish legal documents. *Riding* is I believe a relatively late development. It represents the word *ridding* or *redding* (see REDD, XV), here meaning settling with precision the correct boundaries of a piece of land. At one stage *rid* was a variant form of *ride*, so that when horses became an essential part of the ceremonial, it was easy to change *ridding* to *riding*. In Lanark the *Riding of the Marches* takes place on *Lanimer Day*. *Lanimer* is derived directly from two Old English words, *land* and *gemaere*, meaning land boundaries.

scoor-oot The custom, now less observed than formerly, of scattering coins at or after a wedding to be scrambled for by children. Also shortened to *scoorie*: in 1952 there was 'a *skoorie* of coppers thrown amongst [the children] by the best man before the wedding actually took place'. In 1964 a mother commented ruefully, 'It'll no be the first time he'll have lost the knees oot 'is BREEKS (trousers) at a *scoor-out*'. Both examples come from Fife. *Scoor* corresponds to English *scour*, but is here used in the sense of to scatter, to throw in all directions. In other parts of Scotland *scatter*, *scramble* and *poor-oot* may be used in the same sense. In 1967 an Edinburgh church magazine commented that 'the increasing volume of traffic today makes the traditional *poor-oot* or *scatter* a hair-raising experience.'

strathspey is short for *Strathspey reel*, a kind of dance similar to a reel but performed at a slower tempo and with slightly different steps. *Strathspey music* is best played on the fiddle; its rhythm is distinctive because of the varying pattern of short and longer notes (e.g. semi-quavers and dotted quavers), and the thrust or BIRL (VI) given to the bow on certain strokes. When alternating with pieces in faster reel time, the strathspey provides a pleasing contrast. In 1749 the dancing of a '*strathspey reel*' was recorded for the first time. About twenty years later an English visitor described 'a kind of quick minuet, or what the Scots call a *straspae*'. The dance is named after Strathspey in Morayshire, where it may have originated.

sword dance A traditional Highland dance, usually performed solo. Two swords are laid crosswise on the ground, and the dancer must dance above them without letting his feet touch either. In 1844 a performance of the dance was witnessed by the King of Saxony: it had, he thought, 'something savage, but at the same time natural and primitive in its character'.

Trades Holiday(s) see FAIR, THE (IX).

Uphellya A festival held at Lerwick in Shetland on the last Tuesday of January. It is a survival of the fire festival anciently held to honour the sun at the time of the winter solstice, and to mark the end of the celebrations of Yule. Until about a hundred years ago the occasion was marked only by the lighting of large bonfires, but since 1882 it has been organised by an *Uphellya* committee presided over by an elected official known as the Guizer Jarl (chief masker; see GUISER, IX). The culmination of the modern event is a torchlight procession of maskers in Viking costume through the streets, accompanied by bands and headed by a newly-constructed Viking ship. At the conclusion of the march the torches are hurled into the ship, which is soon consumed by fire. 'In this way', wrote Marian McNeill in 1968, 'the spirit of *Up-Helly-Aa*, which is basically a sense of pride in Shetland's Norse heritage, is passed on to succeeding generations.' In 1884 '*Uphelya*' was explained as 'the 24th day after Yule, and that on which the holidays are supposed to be *up* (i.e. finished).' If the final syllable represents *a* (all), we can break the word down into three elements – *up, holy* and *all*. In 1774 the festival was referred to as *Uphaliday*, which by altering the last element links the Shetland name to the Lowland Scots *Up-halie-day*, the name formerly given to the feast of the Epiphany, the Twelfth Night or end of the Christmas festival. *Uphelli nicht* was the eve of the Epiphany, and in the middle of the 19th century it was believed by some in Morayshire that 'a woman could cease to be a witch by saying the Lord's Prayer every night from *Hallowe'en* to *Uphellie-night*.'

tossing the caber (X)

shinty (X) **gird and cleek** (X)

guddling for trout (X)

X

Sports and Games

ba, baw Ball. In words endng in *-all*, the *-ll* is eliminated in Colloquial Scots; hence *fa* for *fall*, *a* for *all*, and so on. Football becomes *fitba*. In certain traditional uses, *ba* stands for the game played as well as the ball played with. Such games were often annual events which took place on recognised festivals. Everybody eligible joined in, and teams selected themselves, as they were based each year on the same easily recognised division of local society. Until the end of the 19th century, in Scone in Perthshire, a football match was played every Shrove Tuesday between the married men and the bachelors: it was known as 'The *ba* of Scone.'

Shrove Tuesday, or (to give it its older Scots name) Fastern's Een, was a favourite occasion for such contests, preceding as it did the season of Lent. A robust game of *hand-ba*, more like rugby than handball, was often played instead of football. It has survived longer in the Borders than elsewhere, and in Jedburgh 'the Fastern's Een Handball ... known as The Men's *Ba*' (1916) still takes place. But in Kelso the annual *ba' day* has died out. In Orkney the Kirkwall *Ba* game still takes place on New Year's Day. The opposing sides are called the 'uppies' and the 'doonies' – a distinction based upon the part of Kirkwall from which they come.

barley see KEYS (X).

bed see PEEVER (X).

bogie '*The gem's* (game is) *a bogie*' is shouted by children when for one reason or another the game they are playing has broken down. The call requires the game to come to a sudden end, and a fresh start to be made. In '*The Game's a Bogie*' (1975), a play by John McGrath dealing with social inequalities, it might be loosely translated as 'enough's enough.' *Bogie* is an English word for a goblin: a Scots equivalent would be *bogle*.

bonspiel A match or contest between two opposing teams in CURLING (X). When first recorded in the 16th century it meant a contest of any kind, as in archery or golf. But when in 1773 we read of 'many a bonspiel gaind Against opposing parishes' we are on curling trritory. The biggest event in the Scottish curling calendar is a **Grand Match** between the North and South. This is, when the weather permits, held at the Lake of Menteith in Perthshire, so long as the ice is at least six inches thick. The first Grand Match took place in 1847, and the most recent was held in February 1979, after a lapse of sixteen years. It was attended by 6000 people, nearly half of them players. The origin of *bonspiel* is not certain. It may be from early Dutch *bond*, a league or alliance, and *spel*, a game. There is also an independent word *spiel*, which once meant any kind of game, but now is only a curling match.

bunker is best-known today as a hazard on a golf-course: it was first recorded in this sense in Fife in 1812, in a description of how to play a ball lying 'on sand or in a *bunker*.' It also meant a sand-pit more generally: in *Redgauntlet* (1824) Scott writes of 'what you might call a *bunker*, a little sand-pit.' *Bunker* was first recorded in Scots in 1540, in the sense of a box or chest. It was in a development of this sense that it first appeared in English in the 19th century as a 'coal bunker' on a ship. In Scots a coal *bunker* was a domestic storage place for coal, sometimes fitted into an indoor cupboard, sometimes outside the house: in parts of Scotland it is still used in this sense. It is also widely used to mean the 'work-top' beside a kitchen sink. The origin of *bunker* is uncertain: it may have a common origin with English *bunk*.

caber A long heavy spar or pole, usually made by stripping down the trunk of a slender tree. In the 16th century the *caber* was regarded chiefly as a rafter for use in building, though in 1624 someone was in trouble for striking a neighbour 'with a great *caber* in his hand'. In modern times it is best known for its use in the contest of strength and skill known as *tossing the caber*. The caber must be thrown in such a way that it lands on the heavy end, and when it does so topples away from the thrower. The event is one of the high spots of any Highland Games (see GAMES, X), and the prize goes to the competitor who throws the *caber* furthest. *Cabar* is the Gaelic for a pole or rafter.

caddie, someone who carries a golfer's clubs for him when he is playing, and gives advice when it is asked for, comes from the French *cadet*, a military cadet. It was in this sense that it first appeared in Scots as *cadie* (and in English as *cadee*) in the 17th century. But in 18th century Scotland it came to mean someone who earned his living in a town by offering to perform almost any service for payment. In Edinburgh and other large towns the *cadies* were organised into a body – what Captain Topham, an Englishman residing in Edinburgh in the 1770s, described as 'a society ... as useful ... as ever existed ... It contains persons for every use and employment, who faithfully execute all commands at a very reasonable price.' Their reputation cannot always have been so good, however, for from the late 18th century *cadie* was often used for a ragamuffin or rough; and it was still used in this sense in the 1930s. The golfing *cadie* is first noticed in 1773, when a local rule of golf laid down that 'no golfer or *cadie* shall be allowed to make any tee within ten yards of the hole'. In 1845 it was noted that 'many of the young ... are employed as *cadies* or golf carriers.' *Caddie* can also mean to act as a caddie. It is part of the golfing jargon that has passed into general English.

carpet bowls Indoor bowls, a game similar to bowls, but played on a carpet so that the playing surface may resemble a lawn. According to the 1909 *Handbook of the Scottish Carpet*

Bowling Association the game was most popular in the southern counties, where it was adapted from English alley bowling. Locally, the game is known as 'the *carpit boolin*' or, sometimes, 'poor man's curlin' (*Scots Mag.*, 1975).

chuckiestanes A game which requires the simplest of equipment but great quickness of hand. Five pebbles are laid on a surface: one of them is taken up and tossed into the air. Before it comes down the other four pebbles must be picked up in one hand. The player must then with the same hand catch the fifth stone as it descends. The game is also known as *chucks* or *five stanes*. A **chuckiestane** is a pebble: colloquial and occasional Scots. It was first recorded in the 19th century, and probably comes from English *chuck*, to throw. Also known as a *chuckie*: in 1988 someone covered his garden path with 'granite chips and *chuckies.*'

collie-buckie A pickaback. Localised Scots. On a hill walk in 1986 one walker jokingly asked another, 'Will you give me a *collie-buckie?*' An alternative form, *coalie-backie*, suggests the origin – coal carried on one's back. Probably a children's term; first recorded in the 20th century.

curling The game of *curling* is played on ice, on a rectangular course or RINK (X). The object of the game is similar to that of bowls: one team tries to defeat another by getting as near to a target as possible more 'STONES' (X) than the opposing team.
    A match is played between two teams of four players, each captained by a SKIP (X). The players take it in turn to slide a stone along the *rink*. Each *curler* has two shots, and when all sixteen stones have been delivered a count is made to see how many stones one side has got nearer to the TEE (X, target) than any opposition stone. A team may, by winning an END (X), gain from 1 to 8 points. Another *end* is then played in the opposite direction. A match continues for at least ten ends, and is won by the team gaining most points over the whole contest. Each curler is armed with a BESOM (XIII) or broom, and with this members of a team try to SOOP (X, sweep) the ice clear of minor obstructions.

The antiquity of curling is uncertain. There is a reference to curling stones in a poem dated 1638, and the game is mentioned several times before 1700. It has been pointed out that in Bruegel's painting, 'Hunters in the Snow' (1565), a game resembling curling is in progress on a frozen pond; so the game may have originated outside Scotland. But in its modern form, and for its international organisation, the game is indebted to the Royal Caledonian Curling Club, founded in Edinburgh in 1838. Curling is now played in many countries, and the modern ice rink allows it to be carried on indoors on a prearranged date, unaffected by the vagaries of the weather. The word is apparently derived from a special use of to *curl*, to give a curling motion to the stone when delivering it. This is an important skill in the game, though one authority claims that '*a curler* who cannot shoot straight cannot put on the proper curl.'

den[1] As well has having the common standard English sense of an animal's lair, *den* in Scots is the 'base' or 'home' in certain games – a place from which a 'hunter' may set out or in which the 'hunted' may find sanctuary. In the game of TIG (X), the 'toucher' has to stay in the *den* while the others go and hide. At the beginning of some 'hunting' games the players choose a *den* large enough for the whole side who are 'in'.

drive in golf was originally to hit the ball as far as was possible or necessary. It was first used in this sense in Scots, in a poem written about 1460. The club used for this purpose was called a *driver* from 1674, and also sometimes a 'play-club' (1685). If an iron club was used it was called a *driving* IRON (X), but for shorter shots a player could at one time call on a *driving cleek* (1891) and even a *driving putter* (1857).

end A unit of play in a CURLING (X) match. In the course of one *end*, each player delivers both his stones from one end of the RINK (X). A match usually consists of ten ends.

games An outdoor gathering at which contests are held in athletics, piping and dancing. Frequently, and justly, known as **Highland games**, for it was in the Highlands that such 'games' were first held, though now they are also held in Lowland towns: for example, they are now a feature of the Edinburgh Festival each summer. There is, moreover, 'a *Highland Games* in nearly every state' in the U.S.A.

Though believed to have existed in some form for centuries, Highland Games first received outside attention in the 1820s; in 1831 '*The Games*' was a sufficient mode of reference to the Braemar Gathering, 'one of our oldest meetings for ... the practice of Highland games' (1853). Common events at such meetings are 'tossing the caber' (see CABER, X), 'putting the shot' (see PUTT, X), 'throwing the hammer', Highland dancing, and a more everyday diet of foot races. See also GATHERING (IX).

gird and cleek A children's game played with a hoop (the *gird*); the *cleek* is the hook-shaped piece of iron or strong wire used to guide and control the rolling hoop. Once popular playthings, but now seldom seen, though they were photographed for the *Scotsman Magazine* in 1987. *Gird*, or *girr*, can also mean a hoop or band more generally; it has been in Scots since the 16th century, and is related to English *girth*. See also CLEEK (XII).

golf, Sc **gowf** was defined in Jamieson's *Dictionary* (1808) as 'a game in Scotland in which hooked clubs are used for striking balls, stuffed very hard with feathers, from hole to hole.' Arguably, Scotland's greatest gift to the world, especially to the new world, though derivation from Dutch *kolf* (a club used in a similar ball game) is generally conceded.

The first known reference to the game is in an Act of the Scottish Parliament in 1457. We know from this that '*the gowf*' was already popular in Scotland, as the intention of the Act was to discourage golf in the belief that it distracted men from weapon-training with the bow and arrow. But its popularity continued, and numerous offenders were summoned before Kirk Sessions after the Reformation for playing golf on Sundays 'in time of sermon.' The novelist

Tobias Smollett noted, in 1766, 'Of this diversion the Scots are so fond that, when the weather will permit, you may see a multitude of all ranks, from the senator of justice to the lowest tradesman, mingled together ... following the balls with the utmost eagerness.'

A century ago *The Times* claimed as one attraction of golf that it was 'one of the cheapest recreations'. In Scotland, even today, this may be true, though it is no longer possible, as it was till 1913, for all comers to enjoy their golf free at St Andrews. In Edinburgh, fifty years ago, eighteen holes on the Braids No 2 Course cost a schoolboy sixpence. Now, in 1986, a schoolboy pays 35 pence, an adult £2, for a round over the same course. The game proved equally popular at the other end of the social scale. James IV was an early exponent. Mary Queen of Scots, it was reported with disapproval, played golf in the fields near Seton shortly after the murder of her husband Darnley, in which she was believed to be implicated. When the North Berwick Golf Club was formed in 1832, membership was limited to 50, consisting of 'nobles and gentlemen from all parts of the country.'

At first golf was played on unproductive land near towns – a requirement that made LINKS (X, sandy ground near the coast) an eminently suitable venue. In St Andrews the course on which the game was played was 'covered with a peculiarly soft and scrubby grass, interspersed with whins (gorse), sand-holes, etc.' Far from being a disadvantage, a 19th century apologist argued, 'the inequalities of surface which the course presents ... tends materially to increase the interest of the game.' These natural features, and the initiative of its citizens, made 'the antient city of St Andrews' pre-eminent among Scottish golf courses. See also ROYAL AND ANCIENT (X).

Golf was introduced to England by James VI of Scotland after he became James I of England in 1603. Blackheath was found to be the nearest equivalent to Scottish links in the London area, and James recognised the terrain there as entirely suitable for his favourite game. Hence the Royal Blackheath Golf Club's claim to have been established in

1608, and its entitlement to use 'Royal' in its name. In 1874 *The Times* recognised that 'Golf has been played by Scots literally from time immemorial ... We hear of golf ... in all the colonies that are most affected by Scotchmen ... while in England it has been acclimatised from the bleak coasts of Northumberland to the sunny shores of Devon.'

Over the centuries when it was 'peculiar to Scotland' golf developed a terminology of its own. The original names of nearly all the clubs (brassie, spoon, baffie, mashie, niblick and putter) originated in Scotland; see also DRIVER (X), CLEEK (XII), IRON (X). So did such golfing terms as dormie, round, and BUNKER, CADDIE, GREEN, HOLE, PUTT, STYMIE and TEE (all X). To this day one club in Ayrshire is proud to display as its title Lowdon *Gowf* Club.

Grand Match see BONSPIEL (X).

green as used in golf originated in Scotland, in both the more usual modern sense of a putting *green*, and in the older sense of the whole playing area of the course (retained in *green-fee*). In 1744 there was a reference to the 'fair *green* (fairway)' and in 1817 someone was indulging in 'open swiping thro the long *green*.' Most tenements in Scotland are provided with a *back-green* or *drying-green*, sometimes dignified by the name of a rear garden, but more often simply referred to as 'shared *drying-green* to rear' (1987). Conversely, the back garden of a house is sometimes known as a *green*.

guddle To catch fish with the hands by feeling the way into places in a stream where the fish are likely to lurk. The ability to *guddle* trout, or to *guddle for* trout, is an admired skill. 'He is an expert *guddler*.' Figuratively, only the messy aspect of *guddling* is taken into account. Applied to other activities, to *guddle* means to mess about, to cause a muddle. To be *in a guddle* is to be in a mess, or in a state of muddle. To 'mak a richt *guddle o* a job' is to make a bad mess of it. *Guddle* was not recorded in Scots till the 19th century. It is probably sound-imitative in origin.

hole developed special senses in Scots to meet the needs of golfers: one of these is the unit of play by which success or failure against an opponent is measured. We find this last use celebrated in verse as early as 1743: 'Thrice three *holes* to great Castalio fall.' You have been able to *hole* the ball since 1744, and 'the putter is usually considered the best club for *holing out* the ball' (*1857*). All these senses are now general English – if you play golf.

iron as a name for a golf club is first found in Scots, in 1807: 'the iron [is used when the ball is] among gravel or sand.' But much earlier than that, in 1685, there is a reference to '3 *iron-clubs*'. Irons in the past were classified as *driving-iron, mid-iron, lofting-iron* according to their specific purpose.

keepie–up(pie) A game played by a boy or a football fanatic. The aim is to keep a ball in the air without using the hands – feet, knees, chest and head are all permitted. A variation is to keep on heading the ball against a wall, returning the rebound. General Scots for those skilful enough so to indulge themselves.

keys In children's games, a call for a truce or for safety. It is usually accompanied by a sign made with the hands, presumably to represent keys – crossed fingers, the thumb held between the two nearest fingers, or both thumbs held up. Rules may be strict: you can't call '*Keys*' unless you're really hurt.

A similar truce word is **barley**. In 1902 someone described how an assailant 'fair choked me ... afore I could cry a *barley*.' The word may be connected with 17th century Scots *parlie*, a truce between armies, from Middle English *parley* or perhaps directly from French *parlez*! (speak).

Both terms are now localised Scots.

links In general English, a golf course (especially one beside the sea, which is also often called a *links course*). In 1769 Daniel Defoe, describing a visit to Scotland, wrote of 'the sandy downs, or *links* as they call them here', and one of

Scott's English characters is made to write of 'sandy knolls, covered with short herbage, which you [Scots] call *links*, and we English downs' (1824).

Stretches of sandy, undulating ground with a growth of rough grass, whins (gorse) etc, are common on the coasts of Scotland. But the use of *links* was long confined to the east coast, though by 1680 there is mention of the 'pleasant fields and *links*' near Ayr. Such land was used in various ways. Sheep were often put to feed on links. In Edinburgh men were appointed to maintain rabbit-warrens on links as a potential source of food. In the 17th century the links of Dornoch were claimed to be 'the fairest and largest *links* . . . of any part of Scotland', and 'fit for archery, golfing, ryding and all other exercises'.

The first mention in Scots of a *golf-links* was in 1797, and it is thanks to golf that *links* has become widely used outside Scotland. In 1986 a commentator on the Open Golf Championship spoke of the special difficulties facing competitors on 'links courses' like Turnberry. Americans claimed earlier in the same year that Shinnecock Hills on Long Island was like 'a British *links*', and that it was the best U.S. example of a British '*links-course*'.

Except in place names, and in golfing contexts, *links* is now rarely heard in Scotland. One context in which the word has survived is *Links Market*, the name given to a popular fair held each spring in Kirkcaldy on the town seafront. The 'sea-blown *links*' (1925) have now made way for a sea-wall and a broad roadway. Though always plural in Scots, *links* derives from an Old English singular noun meaning rising ground, a slope; and as late as 1836 *link*, meaning a green or wooded bank, could still be found in the dialect of Sussex.

menage, menodge A friendly society or savings club. Localised Scots. Members contribute a small sum each week to save for a specific object, or in the hope of winning the 'jackpot' in an occasional draw. Sometimes members of a *menodge* can obtain a loan from the common pool, or may obtain sick benefit when ill. In 1959 an Edinburgh shop advertised for a 'girl to take up *menages* (contributions).' First recorded in Scots early in the 19th century. From French *ménage* meaning (among other things) thrift.

Munro The name given by climbers and hillwalkers to any Scottish peak that is 3000 or more feet in height. A list of such peaks was drawn up by Sir Hugh Munro, and published in the *Scottish Mountaineering Club Journal* in 1891. Though changes have been made in the list from time to time, the *Munros* (which in 1986 numbered 285) are substantially those nominated by Sir Hugh. With the growing popularity of hillwalking and climbing, the list is now less a statement than an incitement. Many walkers set themselves the task of climbing all the *Munros* – at least one person I know has climbed them all three times. This activity is called – chiefly by those who disapprove of it – *Munro-bagging*, and those who indulge in it are *Munro-baggers*. There are also lists of *Corbetts* (mountains between 2500 and 3000 feet) and *Donalds* (Lowland hills of 2000 feet or more).

Old Firm The name given to Rangers and Celtic, the two biggest football clubs in Scotland, when thought of as a unit, united like Punch and Judy by their opposition to each other. Both are Glasgow clubs, and each has a large, devoted and noisy following. Their rivalry is strengthened by the long association of Celtic with Ireland and Roman Catholicism, and of Rangers with a militant version of Protestantism. *Old Firm* matches draw large crowds, and are perhaps the most emotionally charged occasions in the British sporting calendar.

pallally see PEEVER (X).

peerie A spinning top. A Scots traveller in France in 1676 noted that 'the *bairns* (children) of France' played at 'the tap (top)' and 'the *pery*', but the toy is not recorded in home use till 1756, when in Ayr boys were 'scourging their tops and casting their peeries'. The difference between top and *peerie* was explained by a much later writer; 'a top was flogged into spinning life' whereas 'a *peerie* was spun by means of a string'

(1931). *Peerie-heidit* means that your head is in a whirl: 'What a day! ... I'm just about *peerie-heidit*' (1953). Even more modern is *peerie-heels* for stiletto-heels. *Peerie* is perhaps from *pear* (pronounced *peer* in Scots), and if so will mean 'pear-shaped'.

peever A flat stone or disc (for example, an old shoe-polish tin filled with earth) for use in the game of *peever* or *peevers*. 'Hopscotch is an English game. We Scots called it *peever* or *pallally* or *pot*' (*Glasgow Herald*, 1936). *Peever*, or *peevers*, is a street game, and as such it was sometimes condemned for being the occasion of 'chalking and disfiguring the streets' (1921). In 1986 I passed some little girls playing it during their school interval. They had chalked out their series of '*beds*' on the pavement, and were throwing the *peever* into each **bed** in turn, then kicking it back to the base with the foot on which they were hopping. The game is in some places (e.g. Glasgow) known as '*beds*'. Another alternative name, **pallally** (in parts of eastern Scotland also *pallall*, *pallie* or *paldy*), has an interesting origin. It is from French *palet*, a stone or metal disc thrown at a target in certain games.

putt To propel a ball or heavy stone in the direction desired in a contest; an action that does this. In golf *putts* are successful when balls 'with *putt* well-directed plunge into the hole' (1743). Nowadays a *putter* is a club reserved for putting, but in 1857 a golfer might possess both a *green putter* and a *driving putter*: the latter was used 'to drive the ball up to the *putting green* when no hazards ... intervene to prevent the roll of the ball' (1857). *Putting the stone* calls for effort of a different nature. In 1711 a writer, lamenting the disappearance of many of the old Highland games, found comfort in the survival of *throwing the putting-stone*'. In this sport a heavy stone (weighing between 16 and 23 lbs) has to be hurled as far as possible by a thrust from the shoulder of the competitor. The event, now more often billed as *putting the shot*, is still a feature of GAMES (X). *Putt* has developed from *pit*, which is the Scots form corresponding to English *put*.

rink An area marked out for some particular activity or contest, especially CURLING (X) or bowling. The most common use in standard English is in *ice-rink*, first recorded in 1867. The word was probably carried south by Scots curlers, and the association with ice did the rest. In curling, the rectangular area marked out on the ice for a match is called *the rink*, and the official who presides over a contest is called *master of the rinks*. *Rink* is also the name given not only to a contest between two teams, but also to each team of four that takes part in a curling match. *Rink* and standard English *rank* both come from French *renc*, a row of fighting men, and both had at first the same meaning as the French. But *rink* soon came to mean the place of battle, then a single onset in a mock battle or joust, and after that a course marked out for a contest or race.

royal and ancient The '*royal and ancient* game' is the game of GOLF (X). It acquired this title indirectly. The authoritative legislative body for golf in the British Isles has long been The Society of Golfers of St Andrews, which was formed in 1754 when a group of 'Noblemen and Gentlemen', after stating their admiration of 'the ancient and healthful exercise of the golf', drew up a set of rules for the game. These were in fact copied from the rules drawn up for the Honourable Company of Golfers of Edinburgh in 1743, but in the long run it was St Andrews that achieved primacy in authority. In 1834, to confirm their status, the Club petitioned William IV for the right to be known as the 'Royal and Ancient Club of St Andrews'. Since the King granted this request, the club, and later the game itself, came to enjoy the distinction of being called '*royal and ancient*'.

sclaff In golf, to *sclaff* is to hit the ground a glancing blow with the club before striking the ball. A *sclaff* is a shot thus imperfectly executed. In this sense *sclaff* is also used in English. A Scots football commentator recently described a muffed shot as 'more a *sclaff* than anything else' (1986). The earliest recorded use of *sclaffing* referred to blows given with the palm of the hand or with a flat implement. A rarer sense is to walk in a shuffling way, and a *sclaff* is sometimes used for a badly-fitting shoe or slipper. A *sclaffer*, or *sclaffert*, is a clumsy or flat-footed person, and *sclaff-fittit* means flat-footed: all these uses are localised or dialect. *Sclaff* is probably onomatopoeic in origin.

seven-a-sides Seven-a-side rugby was devised in Melrose, and the first tournament took place there in 1883. At first limited to the Scottish Border clubs, this 'abbreviated code' is now internationally popular. The Melrose '*sevens*' are regarded as the most prestigious of the Scottish tournaments.

shinty A game played with ball and sticks, and so often likened to hockey and the Irish game of hurling, though it differs substantially from both. It is now rarely played outside the Highlands. The Gaelic name for the sport is *camanachd*, from *caman*, the Gaelic name for the stick, also called a *cammock* in Scots. The game is played between two teams, each of twelve players, on a large field (up to 170 yards long by 80 broad). The stick-head has a slightly angled face on both sides, which permits lofted shots to be made from the ground, and the ball is small and hard. At either end of the field are goals, or *hails* as they are called, like those used in soccer. Scoring is by goals. There is no offside, but there is a semi-circular line 9 yards from the goal: no attacker may cross this line until the ball is inside the circle. The game is played with great, sometimes excessive, vigour. In the *Statistical Account of Scotland* for 1795 it was noted that, in Argyll and Perthshire, 'on holidays all the males ... young and old, met to play at football, but oftener at *shinty*.' But in 1876 a more cautious note is sounded: 'the rough but manly game of *shinty* has not yet fallen into desuetude.' Neither has it yet, and (thanks partly to the formation in 1893 of the Camanachd Association) every year there is keen rivalry, especially for the Camanachd Cup.

skip The 'captain' of a team in curling or bowling. The word is shortened from *skipper*, and the title is not an honorary one. The *skip* has to control the strategy of his team so that individual skills are made to serve the common cause. As an account of *curling* written in 1933 puts it: 'Each *rink* has its *skip* who directs the sooping (sweeping) of the besoms (brooms) and the play generally.' As a verb, to *skip*, or to *skip a rink*, means to act as *skip* or captain. In December 1986 someone was appointed to *skip* 'England's team of Scots against Japan'.

soop Scots form of *sweep*, by which it has now been almost entirely displaced. It survives in one particular situation – in a game of CURLING (X). The task of sweeping the ice to allow the curling-stone to glide more easily over its surface is still often referred to as *sooping*, and during a match players may be urged on to greater effort by cries of '*Soop!*' or '*Soop up!*'

stone, *Sc* **stane** The rounded polished stone, fitted with a handle, that is used in the game of CURLING (X). It was laid down in 1739 that every member of a club 'shall provide himself with a curling *stone*'. A stone, 'including handle and bolt' (1940) weighs about 40 lbs.

stymie In general English, *to be stymied* is to be prevented by circumstances from carrying out one's plans, to be thwarted. But *stymie* is of Scottish and sporting origin, as may be seen in these verses: 'It's aye the same in life an' gowf (golf), I'm *stymied* late an ear (early)' (1892). A golf *stymie* occurred when a ball landed on the green six inches or more from an opponent's ball, and in such a position that the line between that ball and the hole was obstructed.

With many golfers the *stymie* was unpopular, and many sighed with relief when on 1st January 1952 the *Scotsman* could report that for the last time a player had been '*laid a stymie*'. The stymie had been outlawed. The origin of *stymie* is uncertain. There is a Scots verb *stime*, to blink, peer; and *not so see a stime* is to be unable to see the least thing. It seems quite probable that this gave rise to the golfing use of *stymie*.

tee Originally a golf *tee* was a small heap of earth or sand on which the ball was placed for the first shot at any hole. One of the rules drawn up in 1754 laid down that 'You must *tee* your ball within a club-length of the hole.' The earliest mention of a tee is in Allan Ramsay, who describes golfers as 'Driving their Baws (balls) frae whins (from gorse) or *Tee*' (1721).

In CURLING (X) a *tee* is the mark on the ice in the centre of the HOUSE (XIII) at which the curlers aim their stones. A stone which settles on the tee is said to be *tee-high*, and a *tee-shot* is one that reaches the tee. A *tee* is also the mark, or jack, set up as a target in quoits or CARPET BOWLS (X). *Tee* first appeared in 1673 in the form *teaz* (perhaps a plural form) in a glossary as a golfing term. Its origin is not known.

tig A children's game in which one player, the '*tigger*', chases the rest until he touches with his hand, or *tigs*, one of the others, crying '*Tig!*' as he does so. The person so *tigged* then becomes the chaser or *tigger*. There are of course variations. In one 'the *tigger* or toucher stays in the DEN (X) until the others go and hide' (1905). In a non-stop version the *tigger* could not immediately be tigged back, or '*tug*', by the person he had touched.

The game, also played in England though more usually called 'tag', has been known since 1816, but as a verb it has a much longer history. In the 15th century to *tig* with someone was to touch in a loving, but also sometimes in a teasing or annoying way. A nursery song complained: 'He's aye *tig-tagging* And winna (will not) let me be' (1844). Among boys tigging might be more robust: 'They fell to *tigging* and horse-play which sometimes ended in a spar' (1955). It seems likely that all these senses grew from the idea of touching or tapping someone with the hand, and that *tig* is an attempt to express this action in sound – as does the cry '*Tig!*' in the game.

Highland cattle (XI)

loch (XI)

XI

Countryside Nature
Time and Weather

airt A direction, point of the compass. Most widely known in the lines of Burns, 'Of a' the *airts* the wind can blaw I dearly like the west,' and in such phrases as 'fae a the *airts*,' from every quarter. Now in learned rather than colloquial use. First recorded in a 14th century northern English poem. Of uncertain origin.

auld lang syne see LANG SYNE (XIV).

ben¹ A high mountain or mountain peak. *Ben* is an Anglicized form of one of the Gaelic words for a mountain or hill, and is most commonly heard in place names, as in *Ben Nevis*. But it is also heard on its own: 'Shall we go up the *ben* tomorrow?' (1973). Highland scenery has been shortly described as 'bens and glens'.

birk Birch tree. A small wood consisting mainly of birch trees is sometimes called 'the *birks*', as in the Birks of Aberfeldy, celebrated in song by Burns, and still open to visitors. *Birk* was first recorded in Scots in 1348: it is also found in northern English dialect.

blaeberry Bilberry (both fruit and plant). General Scots. *Blaeberries* are sometimes called *blaes*. **Blae** means bluish or blue-grey. *Blaeberry* is also found in northern and some other English dialects. Of Scandinavian origin. See also BLAES (XII).

bluebell The '*bluebell of Scotland*' is 'the bonnie harebell blue.' Until the 18th century the harebell was also known as the blubell in England, but it has continued to be so only in Scotland. The English bluebell is called the wild hyacinth in Scotland. There are at least four songs whose titles make reference to Scottish *blue bells* (witten as two words in each case). The best known of these, 'The *Blue Bells of Scotland*,' may have popularised the phrase. Its main concern is however with the whereabouts of a certain 'bonnie Hieland laddie,' and the '*blue bells*' are mentioned only in passing.

Borders, the The area between the Lothians and the Scottish-English border; now, since Scottish local government was reorganised in 1975, given a form of official recognition as Borders Region. *The Borders* are famous, among other things, for ballads, sheep-farming, tweed, hill-walking and rugby. One of the world's greatest lexicographers, Sir James Murray, the first editor of the *Oxford English Dictionary*, was a *Borderer*.

brae A hill slope. The commonest sense since the 14th century has been a hill or hillside, as in the 1916 poem which described Scotland as the 'Land o' ben (mountain) and *brae*'. It also means the ground sloping up from the bank of a river, as when Burns writes: 'Ye banks and *braes* o' bonnie Doon.' A later sense is a road going up a hill with a fairly steep slope. Finally, the plural *braes* may refer to an area dominated by hills, as in the *Braes* of Balquhidder. *Brae* is from an Old Norse word which meant first the eyelash, then the eyelid, and then the eyebrow. The idea of 'brow' was transferred to the appearance of the crest of a slope – the brow of a hill. *Brae* also occurs in northern English dialect.

bramble, *Sc* **brammle** General Scots for a blackberry or a blackberry bush. Also used in this sense in English dialect.

brock The badger, which was regarded as an evil-smelling animal. In the 16th century guardians of the law once complained that men they had arrested 'stink as [if] they were *brocks*'. It was therefore easy for *brock* to become a term of abuse: in Ulster in 1901 a *brock* was defined as 'a dirty malodorous person ... and hence, a skunk, that is, one given to dirty tricks.' In fact, *brock* developed in meaning in the same way as *skunk* did in American English. *Brock* also occurs in northern English dialect, frequently accompanied by the adjective *stinking*. It is of Old English origin.

capercailzie The wood-grouse, also sometimes known as the Cock of the Woods. The first reference to it in 1533 suggests that it was once almost as much myth as bird: a fowl larger than a raven, which lives only on the barks of trees. The *capercailzie* was indigenous to Scotland, but became extinct. In 1795 the *Statistical Account of Scotland* noted that the '*caper coille*, or wild turkey' had not been seen for 40 years. It was however reintroduced from Sweden, and can again be seen, though rarely. The name is from two Gaelic words meaning 'horse of the woods', *horse* being indicative of size, as in *horse-radish*. The apparent *z* is pronounced like a *y*, because at one time the symbol used in Scots for *y* was much the same as an English *z* (this explains, in part, why the name Dalziel is pronounced *de-yéll*). Some however take the easy way out, ignore the *z*, and say *-kaily*.

carse A stretch of low-lying land on the bank or banks of a river. *Carse* has been in Scots since 1292, when it was recorded in a place name, and to this day it is more often heard in place names than elsewhere. It may be that at first a *carse* was noted for the wetness of its soil, but later its potential fertility was realised, and now 'the *carse* [of Forth] is an area of flat rectangular fields' (1970). The word is probably connected with the English dialect word *carr*, a bog or fen, which is of Scandinavian origin.

cleg A gadfly or horsefly. In the summer both cattle and people may be 'tormented by *clegs* and flies.' General Scots, of Norse origin. Once standard English, but now heard only in dialect. Appeared in Scots in the 15th century.

corrie A roundish hollow, often of considerable size, in the side of a mountain or between two mountains; a cirque. The 'great corrie' to the north-east of Ben Lui (near Crianlarich) 'gives the mountain an Alpine character' (*The Munros* ed. Donald Bennet, 1985). *Corrie* is from a Gaelic word for first a cauldron, then a cauldron-shaped hollow. It must have gained wider currency in English through the increased popularity of hill walking.

craig A cliff, or a projecting spur of rock. Common in place names, but otherwise rarely used, probably because it has largely been displaced by *crag*. *To be at the craigs* is to be fishing from the rocks; in Fetlar in the Shetlands 'a man at the *craigs*' means a man fishing with a rod and line. *Craig* is related to the Gaelic word for a rock.

craw Scots form of English *crow*, but in Scotland applied to the rook as well as the crow. The hooded or carrion crow is known as the *hoodie craw*, or simply as the *hoodie*. 'The carrion crow of the Lowlands is called *hoodie* . . . by a great many countrymen' (1956). The Scots spelling would be **huidie**, from *huid*, a hood.

See also CRAWSTEP (XIII).

den² A narrow valley, usually with wooded sides; well defined in Scott's *Redgauntlet* as 'a deep dell or dingle, such as they call in some parts of Scotland a *den*, and in others a cleuch or narrow glen' (1824). The word has been in Scots since the 16th century: it has developed from the same origin as English *dean*, a small valley, and is also found in some English dialects. Many pupils of Kirkcaldy High School take a short cut through '*the den*' on their way to and from school, and there is a *den* in nearby Kennoway.

divot A turf, a piece of earth with grass growing on it. Known to many chiefly from notices in golf clubs, asking members to replace *divots*. *Divot* has been frequently recorded in Scots since about 1500, and *divots* were long in demand as floor coverings, roofing materials, and for making DYKES (XIII). The origin of *divot* is unknown.

doo A dove or pigeon. Colloquial Scots. A pigeon fancier is a *doo* man, dedicated to 'a poor man's sport' (*Scotland on Sunday Mag.*, 1989). The same word as *dove*, but Scots has had *doo* since the 14th century. See also DOOCOT (XIII).

drove road Originally, in the days when the cattle trade was a mainstay of the Highland economy, one of the tracks down which cattle, also sheep were driven on their way to markets in the Scottish Lowlands or in England. *Drove roads* are of more than merely historical interest, for they provide attractive routes through the hills for walkers in many parts of Scotland.

dub A small pool or puddle. Colloquial Scots. After heavy rain, *dubs* may lie all along a country lane. A writer in the *Scotsman* in 1986 described how some walkers set out on a rainy day, undeterred by '*dubs* and glaur (mud) beneath their feet.' Burns's Tam o' Shanter, on his way home, 'skelpit (here, galloped) on thro *dub* and mire' (1791). *Dub* was first recorded in the 18th century: it came to Scots from the Low Countries.

firth An arm of the sea, more particularly one that is the estuary of a river, as are the *firths* of Forth and Clyde. The word has been used in Scots since before 1400. An Act of the Scottish Parliament in 1607 was designed to preserve for Scots 'their trade of fishing within their lochs, *firths* and bays'. *Firth* is now accepted as standard English, though chiefly in Scottish contexts. The word is of Scandinavian origin; *firth* and *fjord* can be traced back to a common ancestor.

flee A fly. Colloquial Scots. *Flee* is of the same origin as *fly*, but the two words have diverged in sound. The word has been in Scots since the 14th century, and was early taken as a type of worthlessness: things are often dismissed as 'not worth a *flee*.' 'Let that *flee* stick to the *wa* (wall)' means say no more on that matter.

forenoon is differently, and more frequently, used in Scots, as a distinction is drawn between the morning and the forenoon. You get up and have breakfast in the morning, but when you have settled down to your day's work you enter the *forenoon*, which lasts, say, from 10 a.m. till noon. Someone has suggested that the first half of the day is in Scotland divisible into three – the SMA OORS (XI), the morning and the *forenoon*.

fulmar A bird of the petrel species. It has sometimes been called the *fulmar petrel*, as in a book written in 1840 which claimed that St Kilda was the only breeding place in Britain of the '*fulmar petrel*'. It was first recorded there in 1698. The word has been in English usage since early in the 19th century, and was the name given to one of the Coastal Command planes during the Second World War. *Fulmar* is a Gaelic borrowing from two Scandinavian words – *full* meaning foul (in this case, evil-smelling) and *mar*, a gull.

gean The wild cherry. General Scots, but as rare as are such cherries themselves, though Almondell near Edinburgh is 'thickly wooded with *gean*, oak and hazel.' The *g* is pronounced as in *go*. First recorded in the 17th century from an early form of French *guigne*, a heart-cherry. Also found in English dialect, particularly in northern dialect.

glaur Soft, sticky mud. Colloquial Scots. '*Glaur* far more accurately expressed what I was standing in than the word mud, because *glaur* gave that feeling of blackness and stickiness' (*The Listener*, 1985). A walker who fell when crossing Rannoch Moor found himself 'covered with *glaur*' when he stood up. *Glaur* is also known in northern English dialect. First recorded about 1500 as *glar*. Of unknown origin.

glen A valley between steep hills, usually with a stream or river flowing through it. Most glens tend to be narrow: cf. STRATH (XI). *Glen* is from the Gaelic for a valley, and is most naturally used of valleys in the Highlands, where Gaelic was long the chief language, and where *glen* is common in place names. It entered Scots in the 14th century, and may now be regarded as general English.

gloamin(g) Dusk. Made widely popular earlier this century by the Harry Lauder song 'Roamin in the *gloamin*,' but adopted into standard English a century before that, perhaps partly because of Byron's use of the word (a reminiscence of his early days in Aberdeen?). *Gloaming* comes from an Old English word for twilight that was lost in Middle English, but not in Scots. It is connected with the word *glum*.

gowan The common daisy. Also used for the marguerite or ox-eye daisy. Localised Scots. In 1929 it was noted that among school-children *gowan* had been almost entirely superseded by *daisy*, though it survived among older folk. When used today, it is chiefly in literary Scots: Burns's words in *Auld Lang Syne*, 'We twa hae pu'd (two have pulled) the *gowans* fine', help to keep the gowan in mind. *Gowan* came into Scots in the 15th century: it was an alteration of the northern English word *gollan*, the name for several yellow flowers.

gowk The cuckoo (as it is in some English dialects). In this sense, it is now localised Scots, but it is more widely used in the figurative sense of a fool or simpleton. This last sense came to be specially associated with April fool's day; a character in one of Scott's novels suggested that Cockneys were made 'April *gowks* ... every month in the year' (*Fortunes of Nigel*, 1822). To send someone to *hunt the gowk* is to send him on a fool's errand, or more narrowly to make an April fool of him. When someone is so tricked, the deceiver may give a triumphant cry of '*hunt the gowk*' or '*huntygowk*', the latter a slurred version of the phrase. In the sense of cuckoo, *gowk* was first recorded in Scots about 1450; it is of Old Norse origin.

haar has two different but related meanings. The first, rarely if ever heard nowadays, is a cold east wind, usually one coming off the North Sea. The second sense (heard, alas! only too often) is a cold mist which drifts across the east coast and hangs on the grass, often while the rest of the country is basking in warm sunshine: 'The last week of May was spoiled by a persistent *haar* which came in from the Firth of Forth' (1987). *Haar* is from a German or Dutch word for a bitterly cold wind.

heather The Scots name for *ling*, and also two species of *Erica*; first recorded about 1400 as *hadder*, but in the altered form *heather* accepted in standard English from about 1600. In the heather moors in the Highlands *ling* (*Calluna vulgaris*, which is the true heather) is dominant. In drier places *bell-heather* (*Erica cinerea*) is also found; *cross-leaved heath (Erica tetralix)* prefers damp or boggy areas. *Heather* has always been an important factor in the economic life of Scotland, but never more so than today. Its abundance on hillside and moorland when it is in flower in August and September is one of the attractions that brings tourists to Scotland. It also attracts bees, so that of honey there are 'two kinds, *hedder* kind and home kind' (1820). *Heather honey* is deservedly widely popular. In earlier times *to take to the heather* was to seek refuge from pursuers in the heather-covered hills. To *set the heather on fire* means to cause a great stir or sensation The origin of the word is unknown.

Highland, *Sc* **Hieland** (pronounced *hee–*) The *Heland* (1503) of Scotland, long known as The *Highlands* or, in Scots, The *Hielands*, is the mountainous part of the north of Scotland. The Highlands lie north-west of an imaginary line, known as the *Highland line*, which begins a few miles to the west of Glasgow, runs north–east across the country, and ends a few miles east of Inverness. The culture of the Highlands is still largely Gaelic. *Highland* is used to identify many products and activities. *Highland whisky* is malt whisky. PIPES (IX) are more accurately called the *Highland bagpipes*. The KILT (III) properly worn is *Highland dress.'Highland games* are a traditional feature of Scottish life. They have kept alive the arts of piping and *Highland dancing* and the Highland forms of athletics' (*The Scotsman*, 1954). The *Highland Show*, no longer exclusively Highland, is the agricultural show held annually in Edinburgh by the Royal Highland and Agricultural Society. Among the most attractive exhibits to be shown there are the *Highland cattle*, a native breed distinguished by their shaggy brown coat and long curving horns. The *Highland Regiments* and the *Highland Division* have the right and the privilege to wear the kilt as their uniform, and they have made it famous throughout the world. Someone who comes from the Highlands is a *Highlander* or *Hielander*. The alternative *Hielan(d)man* is now rarely heard. All these words can also mean a soldier in a Highland regiment.

hoolet An owl or owlet. French *hulotte* was taken into Scots and English at the same time (about 1450), but only Scots retained the *h-*. In 1956 someone found himself unable to sleep because of 'the bloomin *hoolets*'.

howe A hollow, a piece of low ground surrounded by higher ground. Thus 'rivers run Thro' hills and *howes*' (1934). On a larger scale, we have the *Howe* of Fife, a low-lying area surrounded by hills; on a smaller, workmen may be engaged to fill in '*howes* in the road' (1922). *Howe* can also mean depression of mind: 'Nane o' yer heichts ('highs') an *howes*' (1951) means 'None of your tantrums!' A sense of depression is also conveyed in such phrases as 'the *howe* o' the nicht,' the deepest part of the night, or the '*howe* o' winter,' midwinter. In older Scots *how* originally meant a hole; it is in fact an altered form of the Scots for hole.

huidie see CRAW (XI).

kittiwake was adopted from Scots into English as a name for one species of gull. It is first mentioned as nesting on the Bass Rock near North Berwick in 1661. Like other seabirds, *kittiwakes* were at one time an acceptable food: in 1769 they were 'sold at Edinburgh for twenty pence apiece, and served up roasted'. The name is, at least in part, imitative of the cry of the bird.

kyle A narrow strip of water. Almost entirely in place names, as *Kyle* of Lochalsh or the *Kyles* of Bute. Accepted in standard English to describe Scottish conditions, as when in 1935 the *Times* reported that a new boat had 'steamed south through the kyles and sea-lochs of the west'. *Kyle* is an attempt to represent in Scots the Gaelic word for narrow.

laverock The lark. *Laverock* was at one time recognisably the same word as *lark*, which in 13th century English had the form *laverke*. There are Scots forms closer to *lark*, as in '*larrik's* nest' (1957).

lift The sky, the heavens. Now chiefly literary Scots. Often used by W.L. Lorimer in his *New Testament in Scots* (1983): 'They will see the Son o Man comin on the clouds o the *lift*.' Recorded in Scots since the 14th century, *lift* came from northern Middle English: it is related to German *Luft*, as in *Luftwaffe*.

linn A waterfall. This is well illustrated early in the 16th century by a statement that Scottish rivers are 'full of *linns*; as soon as salmon come to the *lin*, they leap.' This sense is common in place names (as *Linn* of Dee). In the 18th century in the south and south-west of Scotland there developed a second meaning of a deep narrow gorge. The word is of Old English origin, and is also found in northern English dialect.

A quite different word **linn** is from Gaelic *linn*, a pool, and means a pool beneath a waterfall. So, in 1951, 'there's a *linn* further up that's good for fishin.'

lintie The linnet. Occasional Scots. The liveliness of the linnet's song is reflected in 'singing like a *lintie*', and also in the occasional description of a lively, cheerful girl as a '*lintie*'. *Lintie*, which is an altered form of older Scots and northern English *lintwhite*, is also found in northern English and Ulster dialect. The first syllable may be from *lint*, as the linnet feeds on flax seeds, but -*white* has nothing to do with colour. It is possibly an imitation of the bird's call.

loch A lake, or an arm of the sea. *Loch* is a Gaelic word that first appeared in Scots in the 14th century, and it has almost entirely ousted the word *lake* from the usage of Scots in speaking of their own country (they do not say Loch District). Many of the best known Scottish lochs are inlets of the sea, and have been compared to Norwegian fjords. The most famous, Loch Lomond, is an inland *loch*. In 1845 a writer glossed 'little lagoons' as *lochans*. *Lochan* is the Gaelic diminutive of *loch*; tarn is a better translation of it than lagoon, though a *lochan* may be as small as a pond. The *lochan* can be a welcome landmark for mountain-walkers.

machair A stretch of low-lying, sandy ground close to the seashore and covered with coarse grasses. This is an instance of a Gaelic word being adopted into Scottish speech because it identifies a feature of, chiefly, the Hebridean landscape for which no exact Scots or English equivalent existed. A *machair* can be quite fertile or used only for rough grazing. In North Uist in summer 'the *Machair* is carpeted with wild flowers and bordered with sand dunes . . . it is tenanted by thriving communities of crofters' (*The Western Isles. Official Guide.* About 1970). Gaelic *machair* originally meant low-lying country.

maw is the Orkney and Shetland word for the **sea-maw** or sea-gull. It has been recorded in Scots since about 1500, and is of Old Norse origin. The black-headed gull is known as the **pickmaw** or, chiefly in the south of Scotland, as the **pickiemaw**. *Pick* is the Scots for pitch.

mirk Dark, gloomy. General Scots, corresponding to English *murk*. Since in standard English the two words would be pronounced in the same way, it is worth noting that Scots speakers clearly distinguish between the *u* and the *i*, and moreover pronounce the *r* with varying degrees of emphasis. *Mirk* also means darkness: 'In the *mirk* it was hard to follow the track.' Recorded in Scots since the 14th century: from a northern Middle English word for dark.

moorfowl, *Sc* **muirfowl** Since at least the 15th century, the Scots name for the red grouse. Curiously enough *moorcock* (the male of the species) was used in the north of England for the grouse about a century before it appeared in Scots; whereas *moorhen*, in Scots the female of the red grouse, in English refers to the water-hen. See also MUIR (XI).

moss An area of wet, boggy land. In 1798 it was pointed out that '*moss* in Scotland is equivalent to *morass* or *bog* in England.' The so-called 'debatable lands' between Scotland and England were marshy, and the men who in the 17th and 18th centuries crossed the mosses on cattle-raids into England were called *moss-troopers*, a name commemorated in the annual Mosstroopers' Race Meeting in Hawick. Further north 'the high *mosses* of the Cairngorms' are claimed as 'a unique topographical feature of the British Isles' (*Scots Magazine*, 1953). *Moss* comes into the name of several plants and birds: for example, the *moss oak* is the bog oak; and *moss-cheeper* is another name for the meadow pipit, not only in Scotland but also in Ulster. *Moss* is from the Old English word for bog; but the Scottish and English uses have diverged considerably, English tending to concentrate on *moss* as a plant name.

muir The Scots form of *moor*, moor or moorland. As a straight equivalent of English *moor*, *muir* is common in Scottish place names. A uniquely Scots usage is *muirburn*, which is the deliberate burning of the old growth on a piece of moorland in order to clear the ground for fresh growth. *Muirburn* was first recorded in 1424, and was long done in defiance of the law. Even now, it is permissible only if great care is exercised: an Aberdeen paper reported in 1956 that certain persons 'made *muirburn* . . . and failed to control and regulate it . . . whereby damage was caused to woodlands (etc.).' A '*muir*' was also the area of common land belonging to a town or village, so that '*burgh muir*' is often found as a place name in Scotland. The Scottish army in 1513 mustered on the '*burgh muir*' of Edinburgh before the battle of Flodden. See also MOORFOWL (XI).

mull A headland or promontory. 'The shores [of Scotland] extend into lengthened headlands or *mulls*' (1846). The word is now heard chiefly in place names, as in the *Mull* of Kintyre. *Mull* is from a Gaelic word which as a noun means a headland, but as an adjective means bald, bare.

next when referring to days of the week or months can cause misunderstanding between Scots and incomers, and even between Scots themselves. Some years ago a University department issued to some of its students a questionnaire designed to find out what they understood by '*next* Monday'. A possible explanation was offered as early as 1787: 'Scots . . . are shy of saying Monday *next* when they mean the nearest Monday: instead they say Monday first.' So, in a week beginning on Monday 1st, Monday 8th is referred to as 'Monday first', and Monday 15th as 'Monday *next*'. But though the standard English sense of 'next Monday' has gained ground, there is still as much scope as ever for misunderstanding in this use of *next*.

peat has been used as a fuel in Scotland since before any records were kept. *Peat* is the substance, and *a peat* is a piece of peat, shaped rather like a large brick. Peat is dug from a *peat-bog* with a specially-shaped spade called a *peat-spade*. Then come the tasks of 'cairtin *peats* fae e moss' (1932, carting peats from the peat-bog) and building them into a *peat-stack* from which they can be taken when needed. The sharp, pungent odour from burning peat is credited with giving the *peat reek* (smoke) flavour to malt whisky. Highland streams often have a brown *peaty* colour. The origin of *peat* is not certain. It is thought to come from a Gaelic word, which in turn derives from the Latin word *petia*, a piece, from which comes English *piece*.

pickiemaw, pickmaw see MAW (XI).

plump A heavy downpour of rain. General Scots. 'There's going to be a real *plump* in a few minutes'. A *thunder-plump* is a sudden heavy thunder-shower. Also a verb: 'It'll *plump* later' (*Scots Mag.*, 1965) forecasts that the rain is going to fall suddenly and heavily. The noun was first recorded in Scots in this sense in the 19th century, but the phrase *plump* shower for a downpour dates back to about 1688: 'Like a *plump* shower to be poured down upon us in this land.' A special use of English *plump*, a heavy fall.

pony, *Sc* **pownie** A pony. When the word first appeared in Scots in the mid-17th century, it meant a riding horse as distinct from a working horse. Since it passed into standard English early in the 18th century, it has come to mean a horse of any small breed. In this connection it is perhaps significant that the small 'Zetland *pownie*' (see also SHELTIE, XI) is mentioned as early as 1702. But the sense of a riding-horse lasted long in Scotland and is retained in the modern sport of *pony-trekking*, first recorded in Scotland, in 1952. *Pony* is also applied to a trestle used by a joiner to support planks of wood when they are being sawed. The word is from French *poulenet*, a small foal or colt.

ptarmigan The word is from Gaelic *tarmachan*: the initial *pt* of ptarmigan is a pretentious adaptation of the bird's name by an 18th century English zoologist to connect the word with the Greek for feather. The *ptarmigan* is a member of the grouse family: in Britain it is found only in the Scottish Highlands, and it is rarely seen at heights of less than 2500 feet.

puddock A frog. General Scots, but there are few occasions for using the word in cities except in contrived situations like that of 'The Princess and the *Puddock*', a Scots version of *The Frog Prince*, performed as a play in 1986. In older Scots the word meant a toad as well as a frog. This may explain why *puddock* has often been used as an insult: 'You miserable ragged wee *puddock*.' A toadstool, or mushroom, is a *puddock-stool*. *Puddock* is the name given to an improvised sledge or trailer for transporting heavy loads. Branches or any available pieces of wood are put together in the shape of a rough triangle, and then loaded. The Old Scots word was *paddock*, with *pad* from an Old English, or Old Norse, word for a toad, and the diminutive *-ock*. In 16th century Scots a *padlock* was also called a *paddock-lock*.

rowan The mountain ash (*rowan-tree*) or its red fruit (*rowan-berry*): the tree is the subject of a well-known Scottish song. General Scots: also found in the north of England. The berries can be made into *rowan jelly*, which may be served with game or mutton. In the past the *rowan* and its berries were valued for a different reason: they were believed to ward off witches' spells. Sometimes a rowan tree was planted near the door of a house to protect it from the powers of evil. *Rowan* is perhaps of Norse origin, from a word meaning red.

scree An area of loose stones or gravel on a hill slope. The word is familiar to, if not popular with, hill walkers; *scree*, or a *scree slope*, is a minor but unpleasant hazard, especially when descending a hill. It was first used in the singular by Scott in 1813 in the form *scrae*, defined in an 1868 edition of his poems as 'a bank of loose stones'. In the plural, however, it had already appeared in a glossary of northern English dialect words as *screes*, defined as 'small stones or pebbles'. It derives from an Old Norse word for a landslip.

sea-maw see MAW (XI).

shaws The stalks and leaves of certain root vegetables – potatoes, and also turnips and carrots. General Scots. 'Never lift your potatoes till the *shaws* begin to wither' (1986). In 1798 a visitor to Scotland noticed that the turnip leaves were 'here called *shaws*'. Occasionally the singular may be used with reference to a single plant: 'four carrots grow from one *shaw*' (1935). The origin of the word is given away by 'the withered stalks of the tattie (potato) *shows*'. The Scots for *show* is *shaw*, and the parts of a root vegetable that show themselves above the ground have been called *shaws* since at least 1726.

sheltie The Shetland pony, a breed of very small ponies native to Shetland. First mentioned in the 17th century as a *shelty horse* (1612). In 1750 *shelties* were described as being 'so very small that one may lay his leg over them from the ground'. Shetlanders are sometimes jokingly referred to as '*shelties*'. The word is probably from the Old Norse for a Shetlander.

sma oors, or the *wee sma oors*, are the earliest hours of the morning. Colloquial and occasional Scots. *Sma* is the Scots form of *small*.

smirr Fine rain, drizzle. General Scots, and very common in the phrase *a smirr o rain*, very light drifting rain. Also, rarely, a *smirr* of sleet or snow. *Smir*, or *smur*, is also found in English dialect: its origin is uncertain, perhaps onomatopoeic.

snell Sharp, biting. General Scots, and now virtually limited to comments on the weather. The air, the wind or the winter may each be labelled *snell* when the cold seems to have a particularly penetrating quality, as in 'the *snell* winter blast' (Radio Scotland, 1987). *Snell* derives from an Old English word for quick or active. It was also found in northern Middle English.

solan (goose) The gannet. The Latin name is *sula bassana*: *solan* derives from the *sula*, and *bassana* indicates that the species is specially connected with the Bass Rock near North Berwick, one of the chief breeding grounds of the gannet. The *solan* was a staple of the diet of the inhabitants of the remote island of St Kilda until it was evacuated in 1930, and it is still eaten in some of the Outer Hebrides. Fishermen sometimes supplement their catch by shooting *solan geese*.

spate A sudden rise in the level of water in a stream or river, often leading to local flooding. The word is first recorded in Scots about 1420 in a reference to 'the *spate* of Noah', and it was adopted into standard English in the 16th century. It is most frequently heard in the phrase *in spate*: a river that is swollen with flood water is said to be *in spate*. *Spate* is freely used in figurative senses. In 1923 a rugby reporter wrote of 'a *spate* of tries' in one match, and an eloquent speaker can be said to be 'in full *spate*'. The origin of *spate* is unknown.

spug A house sparrow. Also *speug*, representing an alternative *spyug* pronunciation. General and occasional Scots. Though regarded as a child's word, it is often used nostalgically by adults. As a word, its history is complex. An older word for a sparrow was *spur*, of Scandinavian origin. It had a diminutive *spurrock*, which was shortened in speech to *spurg*. This form was in turn altered to *sprug*, still heard in some districts for a house-sparrow, or *spug*.

stinkin Willie Ragwort, 'an orange-coloured and obnoxious plant' (1879). The name is said to have been given to the plant by the Highlanders after Culloden to mark their hatred for William Duke of Cumberland, whose methods of pacifying the Highlands did not win universal approval. There is a popular belief that his horses brought the seeds of ragwort to Scotland.

strath A river valley. Unlike a GLEN (XI) a *strath* is wide; fertile land may be on either side of the river and stretch for a considerable distance. *Strath* has been in Scots since the 16th century. It is of Gaelic origin, and is common in place names, especially in parts of Scotland where Gaelic was once the principal speech. Learned or localised Scots.

thistle, *Sc* **thrissell** There is some doubt as to which of the thistle family should properly be called the Scottish thistle. This title is often bestowed on the cotton thistle, but the Readers' Digest *Wild Flowers of Britain* (1981) has no doubt that 'the emblem of Scotland is ... derived from the spear thistle, *Cirsium vulgare*.' The thistle, with its spikiness and rough vigour, was adopted as the splendidly suitable emblem of Scotland in the 15th century. The poet William Dunbar celebrated the marriage of James IV of Scotland to the daughter of Henry VII of England with a poem entitled 'The

Thrissill and the Rois (rose)' (1503). The thistle is the emblem worn on the jerseys of the Scottish rugby team. It is also the badge of the *Order of the Thistle*, an order of knighthood peculiar to Scotland, founded in 1687 by James VII (II of England). The form *thrissel* is now localised Scots. It has the same origin as *thistle*. The *r* in *thrissel* may be due to a mistaken notion that the word was related to *thrist*, the Scots for thrust (as with a spear).

whaup The curlew. The Scots name (as is *curlew*) is based on observation of the bird's cry. *Whaup* is from an Old English word for a sea-bird, and that in turn may be related to the word *whelp*, a puppy, but also a yelper or whiner. Other characteristics of the bird that attracted attention were its long beak and its long neck. The beak was called a *whaup-neb* (nose), and a person with a long thin neck might be described as *whaup-neckit*.

whin Gorse, furze. In general use in Scotland, but not to the exclusion of *gorse*, which is quite common, whereas *furze* is rare. *Whin*, on the other hand, is found in both English and Irish dialect. In the plural, it can mean an area in which *whin* is plentiful, as when Burns's Tam o'Shanter rode 'through the *whins*' (1790). The origin of *whin* is unknown.

whin(stone) A hard igneous rock (e.g. basalt). Also used for any hard stone used for road making. Recorded for the first time in Scots as early as 1573; accepted into standard English by the 18th century. *Whin* has been regularly used for building walls and houses, and in 1971 it was announced that a Midlothian quarry was to supply 20,000 tons of *whinstone* for the construction of the M4 motorway. The notorious hardness of *whin* was alluded to by Burns when he criticised the Edinburgh gentry for their '*whinstane* hearts'. *Whin* came from northern Middle English; its origin is not known.

XII

Fishing Farming Industry Crafts and Gear

bing A slag-heap. When originally recorded in Scots in the 16th century, *bing* was a pile or heap of any sort, but in modern times it has come to be limited to the great heaps of waste thrown up from mine workings. In part of West Lothian 'huge tubular *bings* of spent shale' are still features of the landscape. Not long ago Fife was similarly scarred by coal *bings*, but many of these have been levelled or landscaped, and Cowdenbeath is still trying to change its 'outdated *pit-bing* image' (*Scotsman*, 1987). *Bing* is of Old Norse origin: it exists also in English dialect, but with the senses of a bin or a manger.

blaes, blae A bluish-grey clay or soft slate, a by-product of the shale industry once prominent in West Lothian. As a soft clay, *blae* is vividly recalled by the miner poet Joe Corrie, writing of himself at work: 'Crawlin' aboot ... in the mud Covered wi' clammy *blae*' (1928). When the shale oil is extracted by a heating process, there remains a reddish gritty substance. This material, known as *blaes*, has been used for making tennis courts, all-weather football or hockey pitches, and more recently in road-making. *Blaes*, or *blae*, though here used as a noun, is the same word as *blae* (blue, livid), the first element in BLAEBERRY (XI).

bubbly jock A turkey cock. Sometimes shortened to *bubbly*. Colloquial and literary Scots. A Duchess of Gordon early in the 19th century is reported to have said, 'Rax me a spaul (pass me a leg) o' that *bubbly-jock*' (see RAX, VI). How many of her successors would, or could, express themselves in these terms! The turkey-cock was regarded as rather a terrifying creature: hence the saying 'There's a *bubbly jock* at every-body's door' (1936), and a reference to the 'dreaded *bubbly jock*' in 1986. The name was probably an attempt to imitate the sound made by the turkey cock. It seems almost a pity to reject an earlier explanation: 'The name seems to have originated from the shape of his [wattles], which had considerable resemblance to the snot collected at a dirty child's nose' (1808).

buckie A whelk, a (not always edible) shellfish. First appears in Scots at the end of the 16th century. In 1706 the edible kind were being served up at a feast: 'There will be partans (crabs) and *buckies*'. In 1845 they were being used for 'baiting cod-lines'. In 1935 someone enthused over 'those lovely little shells, the John o' Groats *buckies*'. Buckie has also been used this century for the shell of a snail. The origin of *buckie* is uncertain. But it belongs to the genus *buccinum*, and may derive from this Latin word for a kind of shellfish.

byre A cowshed. General Scots. Also in northern English dialect. First recorded in Scots in 1437, in a reference to the gate between 'the barn and the *byre*', two buildings that are often linked to symbolise farm-life in Scotland – the 'work of barn and *byre*.' From Old English *bur*, from which English *bower* probably derived.

cleek A hook or hook-shaped implement. Since first recorded in Scots in the 15th century *cleek* has been applied to, among other things, a crochet hook and a salmon gaff. In 1988 someone admitted 'being in possession of a *cleek* for the purpose of poaching.' It was also until the early part of the 20th century the name of one of the golfing irons. In Leven in Fife a factory where golf clubs were made was known locally as the '*Cleek works*.' Also a verb. To *cleek* arms is to link arms; see also PINKIE (I). *Cleekit* gloves are crocheted. From a northern Middle English word for a hook. See also GIRD AND CLEEK (X).

collie A sheep dog distinguished for its intelligence rather than its pedigree. First appeared in Scots in the 17th century. Since such dogs are often dark in colour it is supposed that *collie* is from *coalie* (black as coal). In English *collie* is usually applied to thoroughbred dogs of the 'Lassie' type.

coo is the Scots form of *cow*, and is used as in standard English. It has two possible plural forms – *coos* and *kye*: the latter is less used than it once was.

creel A basket. Now widely used in general English for an angler's basket, but in earlier use in Scots it was a deep basket for carrying heavy loads. A pack animal could be loaded with two *creels*, one on each side, to carry fish, peat, etc. A man or woman would carry the *creel* on his or her back: it would be supported by a strap around the body, or sometimes round the forehead. A *labster-creel* is a lobster-pot. The origin of *creel* is unknown. It first appeared in Scots in the 14th century, and has been recorded in English since the 15th century.

croft in Scots usage is a small-holding. The *croft* is part of the way of life in the Highlands, and the area covered by what were till 1975 the seven northernmost counties of Scotland is still known as 'the *crofting* counties.' Farming on a croft is basically subsistence farming, and the *crofter* has often had a hard struggle to make ends meet. 'Fewer than 5% of all *crofts* can provide full-time employment in agriculture, so that other forms of employment such as fishing, weaving, roadwork, work as a postman, etc. are necessary' (A. Fenton *Scottish Country Life*, 1977).

cuddie A donkey; also, in some places, a horse. The old proverb 'A *cuddy's* gallop's sune (soon) done' clearly refers to the donkey. In a *cuddie-fight* a boy mounted pickaback on a friend tried to unseat another boy similarly mounted. *Cuddie-lowps* is another name for leap-frog (see also LOWP, VI). *Cuddie* was also applied to the 'horse' used in a gymnasium, and to a trestle used by a joiner. The origin of *cuddie* is uncertain: it may simply be from the short form of the name Cuthbert.

dross in Scotland has the special sense of 'slack', or refuse coal. It can vary in quality from tiny chips of coal to coal-dust. People burning coal sometimes complain that the coal-man has left them 'nothing but *dross*'.

fank A sheepfold. Initially a Gaelic word, and confined to the Highlands, *fank* has come to be accepted further south. First recorded in Scots in 1812, in Stirling: 'a pen, here called a *fank*'. A *fank* can be quite a complex structure, containing several pens, so that 'sheep can be sorted according to their class and age' (*Scots Magazine*, 1949). It has developed the extended meaning of what goes on in the *fank* (i.e. shearing), as in a caption to a picture, 'A sheep *fank* in progress', in the *Western Isles Guide* (*c* 1970). From Gaelic *fang*, of uncertain origin.

girdle A round flat iron baking-plate with a semi-circular handle which could be used to suspend the *girdle* over the fire when baking. In the absence of an oven, the *girdle* was essential for baking, but it meant that baking was limited to things that could be baked on it, like OATCAKES, SCONES, PANCAKES (all IV), etc. In modern times girdle baking has been almost entirely replaced by oven baking, though girdles in more streamlined shapes can still be bought. A person in a state of restless impatience can be described as being 'like a hen on a het (hot) *girdle*'. *Girdle* is originally the same word as English *griddle*; the *r* and the *i* were transposed in Scots.

graip An iron-headed fork with three or four prongs, used on the farm or in the garden. An interfering woman was once accused of 'strikin her *graip* in her neighbour's midden' (see MIDDEN, XII). *Graip* which is of Old Norse origin, is also found in northern English dialect.

graith The tools or equipment needed to perform some

particular job. Colloquial and localised Scots. The general meaning is well summed up by the novelist Neil Munro: before a man starts a job, he 'should hae all his working *graith* aboot him' (about 1930). The man who asks 'Where's ma *graith*?' is looking for his tools, and also perhaps for his working clothes. *Ploo-graith* is, or was, all the gear needed when ploughing, and *graith* can also refer to the harness of a horse. A curious development has made *graith* prominent among terms used in the washing of clothes. It can mean a soapy lather in which to wash or steep clothes; by putting plenty of soap powder in the water, you will get a good *graith* for the wash. It can also mean the action of washing or steeping: dirty clothes must be given a good *graith*, sometimes 'anither *graith*'. *Graith* can also be used of the mass of soap suds left behind when the wash is finished. *Graith* can mean a person's material possessions, collectively: to have a 'good *graith*' is to be well-off or prosperous.

Graith was once commonly used as a verb, but as such it is now rare. To *graith* one's equipment means to make it ready for a job. In older Scots from the 14th century *graith* was very common indeed, both as noun and verb, and with much the same meanings as it has today. It is of Old Norse origin, and was also found in northern Middle English.

hairst A shortened form of *hairvest* or *hervest*, the Scots equivalents of English *harvest*. A possible effect of the existence of two distinct forms of a word is illustrated by this quotation: 'Here in Creiff [Perthshife] *hairst* is used for the grain harvest. *Hervest* is used of the fruit harvest. People . . . would never say apple *hairst*' (1955).

herd To *herd* sheep or cattle is to watch over them to prevent them from straying on to crops, especially in places where there is no fencing. By a relatively recent extension of meaning one can now *herd* crows or rooks, to stop them from feeding on crops. A *herd* is someone employed to do this or to be a shepherd.

hog(g) A young sheep from the time it has been weaned

until it is shorn for the first time. This is also the sense of *hog* in many English dialects, but in standard English a hog refers only to a pig. *Hog(g)* has had this sense in Scots since the 15th century. In 1483 one condition for the sale of some sheep was that none of them should be '*hogs* or clipped sheep', and in 1709 we hear of the theft of a '*hog sheep*'. In 1956 there was a '*Hogg* sale' in Bathgate: 'Gross *hoggs* [were] sold to 139/-.' The spelling with -*gg* is common in such notices, probably to avoid confusion with the standard English sense.

Hog has also been, since 1772, a CURLING (X) term for a 'stone' which is out of bounds. A line called the *hog-score* is drawn across the rink, and every stone delivered must cross it to be in play. A stone which fails to cross the *hog-score* is removed from the ice, or '*hogged off*', and a stone so removed is known as a *hog*. This may be because young sheep at the *hog* stage may be sickly, and perhaps unable to keep up with the flock. The same penalty of being *hogged* also applies in CARPET BOWLS (X).

hutch in technical Scots is a small wheeled truck or wagon used for transporting coal from the coal face. A former miner remembers in his youth 'emptying the *hutches* at the pitheid.' In Fife also known as a box or tub.

ingan An onion. Colloquial Scots. Old French for an onion was *oingnon* or *oignon*, the *(n)gn* group representing an -*ny*-sound. The French sound was treated differently in Scots and English. Hence the contrast between Scots *ingan* and English *onion*, though the two words have the same French origin. In some places the Frenchmen who until the 1960s sold onions from door to door were known as '*ingan Johnnies*'.

joiner, *Sc* **jiner** A carpenter. General Scots. In English a joiner is someone who does lighter work than a carpenter. Advertisement columns in Scottish papers may have a section devoted to 'Builders and *Joiners*' offering to carry out 'all types of *joinery* work' (1987). Until the 19th century the ordinary Scots word for a carpenter was *wricht* (wright, as in woodwright), but it has now been replaced by *joiner*.

kail Borecole or cabbage. *Kail* was a staple of the Scots diet – so much so that at one time *kail* came to mean the main meal of the day, and one way of asking a friend to dinner was to ask him to 'take his *kail* with the family' (1858). As early as the 17th century the summons to dinner was not a gong but a *kail-bell* – a sense remembered by a writer from the north-east in 1933: 'Lassie, ye've a tongue like a *kale-bell*.' *Kail* was so important in the kitchen garden that this was from the 16th century on called the *kailyard* (see also KAILYARD SCHOOL, V), and Burns's Holy Willie called upon God to curse his enemy's '*kail* and potatoes'. The so-called *Scotch kail* has purplish leaves, less wrinkled than those of kail; in Scotland it was called *lang kaill*.

Kail was also the name given to various dishes made with that vegetable as the principal ingredient, either by boiling or mashing the leaves, or by making a soup from kail and other ingredients. The name could even apply to a vegetable soup without any kail in it: 'pea *kail* is broth made with fresh green peas' (1942). The stalk of *kail*, stripped of its leaves, is called a *kail-runt*. At one time it was believed in Orkney that if you went out in the dark and pulled a *kail-runt*, you might see in it the shape of your future spouse. *Kail-runt* was sometimes used as an insult, especially apparently to old women, but there is something refreshing about a reference to 'the sapless *kail-runts* of the SENATUS (VIII)' of a University (1934). See also RUNT (I). *Cauld kail het again* is reheated food, but also is said of a story told so often that it has become boring. *Kail* is the Scots form of English *cole*.

klondyke To export fresh fish to the continent on factory ships, which process them on the way to the continental markets where they are sold. Early in the 20th century *klondykers* came from a variety of European countries in search of herring, but nowadays they come only from East European countries and buy mackerel. Early in 1988 most of the mackerel landed at Ullapool was 'sold to *klondykers*.' This trade brings larger and quicker returns than does landing fish in home ports. Hence the use of the term *klondyke*, from the famous Yukon goldmine of the late

19th century, to suggest the 'get-rich-quick' motive of those involved in *klondyking*.

lazy-bed A method of planting a crop, now almost exclusively potatoes, that does not involve tilling an area of land. A strip of uncultivated ground about 3–4 feet wide is marked out, and is covered with manure – or, as once was the case in the Hebrides and parts of the Highlands – with seaweed. Furrows are then dug on either side of the strip, and earth or sods taken from it are thrown up on to the strip, sometimes over the seeds, but seeds may also be dibbled in afterwards. The method was used chiefly in the Highlands, but also in bad land in the Lowlands. The lazy-bed technique is now rarely used, but it still has its advocates.

lib To geld or castrate (a farm animal). In *Sunset Song* (1932) the novelist Lewis Grassic Gibbon writes of 'the *libbing* of the lambs'. W.L. Lormer's *New Testament in Scots* (1983) translates *Matthew* xix.12 by 'some hes made themsels *libberts* (eunuchs) for the sake of the Kingdom o Heiven.' *Lib* is from Middle English, and is still used in northern English dialect. It was first recorded in Scots in the 16th century.

mains The home farm of an estate, cultivated for the benefit of the proprietor of the estate. In current use, the word is found chiefly in farm names (as Carberry *Mains*, *Mains* of Midstrath), but it is also applied to the outbuildings of a farm. *Mains* is a shortened form of *domain*, which is from French, and is connected (as is English *demesne*) with Latin *dominus*, a lord or master.

mart is a market, in Scots as in English. But in Scots it has also the specialised sense of an auction sale of livestock, farm products and agricultural implements. Thus in May 1987 St Boswell's Auction *Mart* offered for sale on successive days cattle and sheep; tractors and farm machinery; and grazing land. The *mart* was originally the building where such sales took place; it then came to mean the sales themselves. *Mart* is from English *mart*, a market place or hall, an auction, which derived from Dutch *markt*.

mell A mallet or heavy hammer, usually made of wood and so suitable for driving fencing posts into the ground. *Mell*, which existed in both older Scots and northern Middle English, is from the French, and ultimately from Latin *malleus*. Edward I of England was known as *malleus Scotorum*, the hammer of the Scots.

merchant in Scotland, alongside the standard English sense, retains the older meaning of a retail shopkeeper. The Edinburgh *Yellow Pages* for 1986 contains a list of *General Merchants*, and the *Wine and Spirit Merchants* section is divided into two – retail and wholesale. *Provision Merchants* is followed by the direction: 'See also Grocers, Supermarkets and General Stores.' *Merchant* also occurs in the titles of such corporations as the Merchant Company or Merchant Guild of a town. These were once guilds in the historical sense, and they still play an important part in the life of their communities. For example, the Edinburgh Merchant Company makes provision for several well-known schools and also for a 'Home for the Elderly'.

midden A dunghill, as in English dialect. The sense, if not the thing itself, has been refined in Scots, so that a *midden* may also be a compost heap or a refuse heap of any kind. General Scots. It has even in some places come to mean the refuse put out of a house for collection by the local cleansing department. The Glasgow writer, Cliff Hanley, remembers that 'what are called *middens* upper class people described as dustbins' (1958). Sometimes in recent use shortened to **midgie**, which has yielded new compounds like *midgie-bin* (dustbin) and *midgie-man* (dustman). A *midden* is also applied to a dirty and untidy place: 'His bed-sit's just a *midden*.' *Midden* was first recorded in Scots in the 14th century. It came through Middle English from an Old Norse word for a muck heap.

midgie see MIDDEN (XII)

neep A turnip, especially the swede. Colloquial and occasional Scots. The food value of the *neep* for both people and farm animals has long been recognized, and the *neep* field is a common sight. A hollowed-out turnip could be made into a *neep-lantern* for HALLOWEEN (IX). The plural *neeps* often refers to cooked and mashed turnips. It is the vegetable dish most commonly served with HAGGIS (IV). *Neep* is found in Middle and Old English, but since the 16th century it has been only dialect in English.

opencast has been used in Scottish mining since the 17th century, and is now in general English use for extraction of coal by quarrying at ground level instead of mining. *Cast* as here used means an excavation, a meaning developed from the verb *cast* in the sense of to dig. *Opencast* was also found in northern English dialect.

park In Scotland, as in Ireland, *park* has developed the special meaning of an enclosed field: one may have a '*park* o gress (grass)' or a '*park* o tatties (potatoes)', and one can talk about the 'work of *park* and byre'. The attendant at a public park is known to the local children as a *parkie* – a blast on his whistle used to be a sufficient signal to behave correctly.

Park is now commonly used to mean a football pitch. Scots footballers being interviewed insist that it is 'performances on the *park* that matter' (1986), and in 1987 a rugby commentator observed that play was moving 'from end to end of the *park*'. This usage is now also heard in England.

partan A crab – strictly speaking, an edible variety, as when in 1701 'lapster (lobster) and *partans* and brandie' were served for dinner. *Partan pie* used to be a popular dish, and *partan bree* is crab soup. But to small boys intent on bashing '*partins*' with a stone, they were simply creatures which 'nips folk's taes (toes)' (1901). *Partan* is the Gaelic word for a small crab. In Scots it is colloquial, but increasingly localised.

pellock A porpoise. In Scots since before 1500, but in early use perhaps referring to the dolphin. In the 17th century there was frequent mention of *pellock-whales* in Orkney and Shetland records. In 1955 in the north of Scotland 'a *paillag* came up an awa wi wur nets (and made off with our nets).' Now dialect and localised Scots. It is not known where the word came from.

pirn A reel or bobbin. 'A *pirn* o threid' is a reel of thread. Colloquial Scots. In some places *pirn* is also used for the reel of a fishing rod. First recorded in Scots in the 15th century. Of unknown origin.

shed has certain peculiarly Scots usages, based on the idea of dividing or separating. It is used when a flock of sheep has to be divided into different groups, and especially when lambs are being *shed* from ewes. When sheep are being driven into pens, there may be several entries to allow different groups of sheep to be *shed* into appropriate pens. In sheep-dog trials, the *shedding* of sheep into different groups is one of the tests imposed, and sometimes there is a prize awarded to the owner of the most successful dog because it has proved the best *shed* (or *shedder*). To *shed* is also to divide or part the wool along a sheep's back, and to part the hair on a person's head, the parting being known as the *shed*. Before one boy went out, 'he put a *shed* into his hair.' These senses were first recorded in Scots in the 15th and 16th centuries.

shuil is the commonest of several colloquial Scots forms of English *shovel*. A -*v*- tends to be lost in such a position in Scots: one possible past tense of the verb to *love* in Scots is *lude*. An Aberdeen man remembers using a *shuil* for 'turning grain in a distillery'.

smowt in its original sense, from about 1500, is a young salmon or sea trout. It is however more widely known in its transferred sense of a very small person, or a small child. General Scots, and a statement of fact rather than an insult. 'He's just a *smout*' (1986). R.L. Stevenson when a child was known as '*Smout*'.

spurtle A short rounded stick for stirring porridge. Now frequently on sale in souvenir shops during the tourist season, ornamented with carved thistles or saltires. General Scots except in parts of Tayside region, where the same utensil is called a theevil: 'nowadays my *theevil* hangs as an ornament in my kitchen' (*Scots Magazine*, 1984). *Spurtle* was also the name given to a long–handled spatula that could be used to turn oatcakes or scones during baking. It is used in this sense now chiefly in the areas where a porridge-stick is called a *theevil*. *Spurtle* is connected with English dialect *spartle*, which is probably of Scandinavian origin. *Theevil* came to Scots from a Middle English word for a pot-stick.

stirk in Scots is applied particularly to a young bullock (also, less frequently, to a heifer) which has been weaned, but is being kept for slaughter when 2 or 3 years old. In Perth early in 1988 among store cattle on sale were not only 'heifer *stirks*,' but also *stot stirks*. A **stot stirk** is a Scots term for a bullock in its second year. *Stirk*, recorded in Scots since the 14th century, is ultimately from an Old English word for a calf. *Stot*, which also dates from the 14th century, came through Middle English from an Old Norse word for an ox or bull. In Middle English it could also mean a horse or nag.

stot stirk see STIRK (XII).

syboe A spring onion, as in 'a salad of tomatoes and chopped *syboes*'. First recorded in Scots in 1574 as *sybbow*, perhaps directly from the central French *ciboule*. The northern French form was *chiboule*, from which came English dialect *chibol*. All these go back to a Latin word for a little onion.

tattie Shortened colloquial Scots name for the potato. During and after the two world wars the time of the potato harvest or *tattie howkin* (digging) was eagerly awaited in many schools all over Scotland, as some classes were freed for the *tattie-holidays* to work as *tattie-lifters* in fields of potatoes. In some places the week's holiday now enjoyed in October is still known as the *tattie-holidays*. Until the 1950s some of the harvesting was done by Irish *tattie-howkers*, and even today large numbers of *tattie-pickers* are employed to supplement the work of mechanical harvesters. *Champit*, or *chappit*, *tatties* are mashed potatoes, and the unconsumed portion may be made into TATTIE SCONES (IV). The Scots word for a scarecrow is *tattie-bogle* (or *-bogie*). Properly, it guarded the potato crop, but was given other jobs as well.

theevil see SPURTLE (XII).

upset price The minimum price acceptable if the thing for sale is not to be withdrawn. General Scots. Until recently 'property for sale' advertisements in Scotland used to state the *upset price* of a house, but this is now generally dropped in favour of 'offers over'. *Upset* means the same as standard English *set up*, to erect.

waulk, walk To full cloth, that is, to thicken it and give it a closer texture by soaking and beating it so that it shrinks and is thoroughly cleansed. The *walk-mill* or *waulkin-mill* was the equivalent of the fulling-mill, and the workers were called *waulkers* – hence the surname Walker, and the place name Walkerburn on the River Tweed. Until quite recent times the work of *waulking* the cloth was done in the Hebrides by hand. An early description of the process was given by Boswell in 1773: the work was done by women, who knelt on the ground and rubbed the cloth with both hands, 'singing an Erse song all the time'. Other witnesses tell us that the feet too were used. The accompanying song was a *waulking-song*, and was chosen for the suitability of its rhythm; it was not music composed for this particular work. Such songs, many of which have been preserved, deal with a wide variety of themes, and give unique insights into earlier Gaelic society. *Waulk* is originally the same word as *walk* (go on foot). It was used for to full cloth in Middle English, but in modern English is found in this sense only in dialect.

wulk, wilk Scots form of English *whelk*. In Scotland *wulk* is the usual name for the periwinkle, while the whelk is called a

BUCKIE (XII). Perhaps because '*wulks* stick to rocks' there is a saying 'as thrawn (contrary) as a *wulk*'; another saying is 'as fou (full) as a *wulk*', very drunk (see FOU and THRAWN, II). The nose is in some places jokingly called the *wulk*: hence the phrase to *pick your wulk*.

yowe Scots form of English *ewe*. Colloquial Scots. Made more widely known from the opening line of one of Burns's most lovely songs, 'Ca (drive) the *yowes* tae the knowes (low hills)'.

doocot (XIII)

crawsteps on gable (XIII)

pend (XIII)

quaich (XIII)

pig (XIII)

XIII

Construction   House   Household

ashet A large, frequently oval-shaped, plate used for serving food, especially joints of meat. First recorded in Scots in 1725, and retained in general Scots because there is no satisfactory English alternative. In the 20th century *ashet* has in parts of Scotland been used for an enamel pie-dish. From French *assiette*, a plate.

bass A mat of coarse material, especially a door-mat. Colloquial Scots. A letter to the *Scotsman* in 1986 claimed that in one nuclear plant a main precaution was for the worker to 'dicht his shune (wipe his feet) on the *bass*.' Scots form of English *bast*, the bark of a lime tree; first recorded in Scots in the 18th century.

besom, bizom The original sense of a broom or sweeping brush is common to Scots and English, though the English (unlike the Scots) is limited to a brush made from a stick and a bundle of twigs. Where Scots is distinctive is in its frequent application of *besom* to a woman. Sometimes this is quite good-natured and suggests no more than excessive liveliness, as in 'my wild *besom* o' a cousin' (1929). But more often it is abusive or condemnatory, more the equivalent of *bitch*: 'That lassie's a nesty wee *bizzom*.' In this sense it is general Scots. The usual pronunciation in Scots is *bizom*. Sir James Murray, the Scots editor of the *Oxford English Dictionary*, held that in his Border area there were two forms – *besom* for a broom and *bizom* for a low woman. Other areas seem to have been less discriminating.

big To build. The word *build* entered Scots from English in the 16th century. Before that *big*, of Norse origin, was the word in common use, but since then it has lost ground to *build*; even in colloquial Scots it is now less often heard than it was fifty years ago. *Big* has the same range of meaning as *build*. You can *big* a house or a fire; 'wee birds *bigg* by *ilka* (every) bush' (1929); and you are warned not to '*big* your hopes on that'. A building is a *bigging*, a word sometimes found in place names, as Newbigging.

bothy A rough hut or shelter, the use of which is only occasional or temporary. General Scots. A *bothy* may accommodate workmen on a building site, make provision for fishermen near fishings, or offer shelter to climbers on a mountain. *Bothies* were also the permanent communal living-quarters provided for unmarried men working as labourers on farms at the end of the 19th century and the beginning of this one. In this sense, the word has been given wider currency in *bothy ballads*, songs often of the robust kind one would expect in an all-male environment in which there were few other forms of entertainment available. *Bothy* may be from English *booth* or Gaelic *bothan*, both of which mean a hut; or from a combination of both.

brig The Scots form of *bridge*. Now localised and occasional Scots. In the 1960s the advent of the Forth Road Bridge was heralded locally by a song, 'They're gaun (going) to build a new *brig* ower the Forth'. Very common in place names.

broch A large prehistoric round tower or fort with thick stone walls: now a technical term in archaeology. *Brochs* are found in Orkney and Shetland, the Western Isles and on the adjacent Scottish mainland. They were also known as Picts' castles, as it was long, but wrongly, believed that they had been built by the Picts. The circular shape of the broch is alluded to in some other senses. A halo round the sun or moon is called a *broch*. If around the moon, it is a sign of bad weather: when 'the *broch* is far out from the moon' a storm is close, but if 'the *bruch's* near [the moon] . . . the storm's far' (1914). *Broch* is an altered form of the word BURGH (VII) which originally meant a fortress as well as a town. *Broch* too meant a town. In 1826 there was a popular rhyme which claimed that 'Musselbrogh was a *brogh* when Edinbrogh was nane (none).' It survives in this sense in the north-east of Scotland where Fraserburgh is known lc ally as 'the *Broch*', the nearest town of note in the area.

bucket in Scots has developed the special meaning of a dustbin, and there is a twice-weekly ritual of 'putting out the *bucket*' in time for the refuse collection. *Bucket* has survived the introduction of plastic containers. Whether it will outlive the polythene bags now the rule in some areas has yet to be seen: in Edinburgh these still have to be put out on *bucket-night*. *Bucket* can also mean a drink, especially a large quantity of drink: 'He can take a fair *bucket*' is a tribute to a drinker's capacity.

but and ben A two-roomed cottage. General Scots. In the older type of *but and ben* the front door was at one end of the cottage and gave access to the outer room, which often accommodated domestic animals as well as people. The inner room, or *ben*, formed the living quarters. Children were sometimes described as toddling '*but and ben*', from one room to the other. See also BEN (XIV). *But* now scarcely has a life of its own, though at the beginning of this century it still had a full range of meaning. In a *but and ben* the *but* was the '*but* or kitchen end of the house' – the outer as opposed to the inner room. 'Gang *but*' meant go into the other, or outer, room. *But* originally consisted of two syllables – *be* (as in *between*) and *out*, from an Old English word for outside. See also ROOM (XIII).

cairn A pyramid-shaped pile of loose stones, sometimes one erected over a grave or as a memorial. The Scottish gift to Australia to mark its bi-centenary in 1988 was a *cairn*, to be erected in Sydney. A *cairn* is often found marking a summit at the top of a mountain; this practice was adopted by the Ordnance Survey when mapping Britain in the later 19th century. *Cairn* was thus introduced to English usage. A line of *cairns* may also be set up to mark a hill-path or boundary. An early sense was defined by an English traveller in 1730 as 'an exceedingly stony hill.' For hill-walkers this is a definition worth bearing in mind, as in mountain names *cairn* often indicates the stony nature of the summit. From Gaelic *càrn*; first recorded in Scots in the 15th century, and now accepted as standard English.

causey A paved area, as a road, street or farmyard: now sometimes used for a roadway, as in 'crown of the *causey*'. Chiefly localised Scots or dialect. A *causeystane* is a cobblestone. 'A fireside deil (devil) and a *causey*-saint' describes a person who is snappy at home but agreeable in the *causey* or out-of-doors. From the Middle English equivalent of *causey* came *causey-way*, modern English *causeway*, in the sense of a raised way over wet ground. *Causey* itself is now only dialect in English. It is of French origin.

clachan A small village. Since *clachan* is of Gaelic origin, it was at first used only of Highland villages, but is now used more widely, if selectively. In one of his songs written in 1960 Hamish Henderson used 'pitheid (coalmine) and *clachan*' as typical of the springs of Scottish working class life. *Clachan* is from Gaelic *clach*, a stone. It has been suggested that the meaning of *clachan* in Gaelic developed from the standing stones of the druids to mean a graveyard, and then a village with a church.

close A passageway, in general Scots one leading from a main street to several houses, but in Glasgow the entrance to a TENEMENT (XIII) building. The original sense of *close* in Scots and English was the same – an enclosed space or yard. In Edinburgh, a *close* is a narrow alley leading off the Royal Mile into a courtyard surrounded by houses, or running between buildings on either side: it is often retained in street names

– Old Fishmarket Close and Advocates' Close, for example. In Glasgow in 1839 the *closes* were described as 'courts about 15 to 20 feet square, round which the houses, mostly of three stories high, are built.' *Closes* of the last kind were common to many of the older Scottish towns, but by 1952 the *Scottish National Dictionary* could claim that 'such *closes* are tending to disappear through slum clearance.' In Glasgow today a *close* is the entry passage to a tenement; but it can also mean all the flats sharing the same common hallway and stair, so that many Glaswegians are said to live *up a close*.

cludgie W.C., toilet. In the modern ballad *Hairy Mary* at a vital stage in the plot the heroine's mother has to pay a visit to the *cludgie*. The word seems to have originated in Glasgow, and to have spread over central Scotland and Fife in the 60s. Dictionaries dismiss it as 'slang', and suggest that it is made up from *closet* and *ludge*, the Scots form of *lodge*.

couple As in English, two of a kind; but in technical Scots *couple* has the additional sense of one of a pair of identical rafters, raised in the form of an inverted V, and with other *couples* helping to support a roof. Originally a *couple* probably meant both rafters in a pair.

crawstep A feature of traditional Scottish architecture. The gable wall of a house is often along its top edges ornamented by a set of small steps, sometimes interrupted by a chimney stack. These are *crawsteps* or crowsteps (see CRAW, XI).

cundy, condie Scots forms of *conduit*. Used in localised Scots for a street gutter, a covered drain, or the entrance to a drain. English final -*t* has quite often been lost in a corresponding Scots form. Thus, when first recorded in Scots in 1513, *cundy* was written *cundit*. See also STANK, SYVER (both XIII).

doocot A dovecot, an essential feature of any well-appointed property long before an Act of Parliament in 1424 found it necessary to threaten destroyers of '*dowcottis*' with punishment.

In 1933 it was reported that a pigeon-fancier's birds lived in 'dovecots (pronounced locall; *doocot*, but snappily, thus *dooc't*).' See also DOO (XI).

drystane Built of stones without mortar. Also found in the dialect of north Yorkshire. In 1949 an attempt was being made in the south-west of Scotland 'to revive an almost extinct industry – *drystane* dyking.' A '*dry-stone* wall' (1948) hesitates between Scots and English in a way unthought of in this 1861 quotation: 'O Lord, Thoo is like a moose (mouse) in a *dry-stane* dyke – aye keekin oot (always peeping out) at us frae (from) holes . . . and we canna see Thee.' See also DYKE (XIII).

dyke A low wall of stone or turf. 'The low dry-stone wall is a common field fence in Scotland, and is there named a *dyke* to distinguish it from *wall*, which implies a structure of stone and lime' (1890). The word exists in both Scots and English, and has the same origin as *ditch*. In its earliest use in Scots *dyke* meant a ditch, as it did in English; but by the 16th century the emphasis had shifted from the ditch dug to the mound of earth thrown up by the diggers. Instead of wading through a dyke, attackers now had to climb over one. In the south-west of Scotland in the present century *dyke* is sometimes used for a hedge. A *fail-dyke* is a wall made with sods of turf. A secondary use of the dyke is alluded to in *winter dykis*, the name given to a clothes-horse. As a verb, to *dyke* means to build or repair a dyke, and a man doing such work is a *dyker*. In 1921 someone was recognized as 'the best dry-stane *dyker* in the shire o' Dumfries.'

entry A passage or door which allows access to a place. General Scots. In one sense, such an *entry* is a public passage, sometimes leading to a house, sometimes passing between houses: it is usually arched over. In 1914 the novelist Neil Munro described 'an *entry* high-arched and broad enough to pass a cart.' The second sense is the front doorway of a house, or the entrance to a block of flats (a '*common entry*'), including any passage leading from the door to the street. In

Edinburgh *entry* is often applied to the whole group of houses sharing the one common entrance: 'we used to live in the same *entry*'. *Entry* shares the usual standard English senses, but the above senses are found in England only in dialect.

See also CLOSE, STAIR (both XIII).

flat As an apartment, *flat* is now standard English, though as late as 1897 the *Oxford English Dictionary* could comment, 'until recently, peculiar to Scotland [in this sense].' In the 18th century a *flat* first meant a landing on a stairway: 'a stair of 20 steps, interrupted by a *flat*' (1730). In 1735 it could mean a story of a house: people were described as parting from each other and going into different rooms 'on the same *flat*'. Twenty years later an Aberdeen tenement was 'fitted up for setting (letting) in different *flats*, with a kitchen to each' (1759). In Scott's *Redgauntlet* (1824) there is a reference to the situation of dwellers in Edinburgh's old town, who lived 'piled up above each other in *flats*'.

gantree is, as in standard English, a wooden stand for a barrel. From this in Scots it has developed the sense of the shelved stand behind a bar on which the rows of bottles are displayed. One Edinburgh bar is noted for its 'dark wood bar and *gantry*' (*Tollcross Times*, 1988).

harl To coat an outer wall with a mixture of lime and small stones. Scots since late in the 16th century. The process was described by an English traveller about 1730: 'On the outside they face the work all over with mortar thrown against it with a trowel, which they call *harling*.' In 1956 in one case 'a wide slab of *harling* had fallen away leaving the bare stonework visible.' In the 19th century *harl* came to be used as a noun for the mixture of sand and lime used in roughcasting: in 1909 when a wall was being finished the 'hollows were filled or flushed over with lime *harl*.' In 1970 in a series of stamps issued to illustrate varieties of British domestic architecture the fivepenny stamp bore the legend 'Fife *harling*'. The origin of *harl* is unknown.

house Not only a separate building for dwelling in, as in standard English, but also any part of a building that is occupied as a dwelling, e.g. a flat. As Adam Smith pointed out in 1776, 'in France, Scotland and many other parts of Europe, it [*house*] frequently means no more than a single storey.'

House has a special meaning in the game of CURLING (X). Round the TEE (X), the mark towards which curlers direct their 'stones', a large circle 12 feet in diameter is drawn on the ice; this is called the *house*. When points are reckoned, no stone scores unless it is within the *house*. Much of the skill in curling consists in aiming stones into positions in which they help members of your side, and block the aim of your opponents. A concerted team effort to do this is known as *building a house*.

howf A place to which one goes for company or for refuge. General Scots. The wide definition given covers two different kinds of resort. The first, a place where one can meet people, frequently refers to a public house. 'They sought the shelter of a *howff* off the High Street' (1955). In the 1960s the Dunfermline Folk Song Club used to meet in a somewhat inelegant but friendly hall known locally as 'the *Howff*'. The second, related, meaning is a rude shelter or refuge, particularly a shelter used by mountaineers. In 1948 the *Scottish Mountaineering Club Journal* stated that 'the best known example of a mountaineering *howff* is the Shelter Stone of Loch Avon [in the Cairngorms].' *Howf* is probably from Dutch or Flemish *hof*, an enclosed place or courtyard.

ingle An open fireplace; a hearth or the fire burning on it; the fireside. The sense of domestic comfort and intimacy suggested by *ingle* could not be transferred to modern heating methods, and the word is all but obsolete except in remote dialects and literary Scots. We are left with allusions to an '*ingle*, blazing bright' (1920), with pictures of a family sitting 'round the *ingle*' (1885), or of the cosiness of the *ingle-neuk*, the chimney corner or fireside. *Ingle* is from a Gaelic word for fire.

jaw-box A kitchen sink; formerly, a communal one serving several homes. In 1859 the *Glasgow Herald* announced that every one of a group of new houses was supplied with 'a pipe, a stop-cock and a *jaw-box*.' A *jaw-hole* was a form of drain, at its most primitive a hole in the wall through which dirty water or refuse could be ejected. *Jaw* is an old Scots word, now rare, for to splash, spill or pour. Its origin is unknown. *Box* perhaps refers to the fact that the kitchen sink is often housed in a wooden frame.

kist A chest or box, sometimes a substantial and handsome piece of furniture, sometimes a strong-box. *Kists*, like chests, are no longer in vogue: from being one of the commonest articles of furniture in earlier centuries, the *kist* has become something of a rarity. In 1517 the common seal of the burgh of Selkirk was kept in a '*kest* (kist) with four locks' and valued articles were often stored in a '*kist* at the bed end' (1582). In 1986 a visitor to a stately home noticed that 'an ancient *kist* is kept in the entrance hall' for donations. *Kist* is the Scots, and also the northern English, form corresponding to English *chest*.

(k)nock A clock. Localised Scots, and becoming rare. In 1782 a writer presumed that 'clocks are called *knocks* in some parts of Scotland from the noise they make.' The truth seems to be that the *kl–* sound was here changed in daily use to *kn–*; and *clock* and *knock* are really the same word.

land in 15th century Scots developed the specialised sense of land in a town on which some building had taken place. The name of a *land* was then transferred to the building erected, especially to a large building several stories high. In 1926 someone lived in a 'high, high *land*' in Edinburgh, but generally *land* is now heard only in names such as Gladstone's *Land*, a building in Edinburgh's 'Royal Mile'. It is situated in a street called the Lawnmarket: the first element of this is an altered form of the word *land*, and the *land market* was once the market to which sellers of meat from country districts brought their meat. This preserves an older meaning of *land*, the country as opposed to the town.

lum A chimney, in the widest sense – a flue, a chimney stack, even in the past the 'chimney-corner', the area around the fire so often regarded as the centre of home life. In early use, in the 17th century, a *lum* was probably little more than a vent in the roof, but by 1701, when we find payment being made for '*swyping* (sweeping) 7 *lums*', we have a chimney of a modern kind. *Lum* is colloquial Scots; although often supplanted by 'chimney', it is general Scots in the widely known saying, 'Lang may your *lum* reek (smoke),' a wish for the continued good-fortune of the person addressed. *Lum* can also be used for the funnel of a railway engine or a steamship. A *lum-hat* is a top-hat: in the less ecumenical days of 1935 a reference was made to the '*lum-hatted* English Church'. *Lum* seems to have come from northern English dialect (where it is still known), as it is recorded there almost 100 years before it appeared in Scots. It is perhaps derived from an obsolete Welsh word for a chimney.

main-door A door which gives immediate entry from a street or garden to a private house, as opposed to the common entry door to a TENEMENT (XIII). A *main-door flat* is distinguished from other flats in a tenement by having such a door. In Edinburgh in 1987 a 'well decorated *main-door flat*' was advertised in the local press.

mercat cross The market cross of a burgh. *Mercat* is the Scots form of *market*, and *mercat cross* must be accepted as general Scots, since nearly everyone in Scotland knows what it means and where the local one stands. A *mercat cross* is now a historical relic, though on occasion it may still be the scene of a public proclamation.

pend An arched passageway, frequently one running through a building into a court or yard behind it. Technical Scots. It was reported in *The Scotsman* in 1986 that 'two shop fronts, a *pend* and premises to the rear [had been] transformed into a gallery, meeting place and workshops.' A *pend* was originally an arch or a vault, and in 1454 we find a *pend* being raised over a grave. *The Pends* in St Andrews was once a vaulted gatehouse. *Pend* was at first only a verb, to shape into an archway: it probably came from French *pendre*, to hang. Sometimes altered to the form *pen(n)*.

pig A jar or vessel made of earthenware. The word has been in Scots and northern English since the 15th century, but it has enjoyed a more vigorous life in Scots. The *pig* seems to have had as many uses as it had shapes. In 1540 one held wine for the mass; in 1641 ready money was kept in a little *pint pig*; in 1717 honey was sold in an 'earthen *pigg*'; in 1835 we hear of a 'whisky *pig*', and more recently a container for jam has been called a *jeelie-pig* (see JEELIE, IV). The solidly made earthenware jar that in the 19th and early 20th centuries served as a hot-water bottle was known as a *pig*. The enquiry: 'Shall I put a *pig* in your bed to keep you warm?' must have startled some visitors to Scotland. There was clearly room for confusion between the crock and the animal, but never more so than when in about 1650 a man told how he dreamt that 'he was a *lame pig* and that a golden hammer . . . broke him all to pieces.' In older Scots *lame* meant earthenware. *Pig* was also used for earthenware as a material, as in '*pig* bottle', or for a fragment of earthenware. The phrase *pigs and whistles* meant bits and pieces, odds and ends. *To go to pigs and whistles* is to go to wrack and ruin. In the 19th century *pig* also came to mean an earthenware money-box. This was later expanded to *piggie-bank*, in which *piggie* means made of earthenware, though in modern times such money-boxes are shaped and painted to look like pigs (the animal). *Piggie-bank* is now acceptable standard English. *Pig* came to Scots from Middle English *pygg*, the origin of which is unknown.

plat(t) The long flat stone laid on or just above ground level across the doorway of a house. Technical Scots. When upgrading or repairing a house, one of the works to be carried out may be 'Resurfacing entrance *platts*, entrance passages, (etc.)' (*Edinburgh District Council Order*, about 1983). At one time a *plat* was a landing on a stair, a sense still current in parts of Scotland; in Dundee a landing is called a *plattie* (the *t*'s are silent, as in Scots *be(tt)er*). *Plat(t)*, a plate or platter, first recorded in the 16th century, was used for a landing as early as 1650. It may have come through Middle English from French, or directly from Old French.

policy in Scotland developed the special sense of the enclosed park and gardens of a large estate. In this sense it is now almost invariably used in the plural only: one may admire an estate because the house is surrounded by finely laid out *policies*. In older Scots *policy* had the same meanings as in English, including well-planned activity. One instance of such action was the improvement of an estate by adding extra buildings and making the grounds more attractive. As early as the 15th century *policy* came to be applied to the improvements themselves. In 1541 the *policies* of a particular mansion included buildings, woods, gardens, hedges, ponds and other amenities.

press A large cupboard, nearly always one built into a wall, though it has sometimes been applied to free-standing cupboards. In 1986 a surveyor's report noted that a house had 'the usual *press* and cupboard accommodation.' General Scots, but not so widely used as when in 1962 someone wrote 'Our cupboard, like all Scottish cupboards, was called the *press*.'

pulley An indoor 'clothes-line' consisting of a wooden frame suspended from the ceiling of, usually, the kitchen, and raised and lowered on pulleys by a rope. The clothes to be dried are hung on the frame or ropes attached to it. General Scots, though thanks to modern appliances the pulley is not so necessary as it once was. Yet in 1987 someone assured me, 'I couldn't do without my *pulley*.' An ingenious contraption, whereby a pole, rope and pulley were combined to enable tenement dwellers to hang their washing outside the window to dry, is still in some areas called a *pulley-shee* or *pillie-shee*. It has been described as 'not unlike a gallows' (1929), and derives from an older Scots word *pilliescheve*, a grooved wheel, as in a pulley. It is possible that the indoor *pulley* was an adaptation of the *pulley-shee*. Evidence is lacking, since to date dictionaries have ignored this use of *pulley*.

quaich A drinking vessel, now usually an ornament or trophy. A *quaich* is wide and shallow, more like a bowl than a cup. It often has handles, usually two, one on either side. These are sometimes called lugs (see LUG, I), though they project horizontally from the rim. The workaday *quaich* was made from wooden staves bound together with metal hoops: others were made entirely of silver. In 1958 the *Scots Year Book* carried an advertisement by 'Makers of Wooden Scottish *Quaichs*, from drinking size suitable for St Andrews Dinners and Burns Nicht to large carved ones for prizes or presentations.' The *Craigentinny Quaich* is still competed for annually by golfers in the Edinburgh area. *Quaich* is from Gaelic *cuach*, a cup or bowl.

raggle A groove cut in stone (also, sometimes, in wood) so that, in construction, another stone, a slate, or some other material may fit closely into it. A *raggle* may be cut in the stone course at the top of a wall to receive the edge of a roof, or a gutter; and to *raggle* is to cut such a groove, which is also called a *ragglin*. In mining, to *raggle* is to cut a groove in a coal-face, especially when building a ventilation channel into a working. *Raggle* is technical Scots. It was first recorded in Scots in the 16th century, and is perhaps ultimately connected with Latin *regula*, a straight piece of wood.

rone, rhone The gutter which runs along the eaves of a roof and collects rain-water, which is then fed into a vertical *rone-pipe*, also sometimes ambiguously called a *rone*. Scottish householders have regular trouble with the *rones*, which may be blocked by various obstructions: failure to maintain them may bring an order to 'clean out gutters, *rhones* and roof-pipes' (1984). General Scots, of doubtful origin: perhaps connected with *run*, in the sense flow, discharge.

roof, *Sc* **ruif** in colloquial Scots has the extended sense of the ceiling of a room. Some people never call the ceiling anything else, and will talk of 'papering the *roof* of the sitting-room'.

room The 'sitting-room' in a BUT-AND-BEN (XIII), in which it was sometimes called the *room-end*, or other two-roomed house. The other apartment was the kitchen. In 1988 a Glasgow girl recalled that her family 'used to live in a *room and kitchen* (a two-room flat).' The best room in any house was often called *the room*. In 1795 the *Statistical Account of Scotland* noted that in Wigtown, 'the better sort of inhabitants . . . though they use peat in their kitchens, burn coal in the *rooms*.' From this distinction came into being *room-coal*, now obsolete, for better quality coal. At one time, a *room* was also a small holding of land. Otherwise *room* is used as in standard English.

sapple To soak; to wash or steep clothes in soapy water. Localised Scots. 'There's twa three claes (clothes) and I'll *sapple* them through' (1988). *Sapple*, or *sapples*, is also used as a noun for a soapy lather. *Sapple* was first recorded in the 19th century: it is from an earlier Scots verb *sap*, also meaning to soak.

scheme In Scotland since earlier this century *scheme* has been applied not only to the plan drawn up for a new housing estate, but also to the estate itself. To live on a local authority estate is to live in a *scheme*, or in a *housing scheme*. General Scots.

shore A quay or harbour. Localised Scots. This special sense of standard English *shore* is often preserved in what are now accepted as place names, like *The Shore* in Leith. The capital letter is not always correct: in Aberdeen the price of herring 'at the *shore*' or landing-place may be quoted. Since 1498 there has been a society, or even union, of *shore* porters in Aberdeen: this still exists, and from time to time one may glimpse a van bearing the legend, 'The Society of *Shore* Porters of Aberdeen'.

single end A one-room house, usually a tenement flat. The advertiser in the *Edinburgh Evening News* in 1967 who wanted to exchange 'large room and kitchen for *single end*, boxroom and WC' may have had to make do with a communal toilet on the stair. See also ROOM (XIII).

skew One of the stones forming part of the top course, or coping, of a gable wall on which the roof rests; also, the coping itself. Technical Scots. The coping is usually but not invariably on a slope. In 1923 one gable had 'curved *skewstones*' and another was '*flat-skewed*'. *Skew* was formerly common in English, but is now obsolete. It is from Old French *escu* (modern French *écu*), a shield.

sneck The old type of door-latch, which could be lifted from the outside by raising a small lever. Colloquial Scots. In 1966 a writer in the *Huntly Express* described the 'click of the hooked *sneck* into the staple on the doorpost.' To enter a house you had only to *lift the sneck* – that is, if the door had been left *on the sneck* and unlocked. *Aff* (or *off*) *the sneck* meant unlatched. The lever which operated the *sneck* was called a *sneckin-pin*. When the door clicked shut, you knew that it had *snecked*. If there was no click, but a cry of pain, it was possible that someone had *snecked* his finger in the door. Figurative uses are common. '*Sneck* your mouth' means 'Shut up!' So does '*Sneck up*', also used in this sense by Shakespeare in *Twelfth Night*. You can *sneck off* an electric light. A *sneckerdoun* was recorded in Glasgow in 1970 for a cloth-cap with a press-stud on its peak. *Sneck* was first recorded in Scots in the 15th century; it was also known in northern Middle English, but its earlier history is uncertain. It may be connected with English *snatch*, which until the 16th century sometimes meant a fastening.

snib To fasten a door or window with a catch; the catch used is also often called a *snib*. The little device for securing a yale lock is invariably called a *snib*, and many take care at night to lock and *snib* the front door. The novelist O. Douglas told how she was laughed at in London when she talked about '*snibbing*' the windows (1917). The *snib* was originally a small piece of wood which could be used o jam the latch so that it could not be lifted from outside. In older Scots, *snib* meant to rebuke or scold, and then to restrain or check. In these senses it was also found in Middle English.

stair A flight of steps; more particularly, in a TENEMENT (XIII) building, the flight that gives access to all the flats having a common front door. General Scots. In standard English a flight of steps is referred to in the plural as the *stairs*; and someone may be either *upstairs* or *downstairs*. In Scots the singular form *stair* is normal usage, and in colloquial Scots someone is *up the stair* or *doon the stair*. The difference was noted early in the 18th century by an English visitor, who remarked that in Scots 'at the third *stair*' meant 'three stories high'. The staircase in a tenement is often called the *common stair*. In Edinburgh tenement-dwellers are expected to take their turn of scrubbing and sweeping the '*common stair*'.

stank Originally a pond, often a stagnant one, *stank* while retaining this meaning has moved with the times. First of all, the pond became a ditch, and then a small stream, often one helping to carry away drainage. These senses are now chiefly localised Scots, but in the colloquial Scots of the central belt a street gutter was named a *stank*, and in the west the meaning was further developed to mean the iron grating through which gutter-water runs away. See also CUNDY, SYVER (both XIII). It is a sad fact that a coin dropped in the street may find its way *doon the stank*, and this phrase is now used of something that is lost for ever – by accident or folly. Money lost in a bet may be regarded as *doon the stank*. *Stank* was first recorded in Scots in the 14th century. It came from Middle English and ultimately from Old French *estanc*, the ancestor of French *étang*. Through Latin, it is related to the word *stagnant*.

synd (pronounced like *signed*), **syne** To wash out, or to give something a quick rinse in water. Localised Scots. When in a hurry, you can *syne* some clothes in soapy water and squeeze them out under a running tap. You can *synd oot* a dirty dish, or even *synd* your face before going out. A *synd*, or a *syne oot*, is a quick wash or swill: 'Give the pan a *syne oot.*' *Synd* was first recorded in Scots in the 15th century. It came from northern Middle English *sind*, to rinse, perhaps of Scandinavian origin.

syver A street gutter; more particularly (and perhaps more commonly), the drain-hole which carries away the gutter-water, or the metal grating which covers it. The context may decide the precise application. A dropped coin may roll into a *siver* and be picked up again; if it falls 'doon the *siver*', it is beyond recovery. Localised Scots. The older and original sense of a ditch or a field-drain is not dead, but it is naturally enough confined to some rural areas. *Syver* was first recorded in Scots in the early 16th century; it came from a French word for a drain, and is of the same origin as standard English *sewer*.

See also CUNDY, STANK (both XIII).

tenement A large building, usually three or more stories in height, divided up into numerous FLATS (XIII), each of which is occupied by a different proprietor or tenant. A *tenement* block can be subdivided into a number of separate *tenements*, each of which consists of only the flats reached by a common STAIR (XIII) and approached through a common CLOSE (XIII) or ENTRY (XIII). General Scots. The original meaning of *tenement* was, as in English, a holding of land. It came to apply particularly to a holding of land in a burgh; when this was built on, the building erected was called a *tenement* or LAND (XIII).

tolbooth Both word and building survive as historical relics. At one time most Scottish towns had a *tolbooth*, and many still have one, though stripped of most, if not all, of its functions. A *tolbooth* was originally a stall or office where tolls, market dues, etc. were collected on behalf of the town. From this it developed into something more like a sheriff's office in the 'Wild West', and became the centre of the town's administration, frequently with the jail built in. Hence the later meaning of *tolbooth* might be town house, or jail, or both. At one time the Scottish Parliament met, on occasion, in the *Tolbooth* of Edinburgh, now destroyed (see also HERT, I). But in the small border town of Lauder the *Tolbooth*, built in 1318, is still standing, though greatly altered. *Tolbooth* is a combination of the words *toll* and *booth*. It was also known in Middle English.

tron The place or building in or near the market place of a town in which was kept the weighing-machine used for weighing the commodities brought to market from the surrounding areas. Survives only as a street or locality name, usually in the centre of the old part of the town where the market used to be. Hence the *Tron* Kirks in Edinburgh and Glasgow, and the Trongates in Glasgow and Dundee. Until about 1800 *tron* was the name given to a standard weight for locally produced goods: it had different values in different localities. *Tron weight* was finally abandoned in favour of Imperial measure in 1824. *Tron* when it first appeared in Scots in a Latin document in 1317 meant a weighing-machine. It is probably from Latin *trona*, scales; Old French *trone* had the same meaning.

vennel A narrow lane between houses. Now chiefly in street names, though in *Historic South Edinburgh* (1978) C.J. Smith describes Horse Wynd as 'a narrow *vennel* running to the Cowgate.' Not far off is a street called *The Vennel*. *Vennel* is from French *venelle*, an alley.

whirligig in Scots has, in some areas, the meaning of a revolving chimney cowl. Localised Scots. Also known as a *whirlie*.

wynd A narrow and often winding street or alley, usually leading off the main street of a town. In Edinburgh in 1701 the authorities were concerned about how best to eliminate 'the nastiness of streets, *wynds*' and closes. *Wynd* is now used mainly in street names: Kirk Wynd, and several other *wynds*, none of them at all nasty, lead off Kirkcaldy High Street. *Wynd* is ultimately of the same origin as the verb *wind*, to twist.

yett A gate of any kind. Colloquial Scots; also found in northern English dialect. First recorded in Scots in the 14th century: it has the same origin as *gate*. A later sense, which probably developed in the 18th or 19th century, is a pass through the hills: it is now heard only in such place names at the *Yetts* of Muckhart.

XIV
Grammar Words
Number and Quantity

a, aw Colloquial Scots form of *all*, with typical loss of the *-ll* in pronunciation. Use of the apostrophe (*a'*) is common, and sometimes helpful, in printed texts, as in Burns's 'A man's a man for *a'* that.' Used as is *all* in general English except in a few compounds where it means every rather than all: e.g. *a-body* and *a-thing*.

ablow developed in Scots in the 19th century from *a-below*, formed in imitation of *above*. It means under or below. A folk song tells how a condemned outlaw played a tune on his fiddle '*ablow* the gallows tree.' Sometimes combined with *in*, as: 'Yer bunnet's *in ablow* the chair.'

abune Colloquial Scots for *above*. There are local differences in pronunciation, reflected in such spellings as *aboon*, *abeen*, *abin*, etc. A weathercock on a spire is far *abune* people's heads. Has the same origin as *above*, which was *aboven* in Middle English; English lost the *-n*, Scots the *-v-*.

ae Colloquial Scots for *one*: not to be confused with ANE (XIV) or with the definite article (*a* or *an*). The significance of the *ae* in Burns's *Ae Fond Kiss* is that it is not just *a* kiss, but the last *one*. *Ae* is only an adjective: in English you can say 'one book' and 'give me one'; in Scots, it is *ae* book but give me *yin* or *ane*. Yet *ae*, *a*, *an*, *ane*, *one* and *yin* all go back to *ān*, the Old English for *one*.

afore has in Scots continued to be an alternative to *before*, whereas in standard English it is heard only in compounds like *aforesaid*. Colloquial and occasional Scots. Immortalised by the sung warning that if you 'tak the high road . . . I'll be in Scotland *afore* ye' (*The Bonnie Banks o' Loch Lomond*). A very recent Scots song contains the line, 'Have a dram (drink) *afore* ye go.' Recorded in Scots since the 15th century: came through Middle English from Old English.

aiblins Perhaps, possibly. Despite a long history, *aiblins* is now rarely heard. Many Scots know it; few if any use it in speech. It is found most commonly in attempts to recreate Scots domestic conversation in the near past, and in the writings of those dedicated to the revival of Scots language. It is formed from *able*, with the adverbial ending *-lings*, and was once common in the north of England as well as in Scotland.

ain Colloquial Scots for *own*, as in 'she had her *ain* way o' doing things' (1986). A well-known Scots song, 'My *Ain* Folk,' expresses the feelings of an emigrant who wants to return to Scotland. It has the same uses and origin as *own*.

aleeviɲ see NUMERALS (XIV).

ane, yin One; but used quite differently from AE (XIV). *Ane*, or *yin*, is usually a pronoun: '*ane* of the men' can do, or '*yin* o' them' can tell you, something. In the plural, *yins* is often used to emphasise the usual pronouns, as in 'us *yins*' or '*youse* (you) *yins*,' with the accent on the *us* and *youse*. *Yin* can be used almost as a noun for fellow. The Scottish comedian, Billy Connolly, is popularly known as 'the big *yin*.' On one occasion a B.B.C. announcer got the stress wrong and introduced him as the 'the big *yín*' instead of 'the bíg *yin*'. He sounded like someone speaking a foreign language (as indeed he was).

athegither see THEGITHER (XIV).

aucht see NUMERALS (XIV).

ava Of a' (all): used as is *at all* in standard English, often after a negative. It is heard in the chorus of a popular song, 'there's nae luck aboot the hoose, There's nae luck *ava*.' 'He wisna feart *ava*' means he was not at all afraid. Colloquial when first recorded in the late 19th century, but now localised or dialect.

awa, away The *awa* form is colloquial Scots, but the usages described, some with *away*, are general Scots. It is often used with the verb *come*: 'Come *awa* ben (into) the hoose,' or 'Come *awa*, Rovers!' *To be away* (to some place) means to go: '*I'm awa* to my bed', or '*He's awa* hame (home)'. It is often used as an interjection. Someone when told an improbable story may respond, '*Away!*' (I can't believe it!) '*Awa* wi you' would be more dismissive – nearly 'Nonsense!' '*Och awa(y)*' may express incredulity, or impatience with the folly of oneself or another.

awfae, awfu, awfy are all Scots forms of *awful*, and in colloquial Scots they are in daily use as a more colourful intensive that *verra* or *very*: 'She's an *aafae* bonnie lassie', 'He's *awfy* bad-tempered' or 'I'm *awfu* sorry'. It can also be used with a noun: in 'He has an *awfae* lot of money' it means great (deal), but in 'an *awfy* accident' it means dreadful.

ay, aye Yes. General Scots; even those who allow themselves few other Scotticisms will often reply '*Ay*' to a question, and on occasion may even permit themselves an 'Och, *aye*.' It is in common use as a non-committal greeting, like 'Hallo.' In some parts of the country this is extended to '*Ay, ay*.' Formerly in common use in English, but now obsolete except in dialect and in certain formal situations (e.g. to acknowledge an order in the Royal Navy, or for 'yes' when voting in the House of Commons).

See also AYE (XIV).

aye, ay Always, ever. Colloquial and occasional Scots. A mother complained that when Jean was a baby 'she was *aye* greetin (crying)' (1986). Scots speakers do not confuse *ay* (yes) and *aye* (always) in pronunciation. *Ay* is a long-drawn-out sound; it is lingered over. *Aye* is uttered quickly and sharply. *Aye* may derive from either Middle English or Old Norse.

baith Scots form of *both*. Used as in English, except in the common colloquial Scots *baith the twa of them* for *both of them*.

ben[2] In; inside; towards the inside. Colloquial Scots, but in some situations also in occasional use. 'Come away *ben*' is still a warm invitation to a visitor to come into the house – traditionally, into the best room of the house. The *ben* was the inner room of the two-roomed BUT AND BEN (XIII). To go *ben the hoose*, into the comfort of the best room, is also common. *Ben* is the product of the running together of the prefix *be-* (as in *before*) and the Old English word for inside.

doon Colloquial Scots form of *down*. In the Glasgow area '*doon* the watter' means down the River Clyde and into its firth. In the summer, especially during the Glasgow FAIR (IX), pleasure steamers used to carry numerous Glaswegians *doon the watter* towards such resorts as Rothesay, Dunoon, etc. Scots travel *doon* (*down*, not up) to London. In some local games (see, e.g. BA, X) teams represent the *doonies* (those living in the low-lying parts of a town) and the *uppies*.

drap The colloquial Scots form of *drop*, with the same meanings, though when used for a small quantity *of* something, the *of* is usually missed out; e.g. 'a wee *drap* porridge' or 'a *drap* milk'. A *drap* is frequently used of spirits, and then the diminutive form *drappie* is often used, half-humorously: 'She likes a *drappie*' is from 1824, but it could have been said yesterday.

efter is the Scots form of *after*. A small boy who in 1982 used *efter* before a visitor was scolded by his mother: *efter* was 'rude', and in polite company he should say *after*. In or near Gaelic-speaking areas *efter*, or *after*, is sometimes used as it is in Irish-English: to be *after doing* something is to have completed doing it recently 'I'm just *efter* tellin' ye' (Scottish Television, 1987). This usage is a literal translation from the Gaelic, which forms a series of tenses in this way.

fae is an altered form of **frae**, which is the Scots form of English *fro* (from). It was first a dialect form in the north of Scotland, but is now accepted colloquial Scots. The novelist William McIlvanney uses it regularly in Scots dialogue: one of the characters in *Docherty* (1975) comes '*fae* a readin' family.' *Frae* is rarely heard, though it is used in self-consciously occasional Scots: 'he came *frae* the High Street, Leven.'

fair is very common in general Scots as an intensive, meaning very, completely. 'I'm *fair* pleased wi' myself' (Radio Scotland, 1986). The most forceful example is probably '*fair* forfoughen' (exhausted; see FORFOCHTEN, II). *Fair*, when used of the weather in the negative sense of not actually raining, has given rise to the Scots phrase to *fair up*: 'It's *fairing up*' means that the rain has stopped, and that the weather is improving.

for, *Sc* **fur** In Scots, *for* has the same uses as in English, but there is one special use worth noting. *To be for* something is to want it: 'Are you *fur* anither (drink)?' See also ASK FOR (V), FEART (II).

forby The most common meaning in present-day colloquial Scots is besides, as well as, in addition to. In 1986 a lady was worried about going to a party when she knew only the hosts; '*Forby* them, I won't know anybody at all.' In the same year a policeman described a suspicious character seen after a crime: 'This person, *forby* appearing dishevelled, also appeared very agitated.' More rarely, in localised Scots, *forby* can mean except, as in the complaint that you can get nothing 'oot o Fife, *forby* coal' (1951). The idiom *to be forby* oneself means to be out of one's mind (20th century). *Forby* can also be used as an adverb meaning as well, in addition; after a large helping of Christmas pudding, a little boy asked, 'Are we going to get trifle *forby*?' Though it is recorded in the 14th century, *forby* was not very common in older Scots. It was used in Middle English, and is also found in English dialect.

forrit Scots form of English *forward*: the *w* has been slurred over, as in English *forrard*. Common in colloquial Scots, with much the same meanings as in English. In parts of Scotland (chiefly the north-east and south-west) to *cum* (or *gang*) *forrit* is still used for to come (or go) forward to Communion in the Church of Scotland. The motto of the Scottish Tartans Society is 'Bring *forrit* the Tartan.'

fower see NUMERALS (XIV).

frae see FAE (XIV).

furth is the Scottish form of English *forth*. It is very common in occasional or literary Scots, especially in letters to the papers, in the phrase *furth of Scotland* (outside Scotland), often in a context that is otherwise standard English. In the humbler sense of outside, out of doors, it is now localised Scots or dialect.

galore came from Gaelic into Scots, but it probably entered English from Irish Gaelic in the 17th century. It was made more widely known by the popularity of '*Whisky Galore*' (the novel by Compton Mackenzie, and the film), in which it was unquestionably from Scots Gaelic. In Scots *galore* has been used both as an adverb (in plenty) and as a noun (plenty). In both Scots and Irish Gaelic the two words underlying *galore* normally come directly after the noun (as in money *galore*), and this order of words has been retained in English usage.

gar To make (someone do something). Once very common, but now heard less often, though still used in literary Scots. In 1986 a writer in the *Scotsman* admitted that he hated plucking fowls: 'nothing *gars* me grue (sickens me) so violently.' *Gar* is also found in northern English dialect: it is of Old Norse origin.

gey is a common colloquial Scots intensive, sometimes heard in occasional Scots. 'I know her *gey* well – I know her very well' (overheard in a hotel lounge, 1986). The degree of intensity can vary, from rather to very. *Gey* is usually pronounced to rhyme with *high* (in some places, with *hay*). *Gey* is also used as an adjective to express approval or admiration, sometimes with a degree of slyness or malice, as in Eric Linklater's 'His grandfather was a *gey* man for the women.' English *great* can be similarly used. *Gey* is a Scots form of *gay*. It was first used in the 14th century of things or people that were attractive or showy in appearance. It was closer to the modern sense in 'a *gey* convenient number' (1686).

gin (*g* is pronounced as in *gun*) If, which has now largely replaced it even in colloquial and dialect Scots. A teacher I know sometimes startles his class by saying to them: 'I'm going to speir (ask) *gin* you are a' here.' *Gin* was first recorded in Scots about 1600. It is perhaps from *gi'en*, a Scots form of *given*; if so, it has developed in meaning rather like *provided* in standard English.

hauf, half Half. There are a few special usages in Scots. In one, a *hauf* is a half-measure of a particular amount of drink, especially of a gill of whisky. A *hauf* is a half-gill, and a *wee hauf* is a quarter-gill. See also BEER (IV). In telling the time, Scots for long preferred to identify a *half* as meaning before the next hour on the clock: thus, *half four* meant 3.30, a fact noted with pleasure by a German traveller in Scotland, who found Scots usage closer to German than was English. But though *half four* is still frequently heard, it is now likely to mean half-past four, as the older use is dying out.

hoot(s) A colloquial Scots exclamation to express disagreement or incredulity, with a degree of mild rebuke thrown in. '*Hoots*, awa (away) man!' suggests that the person addressed has been talking nonsense. Because it sounds comic – though not as comic as '*hoots toots*', which has the same sense – it has commonly, in the form '*Hoots, mon*', been attributed to Scots in comic strips or farces. In origin, it is a sound intended to express impatience, not unlike French 'zut!' Now rare.

hunner see NUMERALS (XIV).

ilk Same (place). The commonest use is in the names of landed proprietors. For example, one entry in *Debrett's Peerage* for 1984 reads: Sir Iain Kay Moncrieffe of that *Ilk*, of Moncrieffe, Perthshire. This is perhaps easier to understand in early examples, in which 'of that *ilk*' clearly stood for 'of that same place or landed estate.' Thus in 1408 the lord of the estates of Erskine was Sir Robert of Erskine, 'lord of that *ilk.*' Originally 'of that *ilk*' indicated that the lordship was named after the estate – in the above case, that of Erskine. Moreover the words showed that the person so designated was the head of the landed family, since only he was entitled to the addition 'of that *ilk.*' When the family name was no longer the same as that of the estate, *of that ilk* was understood to be a mark of family seniority, and *ilk* developed the secondary meaning of family. *Of that ilk* is now sometimes used in general English for 'of that kind', as in 'other people of that *ilk.*'

ilka Each, every. *Ilka* has lost favour since the days when '*ilka* lassie' had her 'laddie'. It is rarely if ever heard in everyday speech, and survives chiefly in literary Scots. *Ilka* was found in both older Scots and in northern Middle English.

inby, towards a centre, has developed specific senses best understood by comparing them with *ootby*, away from a centre (*oot* is the Scots form of *out*). In its simplest sense *inby* means in, or into, the house: 'Come *inby*' or 'She's *inby.*' This is close to its earliest sense of further into the house (17th century). Outside the house, *inby* refers to the land near the farmstead, and so by extension to the low-lying parts of a farm as opposed to the hilly or upland parts. A COLLIE (XI) will be trained specially to work *inby*; and ewes and young lambs may be kept *inby*. Such lambs may be referred to as *inby* lambs. On one farm in Caithness a wall 'runs between the hills and the *inby*' (Radio Scotland, 1988).

Ootby started from a general sense of outside in the 17th century, but has developed more specific senses. In its first recorded use in 1640, a child was smacked and told to 'go *outby* (outside the house).' It then came to mean out-of-doors or away from home. In 1933 a man could go *out-by* to meet his friends. A man working *outby* in the fields is an '*outbye* worker'. Just as *inby* relates to the parts of a farm near the farmstead, so *outby* relates to the outlying, sometimes quite distant parts. In some areas the *outby* parts of a farm are upland, and call for different skills. In 1957 an advertisement offered for sale a collie with the recommendation 'good *outbye*'. In 1955 it was difficult to find men ready to work in '*outbye* places', i.e. remote and hilly places in the BORDERS (X). In all these senses *outby* is also found in northern English dialect. In fishing communities in Fife a similar distinction was drawn between an *inby* boat, which fished fairly close to the shore, and an '*ootbye* boat, [which] fished in deeper waters far from home' (Mary Murray *In My Ain Words* 1982).

lane is the Scots form of English *lone*. It is found in the peculiarly Scots colloquial usage, *my lane*, *his lane* etc., the equivalents of myself, himself. Hence, 'on the hills, by *his lane*, a body could think for himself' (*Scots Magazine*, 1953), and 'I went hame to be *ma lane* (on my own).'

lang syne Long since, long ago. Colloquial Scots; but general Scots, and almost general English, in '**auld lang syne**', the days of long ago, old times. Burns found this last phrase 'exceedingly expressive', and immortalised it in the words of one of the most widely known of all songs. *Lang syne* has been in Scots since early in the 15th century. *Auld lang syne* was first recorded, in prose, in 1694; when first used in verse it was as *old lang syne* (about 1700). Of two Middle English words close in meaning, *sithence* gave *since*, and *sithen* gave Scots *syne* (since). *Syne* is pronounced like *sign*, with an *s*, not a *z*.

lenth Scots form of *length*. The general Scots phrase *the lenth of* means as far as. It was first recorded in 1715, when someone offered to go '*the length of* Elgin' to put forward a proposal. It is still common, as in 'I got *the lenth* of the front door' (1986).

mair Scots form of *more*. In daily colloquial use, in every kind of context – 'nae *mair* sweeties' to '*mair* discreet'.

maun, man Must. Colloquial Scots. A brand of soap powder used to carry a picture illustrating the legend, 'You *mauna* (must not) tread on the Scottish thistle, laddie.' English *must* comes from Old English; but *maun*, also found as *man* etc. in northern Middle English, is from Old Norse.

morn in the sense of morning is almost as rare as in standard English, but it is still heard in certain colloquial Scots expressions. *The morn* is tomorrow (see THE, XIV), and *the morn's morn* is tomorrow morning. When in 1987 a group of boys agreed to meet again '*the morn's nicht*' they meant tomorrow night.

na, nae, no Although they are used in different ways, these colloquial Scots negatives are best considered together. For a *no* answer to a question, *na* (or *naw*) is normally used.
  For *not* used with a verb, Scots usage is *nae* or *no*: 'I'll *no* dae (do) it', or 'I'll *no* be lang.' But if the *not* is tacked on to the end of the verb (as in *cannot*), *na* or *nae* (never *no*) is used: *cannae* (can not), *mauna* (must not), *dinna(e)* (do not), etc.
  For *no* in *nobody*, *nowhere*, *nae* is preferred: *naebody*, *naewhere*.
  In negative understatement, common in Scots, *no* or *nae* is needed: 'I'm *no* (or *nae*) weel', (meaning, I'm ill), or 'That's *no* (*nae*) bad', meaning that it is quite good.

never As in English dialect, frequently used as an emphatic negative, as in a direct denial: 'No, I *never* (did it)', or in 'I thought she'd be back in a month, but he *never* brought her' (Radio Scotland, 1986).

no see NA (XIV).

noo Scots form of English *now*. Common colloquial Scots *the noo*, just now, in a moment, comes from an older form *eenoo*: its origin is given away by the alternative *evenoo* (now obsolete). It is the same as English *even now*, the *even* in Scots having been by stages altered into *the*.

nor In colloquial Scots commonly used for *than*. A boy, accused of being troublesome in class, answered: 'The rest's waur (worse) *nor* me.' This is not a misuse of standard English *nor*, but a very old usage, recorded since the 15th century, of which the origin is not clear. It appears to be related to the negative *na* or *no*.

numerals Twa, twae are colloquial Scots forms of two: the *w* is pronounced. Of the other numerals, only **fower** (four), **sax** (six), **seeven** (seven) and **aucht** (eight) may cause puzzlement to a visitor to Scotland. Of higher numbers, at least **aleevin** (eleven), **twal** (twelve) and **hunner** (hundred) shoild be mentioned. These, and all other numbers, particularly when stating measures or quantities, are often followed by a singular noun – *twa* pund (pounds), *seevin* year auld, *sax* oor (hours), for example. See also ANE (XIV).
   Twa three means not only 'two or three,' but also several, a few. 'There's *twa-three* hares joukin aboot (running around) in yon field' (*Scotsman*, 1988).

och An exclamation expressing impatience, irritation or even hesitation as to what to say next: '*Och*, don't be silly!' '*Och*, *awa(γ)* (Nonsense!)' or '*Och*, I'm not sure.' In '*Och*, aye' it is fairly colourless. *Och* was originally an expression of sorrow, and is probably derived from the Highland cry of lamentation '*Ochone!*' based on Gaelic.

oor see WUR (XIV).

ootby see INBY (XIV).

outwith Outside, away from, beyond the confines of. General Scots. Many people in the last decade have had to go '*outwith* their home area' (1987) in order to find work. Members of a committee may decide that certain actions are *outwith* their competence. Before 1400 *outwith* was both Scots and northern Middle English, but since the 15th century it has been obsolete in English.

ower Colloquial Scots form of *over*; pronounced as it is spelt. 'He climbed *ower* the wa (wall).' *Ower* is frequently used as a strong intensive – the equivalent of too. A child can be '*ower* wee' to be allowed out alone.

ra is an almost unrecognisable form of *the*, as in 'He stotted ma heid off *ra* wa' (schoolchild, 1986), which means, freely translated, 'He banged my head on the wall.' Generally credited to Glaswegians, but also sometimes heard in Edinburgh.

richt, right Often used in Scots as an intensive instead of very. As with other words for which both Scots and English forms are current, the English form is often adapted to Scots usage: 'I'm *right* jealous of John's chrysanthemums' alongside 'I'm *richt* weary.'

sax, seeven see NUMERALS (XIV).

syne see LANG SYNE (XIV).

thae Those. Colloquial Scots, with a long and honourable pedigree, and not, as casual listeners often think, a wrong use of *they*. The Old English for those was *thā*, giving obsolete Middle English *thō*, Scots *thā* or *thai*. Hence, 'it was *thae* twa (two) did it.'

the may be used in colloquial and occasional Scots in ways obsolete in or unknown to standard English. Before the name of public institutions *the* is often used when it would be omitted in English. 'He's left *the* school, and gone to *the*

university,' and 'They go to *the* church even on holiday,'
may be heard in colloquial Scots. Certain activities are named
in the same way. Someone who has gone to a football match
may be 'at *the* fitba,' or he may prefer '*the* gowf' or even '*the*
chess.*' Dancing as a pastime is usually referred to as *the*
dancin(g). Illnesses are spoken of in a similar way: a child
may be off school with '*the* flu' or '*the* measles.' The
weakness of drinking too much can be spoken of as '*the*
drink': 'He's awfae fond o' *the* drink.' An important group of
uses of *the* has arisen from the alteration of *to* into *the* (see also
THEGITHER, XIV). In phrases expressing time we find *the day*
for today, *the nicht* for tonight, and *the* morra (or morrow)
for tomorrow.

thegither is the colloquial Scots form of *together*. The
opening line of a well-known folk-song is 'We're a (all) met
thegither here tae sit and tae crack (talk).' *Altogether* receives
similar treatment: 'Things have changed athegither' (Radio
Scotland, 1987).

thon That (one) over there. In Scots *that* and YON (XIV) came
together to give this new word meaning much the same as
yon. 'Do you remember *thon* day we went to Perth?' (1988).
'*Thon thing*' was used by fishermen when talking about the
salmon, the name of the fish itself being taboo: 'there is a
superstition about [salmon], and one may speak only of *thon
things*' (*Dundee Courier*, 1968). There is also a word *thonder*
(over there), once quite common, but now localised or
dialect Scots.

twa, twal, twa-three see NUMERALS (XIV).

unco Very, extremely. It is in this sense that the word is now
most likely to be found: 'There's something *unco* Scottish
about blinds' (*Scots Mag*, 1986). But it seems to be passing
from colloquial to literary or occasional Scots. See also UNCO
GUID (VIII). In 1706, in a speech made against the Act of
Union, a speaker accused supporters of the Act of being
'*uncouth* careful' of some Scottish traditions at the expense of

others. As this indicates, *unco* is the same word as *uncouth*, of which it is a shortened form. Its early use as an adjective, meaning unknown or little known, survives, though it is rare: in 1959 a Scottish paper reported that a contract was being awarded to an 'unco firm'. From this developed a second sense – strange or odd. More than one Scottish poet (e.g. Burns, Robert Garioch) have described an '*unco* sicht (sight).' Both these uses survive in north-east Scotland. Middle English too had a form *unkow* as a variant of *uncouth*.

waur Scots form of worse: still used in colloquial Scots: 'He could dae *waur* than that.'

wha(t), *Sc* **whit** What, as in standard English, but with one or two special Scots usages. One is the use of *what* instead of *how* before adjectives in exclamatory phrases like '*What* nice!', '*What* dirty!' *What a* can be used to mean what a lot of: '*Wha(t)* a cars!' or *What a* smoke from the barbecue!' (1987). *Wha(t) way, whit wey* can mean how ('*What wey* are you?') or why ('*Whit wey* are you daein' that?').

wheen A few, several; a fair number or amount (of). Colloquial Scots. *Wheen* can be used in a variety of grammatical constructions – with a singular or plural noun, and sometimes followed by *of*. You can be given 'a *wheen* porridge' or you may have to wait 'a *wheen* o minutes.' In 1988 someone about to move house found that he had 'a *wheen* things' to take with him. *Wheen*, originally spelt *quheyn* (*quh*- was once the Scots equivalent of English *wh*-), was first recorded in Scots in the 14th century. The *wh*- is pronounced *hw*- (not *w*-), as is usual in Scots.

whiles Sometimes, now and then. Colloquial Scots, but commoner in some parts of the country than in others. '*Whiles* I think we were better aff (off) then.' Also northern English dialect. Recorded in Scots since the 14th century. Of Old English origin.

whit see WHAT (XIV).

wi is the colloquial Scots form of *with*. It has a few special uses. One, less heard now except in dialect, is its use instead of *by* after a verb: 'we were chased *wi* the police' (1958) or 'he was run over *wi* a train' (1964). It is sometimes used for *because of*, but only after a negative: 'he wisnae able to sleep *wi* the noise next door.' And to *die of* something is often to *die* (or *dee*) *wi*: 'she *deet wi* the bronchitis.'

wur, wir Colloquial Scots forms of the pronoun *our* in contexts where there is no stress on the pronoun. If there is stress, **oor** (or *our*) would be used. *Oor* was often pronounced almost as if it had two syllables, *oo-wir*; when unstressed, the first syllable was lost: hence *wur, wir*. '*Wur* lads'll dae their best.' *Wur* is one of the markers of a genuine Scots speaker: it is not often heard in occasional or literary Scots.

yin see ANE (XIV).

yon That (or those) over there – a degree further away than *that*: e.g. 'Not that yin – *yon* wee fella wi the red hair.' 'What was all *yon* about?' refers to something that took place a few minutes earlier. Still common in colloquial Scots: not long ago it was in general use. *Yon* goes back to an Old English word that survives as part of *beyond*: it is now found in English only in dialect.

yonder Over there, in that (relatively remote) place. General Scots, but now less common than *yon*. Used in Middle English, but now only dialect in England.

youse An alternative colloquial Scots form for *you* in the plural. The *Scottish National Dictionary* notes regretfully that it has spread, especially in the central belt of Scotland, 'in illiterate use . . . from Irish influence.' Also used as a singular: in Edinburgh dance halls in the 1930s a common opening gambit was, 'Does *youse* come here often?'

XV
Miscellany

auld Scots form of *old*. Common in colloquial use and in some set phrases, notably '*auld* lang syne' (see LANG SYNE, XIV). Before a sports encounter with England, Scottish papers frequently carry references to 'the *auld* enemy' – a phrase that goes back to the 16th century, when there were frequent complaints about the actions of 'our *auld enemy* (or *enemies*) of England.' When the opponents are French, there may be mention of the '*auld alliance*' which existed between Scotland and France between the 12th or 13th and the 16th centuries.

back *At the back of* (a stated time) means not long after; 'I'll see you *at the back o nine*' is common in colloquial Scots. So is the phrase *to come up* (one's) *back*, to feel a desire to do something. 'What's *come up yer back* the noo?' may be asked when someone seems about to do something unexpected or impulsive. *The back of beyond* is now general English, but the phrase was originally Scots. The earliest recorded example is from Scott's novel *The Antiquary*, in which someone was 'whirled . . . away to *the back of beyont*' (1816). The phrase *backs to the wall*, made famous by General Sir Douglas Haig's order of the day in April 1918 – 'With our *backs to the wall* . . . each one of us must fight to the end' – is believed to go back to the Scots phrase *back(s) at the wall*. It was first recorded early in the 16th century: an enemy was to be driven back till 'we may have their *bakis at the wall*,' so placed that they can neither retreat nor avoid battle.

barrie A substitute for 'smashing', 'super' or 'fantastic', now common especially among the under-15's in Lothian and Fife. First recorded in the *Scottish National Dictionary* in 1926: a '*barrie* fellow' was a fine, big, smart-looking man. It is, like CHORE (II), a borrowing from gipsy speech.

bawbee Now heard chiefly in the plural, when *bawbees* is used semi-jocularly for money. 'He's got plenty of *bawbees*.' Promoting tourism is not 'simply a question of plunking down the *bawbees*' (1986). Until earlier in the present century a *bawbee* meant a halfpenny. When first coined in the 16th century a *bawbee* was worth six pennies Scots. It shared in the general devaluation of the Scots currency in the 17th century, when the pound Scots fell till it was worth only 1/12 of the pound sterling. *Bawbee* is believed to be from the latter part of *Sille-bawbe*, the name of the land of Alex Orrok of Sillebawbe, who was for a time master of the Scottish mint in the 16th century.

bide To stay, remain or dwell. Colloquial Scots. In one of the most popular of Scottish songs, the theme is 'We're no awa tae *bide* awa', we're not going away for ever: it is a favourite song at partings. Someone may *bide* just around the corner from her mother, or she may prefer 'to *bide* at hame (home)' rather than go out one evening. See however BIDIE-IN (I). Also means to put up with, endure, usually in negative statements: 'I cannae *bide* fowk (people) like that.' *Bide* has been recorded in Scots since the 14th century. It came from Middle, ultimately Old, English.

ca Scots form of English *call*, with typical loss of the *-ll*. *Ca* has some special Scots usages, as to *ca* (knock) the legs from under someone, to trip him up, or to *ca* a skipping rope, to keep it turning. To *ca* nails *in* a wall is to hammer them in. The older sense of to drive animals, or to drive a vehicle, is now rarely heard: the two senses were combined in an early instance of someone *ca-ing* a wagon in the 14th century. But this usage has recently been adapted, and one can now *ca* (bring home) turnips from a field. These uses are all colloquial Scots; a general Scots one, now often heard in the form *call*, is to *be called to a church*, to receive a formal invitation from a congregation to be its MINISTER (VIII).

ca canny Go carefully, take care. In 1981 the *Scots Magazine* mentioned that one road-sign in Aberdeenshire read, 'Ca *canny* doon the brae (down the hill)'. The phrase was adopted in both England and the United States to describe any Trade Union policy of 'go slow', once labelled '*ca cannyism*' by the *Glasgow Herald* (1921). A headline in the *Scotsman* in 1986 announced: '*Ca canny* mine dispute flares.' See also CA (XV) and CANNY (II).

cat's lick A quick wash, performed more for appearances than for cleanliness. General Scots. A 20th century coinage.

cauldrife see WAUKRIFE (II).

chap To knock. Colloquial and occasional Scots. 'He came *chappin* at ma door at midnight.' When a surveyor is inspecting a house, he may '*chap* (tap) the walls'. In the game of dominoes, if you are unable to play when your turn comes, you *chap* on the table. In some parts, someone who goes around banging on doors to wake people up in the morning is known as a *chapper-up*. *Chap* is also used for the striking of a clock or the sounding of an alarm: 'The church clock *chappit* three.' To *chap* vegetables is to mash them. In the north of Scotland *chappit tatties* are mashed potatoes. *Chap* was first recorded in Scots in the 16th century. It is another form of the slightly earlier *chop*: both came from Middle English.

clamjamfry, clanjamfry A 'mixed bag'. General Scots. Recorded only since the 19th century, and still fluid in meaning. Originally it meant a collection of people, but conveyed some disapproval – a rabble, riff-raff. But in 1986 the *Scotsman*, during the Edinburgh festival, wrote of 'the Fringe at the seaside, a *clamjamfrie* of various events arranged along Portobello Promenade for Fringe Saturday.' In this sense, it is used in the sense of a gallimaufry. Of unknown origin.

clarty Dirty. Colloquial Scots. Your face or hands may on occasion be *clarty*; so may your clothes or shoes, if you've been walking through mud or slush. *Clarty* also means sticky: sweets kept in a bag in a boy's pocket may become *clarty*, and so may his fingers as he puts them into his mouth. *Clarty*, first recorded in a 16th century Scots poem, is from the noun *clart*, mud, mire, or a lump of mud or something dirty. *Clart* is also found in northern English dialect.

cowp To overturn, upset. Colloquial Scots. If someone gets up awkwardly he may *cowp* the chair he was sitting in: if he has been sitting in a small boat, he may *cowp* the boat. A badly balanced bag may *cowp* and its contents spill out. *Cowping* can be deliberate: you can *cowp* a box, empty it of its contents, by turning it upside down or tilting it sharply. Also used as a noun: 'He's had an awfae *coup* (a bad fall).' In some parts of Scotland *cowp* means a rubbish tip. *Cowp* was first recorded in Scots in the 16th century. It came from Middle English and is connected with French *coup*, a blow.

dae Scots form of *do*. In colloquial Scots *does* is often *dis*, and *does not* is *disna*. *Dinna* stands for *do not*: 'I *dinna* ken what ye mean.' I *canna be daein wi* (or in a more Anglicized form, *I can't be doing with*) another person, or a specified kind of behaviour, means I can't bear, I have no patience with.

darg A task – properly and traditionally, the day's work, but since it has often been spoken of as 'the day's *darg*' the meaning of *darg* has been extended. Localised and occasional Scots. In 1987 a friend, telling how the home help had come in to do her 'daily *darg*', attributed his use of the term to his country upbringing. A *darger* is a casual labourer: it is now only dialect. *Darg* is the same word as English *daywork*. When first recorded in the 16th century, it had an alternative form *dark*. This was a reduced form of the older word *dawerk*, from the Old English words for *day* and *work*.

daud A lump. A chapter in J.J. Bell's *Wee Macgreegor* (1902) is entitled 'A *daud* o' potty (putty)', and you may still be given a *daud* of bread or a *daud* of cheese. In my Edinburgh schooldays in the 1920s we spoke not of SWEETIES (IV) but of *daudles* – presumably the same word as *doddles*, lumps of home-made toffee. Both words go back to *daud*.

deid The Scots form of *dead*, but also the Scots word for *death*. Colloquial Scots, pronounced like *deed*. The use of *dead* in golf, for a ball played so close to the hole that the putt is virtually unmissable, is originally Scots, and dates from the middle of last century.

dicht A quick wipe or rub. Colloquial and occasional Scots. Also found in northern English dialect. You can give almost anything a *dicht*. When visitors are due, the careful housewife gives the best room 'a wee *dicht*' with a duster. Before going out you may give your shoes a *dicht* with a pad, and on returning home your face 'a *dicht* (wash)' before going to bed. *Dicht* is also a verb, to wipe clean: '*Dicht* yer feet afore ye come in.' The corresponding English form, *dight*, became obsolete in the 17th century, though it was partially revived in literary use by the example of Sir Walter Scott. *Dicht* was first recorded in Scots in the 14th century. It is from an Old English word for to arrange or compose.

diet, in the sense of arrangements made for a particular day, developed a fuller range of meaning in Scots than it did in English. A meeting or session of any sort was once often called a *diet*, but in modern times it is chiefly heard in localised Scots in the sense of a church service, and then in the phrase a *diet of worship*. This sense is extended further in a *diet of examinations*, a group of university degree examinations taking place over a limited period of time. Recorded in Scots since the 15th century. From Middle English, or perhaps direct from Old French: ultimately derived from Latin *dies*, a day.

dook To bathe, or a bathe. Some people like *dooking* in the local river; others prefer a *dook* in the sea. In *dookin for aipples* immersion is minimal: in this HALLOWEEN (IX) game players must try to lift floating apples out of a tub of water with their teeth without using the hands. A *dook* was once any liquid into which something was dipped. When this was buttermilk it was called **soor** (sour) **dook**, which earlier this century could be bought from *soor dook* carts that went from door to door. *Dook* was first recorded in the 15th century, meaning to dive or push under water. It came to Scots from Middle English.

doot, doubt In Scots, commonly means to fear rather than to doubt in the usual standard English sense. General Scots, and also known in English dialect. 'I'm afraid the weather's breaking'; 'I *doubt* you're right' is part of a 1986 conversation in Scots standard English. The *doubt* conveys fear of an undesirable future event: 'I *doot* he'll nae be in time.' 'I *hae ma doots*' is a common Scots idiom expressing the speaker's fear about a likely outcome. 'Will they win today?' 'I *hae ma doots.*'

dree To suffer, endure (pain, misfortune). General Scots; also found in northern English dialect. Someone in a difficult situation for which there is no immediate remedy is likely to be told, 'You'll just have to *dree* it.' A common form of 'Job's comfort' is 'You have to *dree* your weird', you must put up with what seems to be your fate (see WEIRD, VIII). *Dree* has been recorded in Scots since the 14th century. It is from the Old English word for to endure, and has a common origin with DREICH (XV), which is said of things that are hard to bear.

dreich Dreary, tiresome, dull, long drawn out. Though now only general Scots, once common to Scots and English, with the basic meaning, lasting for a long time. In this, and in more subjective senses (e.g. tedious, depressing) it was well-known in Middle English, and though obsolete in modern English it was still current in Cumberland, in the form *dree*, in the late 17th century. In Scotland *dreich* is almost indispensable when commenting unfavourably on the weather. 'It's a *dreich*, drizzly Monday' (1986) indicates that the day is sunless, and damp or misty. But it can also be applied to almost any period of time, occasion or task that sorely tries the patience. 'It's a *dreich* job howkin tatties (digging potatoes).' A football match has been dismissed as 'a *dreich* 90 minutes' (1986). Sermons, speeches or meetings may be classed as *dreich*, and so may people. Robert Louis Stevenson described someone as 'a *dreich* body', and a writer to *The Scotsman* in 1986 referred to the '*dreich*, grey men of computing, accounting and technology'.

drookit Drenched, soaked. General Scots. A *drookin* is a drenching. A party of walkers who left the main body ran into heavy rain and got a real *drookin*. They were referred to in a subsequent news-letter as 'the *drookit* Ballachulish contingent.' The verb *drouk*, to drench, was first recorded in Scots in the 16th century: its origin is unknown.

ettle To aim, intend or attempt (to do something). 'He *ettled* to gang tae Arbroath', but missed the bus. In 1929 someone complained that lassies nowadays '*ettle* to dae a (all) things that men can dae.' Colloquial Scots, but phrases like *ettle for* or *after* (be eager for) a new coat, once common, are now dialect. *Ettle* was first recorded in Scots in the 14th century. It came through Middle English from Old Norse.

fankle A tangle, muddle or state of confusion. General Scots. It is easy enough to get knitting wool in a *fankle*. In 1986 the *Glasgow Herald* recalled that President Carter had 'found himself in many a *fankle*' because he meddled in foreign policy. Nearer home, in a football match, the 'defence got in a terrible *fankle*' (Radio Scotland, 1987). *Fankle* was earlier a verb for to tangle or to become tangled – a meaning still heard, as when an angler's line becomes *fankled*. First recorded in the 18th century; the original sense was to trap, as in a snare. It came from an earlier Scots word *fank*, a coil of rope.

far enough (*Sc* **aneuch**) 'I could see him *far enough*' expresses exasperation with, sometimes even dislike of, another person by wishing for his removal to some distant place.

fash To annoy or trouble. Colloquial and occasional Scots. Particularly common in to *fash* oneself, to put oneself out, to bother. Someone asked for help may be unwilling to *fash himsel*; if he seems over-willing he may be told, 'Dinna *fash yersel*.' This may be more picturesquely expressed as 'Dinna *fash* yer heid (head)' or 'Never *fash* yer thoom (thumb).' First recorded in Scots in this sense in the 16th century; from French *fâcher*, to anger or annoy.

ferlie A strange sight or event, a wonder. An eclipse, or the appearance of a comet, is a *ferlie*; a piece of surprising gossip or scandal may be thought a *ferlie*. Now largely confined to literary Scots, though someone I know uses it regularly for a surprise gift or an extravagant but pleasing purchase. Until recently also an adjective meaning unusual, wonderful. In this sense it was also found in northern English dialect. First recorded in the 14th century. From an Old Norse word for monstrous, fearsome.

foostie Musty, mouldy. General Scots. Recently a friend spoke of an aged relative who used to live 'in a *foustie* old house', one where there was a stuffy, airless smell. If you entered one of the old second-hand clothes shops of fifty years ago the *foostie* smell, or the *foost*, thrust itself on your senses. *Foostie* is the Scots form of English *fusty*, musty: it was taken into Scots and given its present form in the 19th century.

gie The Scots form of *give*: the past is expressed by *gied* or *has* (etc.) *gien*. '*Gies* is a shortened form of *give us*; recently a leaflet came through my letter box headed '*Gie's* peace.' It is often used by children for *give me*: '*Gies* a sweetie.'

grannie, as well as naming a female relative (as in the song

'Ye cannae push yer *grannie* aff the bus'), has two special uses in Scots. One sense is a chimney cowl, a modern use, though becoming less common. The other usage is in a contemptuous or dismissive response to something that has just been said: a key word is picked out and repeated, followed by a reference to *yer grannie*. 'But I promised to go home early.' 'Promised *yer grannie*', or even 'Early *yer grannie*'. Colloquial Scots.

gunk, to jilt, was in 1986 given some prominence in the B.B.C. series on English language as an example of a Scots word, now virtually obsolete in Scotland, that has survived in Ulster. As a noun, *gunk* means a bitter disappointment, and to *gie* someone the *gunk* is to jilt, or otherwise disappoint him. *Gunk* was first recorded in Scots in the 18th century: its origin is unknown.

hae Scots form of *have*; *haena* is have not. A writer in the *Guardian* in 1988 quoted 'Scots wha (who) *hae*' as if it were a Scots battle-cry. In fact these are the three opening words of a poem by Burns: 'Scots, wha *hae* wi Wallace bled.' They are meant to be Robert Bruce's first words to his soldiers before the battle of Bannockburn.

hail Scots form of English *whole*. Scots retains meanings like healthy and unhurt, once shared by *whole*, but now found only in northern English dialect and in standard English *hale*, and partly preserved in *wholesome*. In Scots one can separate '*hail* eggs' from 'crackit ones.' *Hail* can sometimes be used with a plural noun. This usage is sometimes seen in legal documents, though now the English form *whole* is more likely to be used: thus in 1955 'the *whole* heritors and their agents' attended a meeting.

haim, hem Scots forms of English *hame*, part of a draught-horse's collar. Preserved in the localised Scots idiom to *pit* (put) *the haims* on someone, to curb or restrain him. Marriage sometimes *pits the hems on* wild young men. In a poem by Stephen Mulrine the 'wee Malkies' may '*pit the hems oan* (put out of action) the sterrheid (stairhead) light.'

halve To halve a hole, or a match, in golf was first recorded in Scots in 1807. It is now standard English. A *halver*, or *haufer*, is a half-share. This is frequently heard in the phrase *to go halvers*, to share equally between two, which is common in colloquial Scots.

hap To cover in order to protect or conceal. Colloquial Scots. One may *hap* (wrap) a sick child in a blanket, and when he is *weel happit-up* carry him to another room. *Hap* has also outdoor applications. Seedlings or plants can be *happed in* with earth or straw as protection against frost or rain – a process sometimes known as *happing up*. At the end of his day a mason may cover up his work to protect it against overnight frost. In some places this last part of the mason's day is called the *happer*. *Hap* was first recorded in Scots in the 14th century: it came from northern Middle English.

heelster-gowdie Head over heels, topsy-turvy. Localised and occasional Scots. Slightly easier to recognize in the earlier form *heels ower* (over) *gowdie* if one realises that *gowdie* (goldy; *gowd* is the Scots for *gold*) here means a head of golden hair. In one of his songs Hamish Henderson has described how on a windy day the clouds blow '*heelster gowdie* ower the bay' (1960).

heeze To hoist, raise up. Colloquial Scots. On a boat you can *heeze* a flag, or *heeze up* the sails. If you want to *heeze up* a clothes-line to profit from a good drying wind, you may in some parts of the country use a *heyser* (clothes prop). Also used figuratively. People who *heeze up* (praise highly) health foods are not always the most robust-looking members of the community. In north-eastern dialect *heeze* has developed the meaning of to dance in a lively manner, to have lots of fun. *Heeze* is from a Low German or Dutch word that was also taken into English, but in the different form of *hoist*.

hotchin Crammed with, overrun by (people): 'The conference was *hotchin* wi fowk (people) wi posh accents.' Also, infested or swarming with: in the summer certain remote areas are *hotchin* with midges. General Scots. To *hotch* is to move about in a fidgetty or restless manner, and when this is a sign of impatience with inaction an eager person may be *hotchin(g)* to get up and do something. In *Tam o' Shanter* even Satan '*hotched* and fidged' as he watched the youngest witch dancing. Someone who sees the humour in a situation may be observed *hotching* (rolling about) with laughter. *Hotch* in the sense of to jerk up and down came into Scots in the 14th or 15th century from a northern Middle English word, the precise origin of which is uncertain.

howk To dig or dig up. General Scots. Suggests more effort or difficulty than mere digging. 'I went out and *howked* the spike out of the ground' (1986). You can spend the day *howkin* tatties (potatoes): if you do so professionally you will be a *tattie-howker*. Also used figuratively. I recently had an impacted wisdom tooth *howked* out by a dentist. After much rummaging, you may *howk* a mislaid tool out of a storage cupboard. Also used for to hew. Miners used to *howk* coal from the coalface, and 'in one of the quarries men still *howked* slates' (*Scots Magazine*, 1951). After *howkin* a neep (turnip) out of the ground you may then *howk* it (hollow it out) to make a lantern for HALLOWEEN (IX). When first recorded in Scots early in the 15th century *howk* had the form *holk*. It and northern Middle English *holk* came from an old German word *holken*, to dig.

humph To carry (a heavy load), or to raise it (on to one's back). 'He'd an awfae job *humphin* the case up the stair.' Colloquial Scots. As a noun, *humph* means a hump or a humped back. A *humphie-backit* person is hunch-backed, even round-backed; one Dundonian, looking back to the 1920s, remembered Winston Churchill as being a bit '*humphie-backit*'. Probably imitative, expressing a grunt of effort, in origin.

jag A prick with something sharp. General Scots. The commonest current sense is an injection, a sense widely understood outside Scotland. At primary school children may be given their *jags* if they haven't been already innoculated. Mischievous boys used to administer *jags* to their neighbours with the point of a geometrical instrument. The *jags* or prickles of a thistle is preserved in the nickname 'the *jags*' given to football teams whose name includes the word *Thistle. Jaggy* means prickly and by extension stinging, so that even nettles may be described as *jaggy*. First recorded in Scots about 1500. From northern Middle English.

jing-bang The colloquial Scots phrase 'the *haill* (whole) *jing-bang*' means the whole lot: 'Thieves got away wi *the haill jing-bang.*' Can also refer to people: 'He walked out on *the haill jing-bang.*' *Jing-bang* is occasionally used as an adjective: 'He ran off wi the *jing-bang* lot.' Perhaps from *jing*, to jingle, and *bang*, an older Scots word for a crowd still heard in north–eastern dialect.

jotter A notebook for rough work, especially one in school use. *Jotters* were usually kept in school, and given out for use in class. Now that folders are in common use in schools, the school *jotter* is well on the way to being superseded, but a *jotter* may still be bought on the open market. In the outside world *jotters* are the documents held by an employer of labour for every man in his employ. To *get your jotters* is to be dismissed from a job, or to be made redundant. From *jot*, to note down, first used as a verb in Scots, and later adopted into English.

keek To peep, glance. General Scots. 'He *keekit* at them through his fingers.' Also used as a noun: 'He had a quick *keek* at her.' In some parts *keekers* is used for eyes, and by a further refinement a *keeker* can mean a black eye: 'You've a right *keeker*' (1987). A *keekin-glass* is a mirror, but this usage is now rare. The Scots form of 'peep-bo,' the peeping game played with very small children, is *keekaboo, keekie-bo* or *keek-bo. Keek* first appeared in Scots in the 15th century. It came from Middle English, but did not survive into the modern English period.

ken To know. Colloquial and occasional Scots: in the former it is far more common than *knaw*, the Scots equivalent of *know*, whereas in England *know* has driven *ken* from the field. You can *ken* both facts and people: 'I dinna *ken* what ye're talking aboot', and 'Aye, I *ken* Jock fine.' *Kent* supplies the past forms, and is itself used to mean well-known. 'A *kent face*' is general Scots: in a busy street one hopes to see one *kent face*, one person who is familiar. The ubiquitous English *you know*, dropped in between every few phrases, is in theory supplied in Scots by 'ye *ken*', but more often this is shortened to *ken*: 'The numbers 1–10 are on the other side of the street, *ken*.' *Ken* was first recorded in Scots in the 14th century. It came from Middle English, and before that from either Old English or Old Norse, or perhaps from both.

kenspeckle Conspicuous, familiar. In Scots since early in the 16th century, though never widely used: even today, it occurs chiefly on the literary or learned level. In 1986 on Radio Scotland Vivaldi was described as having been 'a *kenspeckle* figure in Venice,' and a modern poet was named as one of the most '*kenspeckle* makars (poets) o the Scots Renaissance.' *Kenspeckle* is also found in northern English dialect from the late 16th century till the present day. It may be from *ken*, to know, and *speck* (or *speckle*), a mark.

kip To play truant from school. Like most such terms, localised Scots: particularly common in the south-east. It was the term used in the Edinburgh school I attended 50–60 years ago. *Kipping* was not seen by us as delinquency: we had on occasion to walk out of school early to attend to matters elsewhere. The origin of *kip*, which was first recorded in the 19th century, is obscure.

laich, laigh Scots form of standard English *low*, both coming from Old English *lāh*. Scots retained the *h* as a *-ch*, pronounced as in *loch*. The situation is complicated by the facts that *low* is sometimes used in Scottish senses, and that *laich* is occasionally pronounced *lay*. A Londoner was puzzled by a reference to the '*lay* hall in Parliament House' in Edinburgh, not realising that it meant *low*, in a lower part of the building. A popular restaurant in central Edinburgh in the 1950s and 1960s was known as the *Laigh* Coffee House, or more shortly as the *Laigh*: it was a semi-basement, and patrons had to go down several steps before entering it.

landward In or of the country as opposed to the town. General Scots, but in limited use. A parish that contains both town and country areas may be divided into the burghal and *landward* sections: some parishes are entirely *landward*. In the 1936 drought *landward* districts in Fife suffered particularly from the shortage of water.

len To lend; a loan. Colloquial Scots. The Scots form is historically more correct than the standard English one. Originally, *len* was the accepted form in English; but the past *lend* influenced the present form, and after 1500 *lend* became the standard form. In Scots *len* survived, both as a verb and a noun: '*Len* me a pen', or 'He gied (gave) me the *len* o his pen.' To *tak a len o* someone is to take advantage of him, to make him look a fool.

lippen To trust (a person); to depend on someone (to do something). Colloquial Scots. 'I wadna *lippen* Mrs Smith' may be heard; but more usual is to *lippen tae* or *on* her. 'None o them are tae *lippen tae*', or 'Can I no *lippen on* ye tae dae as ye're told?' The motto of Angus is '*Lippen on* Angus'. *Lippen* can also mean to entrust something to a person. It is useful to know someone you can '*lippen* the keys tae when ye're awa (away from home)', though you may be unwilling to *lippen* certain people with them. Another sense of *lippen* is to count on, expect with confidence. 'I *lippened* tae get the last bus to Leven.' *Lippen* has been recorded in Scots since the 14th century: of doubtful origin, perhaps from an Old Norse word for to depend on. At one time there was a verb *lipnen*, to trust, in the English East Midlands, and *lippen* in some of the senses given above is found in northern English dialect.

lowse in many senses follows or develops from the meanings of English *loose*. One such sense is to *lowse* (free) an animal from plough or harness. From this came the colloquial Scots sense of to release a worker at the end of his day's work: 'When the factory was *lowsed*, he went hame.' The time when work ended came to be known as *lowsin-time*. *Lowse* can mean not tied or fastened together. A shop in central Edinburgh in which goods are measured out only when bought was in the 1970s known to many customers as the '*loose* shop,' presumably because nothing was packaged in advance. 'Yer lace is *lowse*' draws attention to an untied shoelace. Recorded in Scots as a verb since the 14th century. From northern Middle English *lowse*.

maukit, maucht Dirty, filthy. After being empty for months, a house may be *maukit*. Colloquial Scots. An older sense, now localised Scots, is infected with maggots: in hot weather, before the days of refrigerators, meat soon became *maucht* or *mauchy*. In some places, a bluebottle is still known as a *mawk-flee* (fly). *Maukit* is from the Scots word *mauk* or *mauch*, a maggot, recorded since the 16th century. It came to Scots from Middle English.

meikle see MUCKLE (XV).

message(s) To *go the messages* is to do the shopping. Someone, remembering her aunt, said, 'I used to *go the messages* for her' (1986). The things bought are *messages*: 'I'll take up your *messages* the now, Gran' (1986). The *message-boy* (errand-boy) on his round was a familiar sight in the inter-war years.

mickle see MUCKLE (XV).

mind The usual Scots colloquial word for to remember or recall. 'I cannae *mind* what he said' (1986) or '*Mind* to put the milk in the fridge' (1987). A small present given as a mark of goodwill rather than for a particular occasion is often called 'a wee *minding*'. *Mind* had the same sense in Middle English, but it is now only dialect in English use.

mingin Evil-smelling, stinking. Colloquial Scots. A recent song has it that 'the bus was *mingin* wi fish and chips.' It can also mean exceedingly drunk: 'Drunk! He was *mingin*.' A development from *ming*, a smell, first recorded earlier this century. Of unknown origin.

miss onesel(f) To lose the chance of some fun by failing to turn up. 'Were ye at Jock's pairty? No? Och, ye *missed yersel*.' The idiom sounds more than ever a contradiction in terms in such examples as 'Ye fair *missed yersel* at Jock's pairty.' Colloquial Scots.

mixter-maxter A jumble, a bringing together of things of different kinds. General Scots. A teacher, after a glance at her new time-table, commented: 'I've been given a real *mixter-maxter* of classes'(1987). Also used to mean in a jumbled or confused state: 'Papers and books lay *mixter-maxter* all over his desk.' Now used more commonly than the slightly earlier *mixtie-maxtie*, though in 1961 someone could still refer to the '*mixtie-maxtie* contents' of a work-basket. Both terms were first recorded in the 19th century, and derive either from *mixed* or *mixter* (the Scots form of *mixture*).

muck Dung; refuse. General Scots. In English now dialect or colloquial – a retreat from the days when Dr Johnson could say, 'Money is like muck; it is best spread.' *Lord* or *Lady Muck* are 20th century Scottish inventions – names given to those who try to give themselves airs and be thought HIGH HEID YINS (I). As a verb, *muck* in the sense of to clean out farmyard dirt is originally Scots, though now accepted standard English. To *muck*, or *muck oot*, *the byre* (or stables), to clear out the dung, has been in Scots use since 1500. *Muck* came to Scots through Middle English from Old Norse.

muckle, mickle, meikle Large, big. Colloquial Scots. A play by Alexander Reid first performed in 1950 was entitled 'The Lass wi the *Muckle* Mou (mouth).' A farmer interviewed on radio thought that in most years grey-lag geese were 'no a *muckle* problem' (1988). Can also mean much, a lot of: 'He hasnae *muckle* money.' As a noun, *muckle* is widely known through the oft-quoted but puzzling 'Mony a *mickle* maks a *muckle*.' Since *mickle* and *muckle* mean the same thing, the saying seems pointless, and it has been argued that the first words should be 'Mony a little'. This would make sense, and fit in with the Scot's reputation for careful husbandry. *Muckle*, *mickle* and *meikle* all go back to a northern English *mikel*, which is ultimately of the same origin as *much*. *Mickle* and *meikle* were both known in Scots before 1400, two centuries earlier than *muckle*.

neuk Scots form of English *nook*; pronounced *nyook*. In the sense of a corner, as in ingle-*neuk* (SEE INGLE, XIII), or a 'corner' or triangular area of land, as in the *East Neuk* of Fife, which sticks out into the North Sea. Something with corners, with an angular shape, is *neukit*. In the north-east of Scotland this developed the sense of cantankerous: in 1950 someone was described as '*neukit* [and] ill-naitured' (SEE THRAWN, II).

orra Odd, in many of the senses of that word. Colloquial Scots, and more commonly used in country districts; also in some senses occasional Scots. An *orraman* is an odd job man, especially on a farm, and the 'odd jobs' he does may be lumped together as *orra* work. In 1955 a newspaper in the south of Scotland carried an advertisement for an '*orraman* or *orrawoman*', and in 1951 a Fife farmer sought for a 'casual, odd, unskilled man for *orra* work.' The poet Robert Garioch recalled that in the 1970s he was employed for a time as *orraman* on a dictionary. At one time *orra* was frequently used in the sense of spare or without a matching partner: a casual visitor could be put up on the *orra* bed, or if someone lost a shoe he was left with the *orra* one. This use is now only dialect. In the 17th century an *orra* woman was one who had never married. Also now dialect is the use of *orra* for shabby or worn-out: a man going out to do a dirty job might put on his *orra* duddies (clothes): or he might pick up *orra* (odd, sundry) garments from here and there for the occasion. *Orra* may be a reduced form of *ower a'* (over all, everywhere, over and above).

pauchle, pochle at one time meant no more than a package or light load. Then in colloquial Scots it developed the special sense of a parcel of something taken home from work, often quite legitimately, as when a fisherman was allowed for his own use some of the day's catch. Then 'perks' came to be regarded as a right and were sometimes taken without permission; or someone used his position to extract a bit extra from customers. The *Scottish National Dictionary* notes that at one time '*pauchles* ... was an old fishing term for backhanders.' A barman might make a *pauchle* by selling a bottle of whisky a few minutes after closing time. To be regularly making a bit on the side was to be *on the pochle*, 'on the fiddle.' When a treasurer *pochled* the club funds he was charged with theft. A shrewd bystander must have realised that the 'three card trick' was a bit of a *pauchle* (trickery). But to *pauchle the cairts* is to shuffle a pack of cards, with no implication of dishonesty. *Pauchle* is from Old Scots *pakkald*, which came from northern Middle English: it was derived from *pack*, a bundle.

peep A tiny light or flame. General Scots. Most commonly used of a gas flame – to put the gas *at a peep* is to turn it as low as possible without turning off the supply. This is the basis of the idiom *to put* (someone's) *gas at a peep*, to make him feel small, reduce him to size. The same word as *peep*, a glance.

pickle, puckle A small amount, or number, of anything; a little, a few. Colloquial and occasional Scots. 'There was only a *pickle* at the foot of his glass' (1987). A girl may be sent next door to ask for a *pickle* milk – the amount is indefinite, and the *of* is often not expressed. The *puckle* form is commoner in some parts of Scotland: 'a *puckle* dirty water' (*Scots Magazine*, 1951). *Pickle* was first recorded in Scots in the 16th century. At first it referred to a grain of corn, but the meaning was soon generalized. Already by 1638 one could say,, 'There is not a *pickle* of hair in thy head.' *Pickle* was also known, though later, in northern English dialect; of unknown origin.

play oneself To play about, amuse oneself. One of the good men who taught me sixty years ago used to cast an eye over the class and ask, 'Who is that boy *playing himself?*' Now colloquial Scots. Common in the impatient response to, for example, unwanted advice: 'Awa an *play yerself*, 'get lost'.

pochle see PAUCHLE (XV).

poke A bag or pack; a shopkeeper's paper bag. Colloquial and occasional Scots. You can take your dinner PIECE (IV) to work in a *poke*, or you can buy a '*poke* o sweeties' at the corner-shop. At one time the *poke* was made before your eyes by the shopkeeper twisting a square of newspaper into a cone and screwing up one end to close the poke. Nowadays a *poke* may be a carrier-bag. In the Glasgow area a *poke-pudding* is a steamed pudding cooked in a bag; at one time the name was extended to mean an Englishman, the English being popularly seen as steamed pudding addicts. *Poke* came from Middle English and before that from French: it has survived in English till the present day in northern dialect, and in the idiom 'to buy a pig in a poke'. An alternative *pock* form is preserved in the diminutive word *pocket*, also in the *pocks* of smallpox. *Poke* was first recorded in Scots in the 15th century.

preen A metal pin. Colloquial Scots, and also northern English dialect. A *pin* was originally, in both Scots and English, a wooden peg, but over the centuries it has been gradually taking over the senses of *preen* and displacing it, so that nowadays in Scots *pin* (also *peen*) is at least as common as *preen*. *Preen* was first recorded in Scots in the 14th century: it came through northern Middle English from Old English.

puckle see PICKLE (XV).

real MacKay, the The genuine article, not an imitation or inferior substitute. The phrase was popularised in both Scotland and England by its use in advertisements after 1870 by a firm of Edinburgh distillers named Mackay.

redd The commonest surviving senses of *redd* are connected with the idea of cleaning up or putting in order. To tidy a room or a house is to *redd* it; after a meal someone may be asked to *redd* the table. Colloquial Scots. Also to *redd up*: a teacher, who had been showing a class some slides, admitted, 'It'll take me a few minutes to *redd up*' (1987). In mining *redding* is an essential part of the work. At one time a *redsman* had to be employed to keep passages in a mine free of debris. The debris thus cleared was heaped on to a *redding-bing* (see BING, XII). These terms are still used in some mining areas.

A connected sense of *redd*, now heard only in the north-east, is to try to stop a fight, often by active intervention. Sometimes the peacemaker is caught by a blow intended for one of the combatants: this is known as a *redding-lick* or *redding-straik* (*lick* and *straik* both mean a blow). When the time came for an occupant to FLIT (VI) from a dwelling, he was expected to leave it in good order. This was required by a demand that he should leave the house *void and redd*, empty of contents and ready for occupancy. The term is still some-times used in legal documents. *Redd* is also used as a noun for tidying, a tidy up. 'Quick, gie (give) yersel a *redd* before they come.' Or you can give a room a hurried *redd up*. *Redd* was first recorded in Scots in the 14th century, in the sense of to put out (a fire). It is partly from an Old English word for to rescue, partly from an older Dutch or Low German word for to tidy up.

reek Smoke. General Scots; also in northern English dialect, and sometimes in literary use in English. A persisting use of the word is in *peat-reek* (see PEAT, XI), the fume of burning peat, believed to impart a special flavour to whisky. *Reekie*, blackened by smoke, smoke-filled, is widely known through *Auld* (old) *Reekie*, a nickname for Edinburgh. As a verb, *reek* has several senses common to Scots and English, the best-known being to vent smoke. The Scots saying 'Lang may your lum *reek*' (see LUM, XIII) is strictly speaking ambiguous, since a chimney can *reek* in two directions – up, or back down into the room. In the latter case, a *reekin* lum can be a curse. Recorded in Scots as a noun since the 14th century, *reek* came from northern Middle English. It may be of either Old English or old Norse origin.

rickle A carelessly or loosely assembled heap or pile. A *rickle* of sticks may be kept in a yard as firing. Colloquial Scots. Often unkindly applied to ramshackle buildings, and in the phrase a *rickle o banes* (bones) to someone who is painfully thin. A well-known folk-song tells of a girl who was once 'a *rickle o banes* covered ower (over) wi skin.' First appeared in Scots in the 16th century; probably of Scandinavian origin.

sair Scots form of *sore*, and often used as is the English word – a *sair* finger, or 'my hert (heart) is *sair*.' A headache is 'a *sair heid*,' a toothache '*sair teeth*.' Discussion of life's troubles often ends with the shaking of heads and the comment, 'Aye, it's a *sair fecht* (fight)', – life is hard. Often used as an intensive: someone may be *sair* affronted by another's behaviour. At the end of a hard day's endeavour a worker may be *sair* FORFOCHTEN (II).

see (oneself) **doing** (or **do**) To remember doing; to have done something often, or on occasion. A doctor, when admitting an elderly patient to hospital, asked: 'Do you get out of the house?' The reply, 'Aye, I've *seen me* gettin oot o the hoose a' right', suggested that such outings were not frequent. This idiom is a 20th century development.

shot The use of someone else's property for a short time. General Scots. When a boy displays a new bike, a friend may ask, 'Can I have a *shot on* (or *off*) it?' Also used more simply for a turn at doing something: 'It's my *shot* next.'

shote! A warning cry to other children to give them time to escape detection. In certain Edinburgh schools in the 1920s and 1930s it was the regular call to make known the approach of a teacher. A poem by Robert Garioch (*c* 1930) called *Fi'baw* (football) *in the Street* begins '*Shote!* Here's the poliss (police).' *Shote* is probably a variant of shoot: if so, it began in this sense as an incitement to prompt action: 'Beat it!'

sicker Sure, safe. Colloquial Scots. Once known to every Scottish schoolboy from the story of one of Robert the Bruce's followers who, on hearing that his leader had stabbed a rival, vowed not to let the wounded man cheat death with the words 'I'll mak *siccar*', I'll make sure (he's dead). This **he** did by stabbing him again. The phrase has been used many times since then. In reports of football matches, when a 'poacher' has helped a rolling ball over the goal-line, he is sometimes said to have 'made *sicker*.' First recorded in Scots in the 14th century. Came through Middle English from Old English. Ultimately of the same origin as English *secure*.

siller Money. Colloquial and occasional Scots, and the Scots form of English *silver*. In 1986 the *Scotsman* disclosed that in the BORDERS (XI) 'much *siller* is spent promoting tourism.'

skelf A thin chip of wood; a splinter, especially when driven in under the skin. Localised Scots. In the entry on PINKIE (I), a small boy was described as running to an adult with a sore finger. A brief but expert examination revealed the source of the trouble: 'Ay, there's the *skelf*.' See also SPAIL (XV). In parts of Scotland *skelf* is applied to a person who is very small and thin: 'He's a right wee *skelf*.' First recorded in Scots early in the 16th century. Probably from a Middle Dutch word for a splinter.

skitter To potter about ineffectively. 'Don't *skitter* aboot – get on wi it.' Colloquial Scots. A *skittery* job is one that calls for time rather than skill – a fiddly job. *Skittery* may also mean trifling, of no importance. From a much earlier date *skitter* has also mean diarrhoea, or to have diarrhoea. From SKITE (VI). First recorded in the 16th century.

skoosh To gush or spurt out; to make liquid do this. Colloquial Scots. If you take a bottle full of fizzy lemonade, shake it vigorously with your thumb over the mouth of the bottle, then pull away your thumb, the contents will *skoosh* over anyone in the line of fire. In wet or slushy weather buses will *skoosh* through the snow or puddles, making a *skooshing* (swishing) noise. Many people, even some Scots, like to add a *skoosh* of soda to their whisky. Any kind of fizzy drink like lemonade can be called *skoosh*, and any kind of sprinkler may be called a *skoosher*. Recorded only since the end of the 19th century: of onomatopoeic origin.

smoor To suffocate for lack of air. Colloquial Scots, and frequently made relevant to Scottish conditions by association with being lost in the snow. In *Tam o' Shanter* Burns mentions the spot 'Where in the snaw the chapman *smoor'd*.' Sheep buried under snow-drifts may *smoor* before anyone can rescue them. Not only '*smoorin* snaws' cause people to be suffocated: one can also be *smoored* in a bog. The process of damping down a fire at night by covering it with closely-packed wet DROSS (XII) or PEAT (XI) which keeps it smouldering all night is when still practised known as *smooring* the fire.

sort as a verb has several uses peculiar to Scotland. One is to tidy, or put in good order: before visitors arrive children may be sent to 'get your room *sorted*', and then to '*sort* your hair'. Even more common is the sense to repair or mend. Happy are those who are able to *sort* the car if something goes wrong. Sometimes an obliging neighbour may offer to do minor repairs: 'I'll soon *sort* that for you.' People too may be *sorted* – that is, dealt with, put firmly in their places: 'I'll *sort* him when he comes home.' All these senses are general Scots.

spail A splinter or chip of wood broken off accidentally when shaping the wood. General Scots. At one time a marketable by-product: in 1937 someone made some extra money by selling *spails* and shavings. More widely known as a splinter through the skin. When doing gym on an old wooden floor one often gets a *spail* in the hand, foot, or even the behind. As a boy I always used *spail* and not the alternative SKELF (XV), as the latter word was not known to me till much later. First recorded in the 15th century, for a thin strip of wood. Of Scandinavian origin.

squeegee Set at a wrong angle, askew. General Scots. A

tablecloth, if *squeegee*, has to be pulled straight. Without squared paper children's sums soon begin to look a bit *squeegee*. A 20th century formation from *skew*, off the straight, and *ajee*, meaning much the same: nothing to do with English *squeegee*, a kind of mop. Pronounced with equal stress on both syllables.

stance has proved more durable and flexible in Scots than it has in English. A common current English sense today is the way one stands when addressing the ball in golf or cricket. This sense first appeared in Scots with reference to golf in the late 18th century. In the sense of a site, *stance* has been common and productive in Scots usage. From referring to a building site in the 17th century, *stance* has developed such senses as the site of a fair, the place set aside for a stall or a stand at a fair, or the place in which a street-trader is permitted by licence to set up his stall. It is also used in *bus stance*, a bus terminus or a place at which a bus waits to pick up passengers, and *taxi stance*. First recorded in Scots in the 16th century: from Old French or Latin.

stand A complete set, especially 'a *stand* of pipes . . . now a very expensive thing to buy' (*Scotsman*, 1954), which includes bags, drone and chanter, all the parts necessary to the instrument. Also in dialect or localised Scots used for sets of other kinds – a *stand* of knitting needles, or a *stand* (suit) of clothes. In earlier Scots, before the Reformation, a *stand* was often used for a set of ecclesiastical vestments.

stave To sprain or bruise (a joint). General Scots. Boys often *stave* a thumb when playing rugby, as this finger is particularly liable to *staves*. In technical Scots to *stave* two pieces of metal is to heat them, then hammer them together to make a joint. The *Scottish National Dictionary* quotes an instance of '*staved* lead joints.' *Stave* was formed from *staves*, the plural of *staff*. It first appeared in Scots late in the 17th century as a verb for to jab.

stoor, stour As a noun, *stoor* means rising dust or a 'dust-up'.

On some of the old country roads, at times a driver could hardly see the car in front of him 'for the *stour*.' Colloquial Scots. The earliest sense of *stour* was a contest or conflict, as in 'the *stour* of battle'. This sense of strife barely survives in localised Scots. To raise or kick up a *stour* is to create a fuss or disturbance – a sense also heard in English dialect. This may however be connected with the idea of dust (to kick up a dust) rather than of strife. Dust also underlies the main sense of *stoor* as a verb, to run hard or rush, hence raising dust. You can go '*stoorin* doon the road on a bike', or you can *stoor* after someone on foot. *Stour* was first recorded in Scots in the 14th century. It came by way of Middle English, from Old French *estour*, conflict. The sense of dust developed a century later.

stot To bounce or rebound. General Scots. Some balls *stot* better than others, and are more suitable for the pastime of *stotts* or *stotting*, bouncing a ball on the ground with the flat of the hand. Other things may *stot*. A vivid comment on very heavy rain is 'It's *stottin*' – rebounding from the ground. A favourite explanation of the breaking of a piece of china when washing up is 'It *stotted* (jumped, leapt) oot o ma haun (hand).' *Stotting* may also refer to human movement: someone who walks with a springy step may be said to *stot* down the road. It is perhaps this sense that suggested *stotter* as descriptive of an attractive young woman: 'Aye, she's a *stotter*.' But the comment 'He was fair *stottin* last night' indicates that the person concerned was staggering under the influence of drink. You may *stot* more than a ball against a wall. There are recorded instances of one boy *stottin* another's head off a wall. *Stot* has been recorded in Scots since the 16th century. Its origin is perhaps partly a Middle English *stut*, to stumble, and partly a Dutch word for to push or recoil.

stoun(d) (pronounced *stoond*) A pang of pain, physical or emotional. Colloquial Scots. Rheumatism may send *stouns* down your legs, or you may feel a *stoun* of sorrow. Someone, asked if she still had pain a month after an operation, replied, 'To use a Scots word, it *stounds*' (1986). An older sense, now heard only in Shetland dialect, is a period of time. This is probably the base meaning of the word, which came to Scots from Old English through Middle English. It is connected with German *Stunde*, an hour.

swick Cheat, swindle. Colloquial Scots. It is only too easy to be persuaded to buy a gadget from a fast-talking salesman at a market. Friends are quick to point out, 'You were fair *swickit* when you bought that!' or to exclaim in sympathy, 'What a *swick*!' It may also, in some parts, be used of a swindler. First recorded in Scots as a noun early in the 15th century. From an Old English word for deceit or a deceiver.

tent Attention, heed. Also, more rarely, a verb, to pay attention. Colloquial and literary Scots. To *tak tent* also means to pay attention, or to take care. 'Let Wives *Tak Tent*' was the name given by Robert Kemp to his translation into Lowland Scots of Molière's play *L'Ecole des Femmes* (1948). Recorded since the 14th century: shortened from the obsolete English word *attent*.

thole To suffer from; to bear without complaint. General Scots. The first sense is also heard in northern English dialect. If you tell someone you are *tholing* backache, you no doubt hope for some sympathy for your suffering. The other sense of *thole* belongs rather to a listener's response to suffering, and is less sympathetic: if you complain of some trouble, you may be told, 'Ye'll just hae to *thole* it', grin and bear it. It is reported of R.L. Stevenson that he 'couldna *thole* respectable Heriot Row', the street in Edinburgh's New Town in which he was brought up. *Thole* has been recorded in Scots since the 14th century. It came from Old English through Middle English.

thraw Scots form of English *throw*. In Scots *thraw* has retained a group of meanings which have in common the idea of twisting or turning; these are now largely obsolete in standard English except in special contexts, as 'throwing pottery' on a throwing-wheel. In Scots to '*thraw rapes*' is to make rope by twisting strands together, and the person who '*threw* the key in the door' (1955) was turning the key in the lock: both these usages are now chiefly localised or dialect Scots. To *thraw* the neck of a fowl is to wring its neck. As a noun too *thraw* is largely confined to dialect use. One sense, that of a fit of perversity or ill-humour, is more often expressed in the adjective THRAWN (II).

tim see TUME (XV).

tocher A marriage portion, usually the bride's dowry. Now chiefly literary Scots. A publication issued annually by the School of Scottish Studies to put on record Scotland's heritage of folklore, song and story in both Lowland Scots and Gaelic is aptly named *Tocher*. The word *tocher*, recorded since the 15th century, passed from Gaelic into Scots.

toom see TUME (XV).

tryst in its now accepted standard English sense of an appointment or rendezvous, or the place arranged for a meeting, was originally Scots. It passed into English in the course of the 19th century, and is common in such romantic phrases as a lovers' tryst. In Scots a *tryst* was in the past a meeting–place in more utilitarian senses. Huntsmen would meet at a certain well-known point: hence such a place name as Hunter's *Tryst* near Edinburgh. Farmers used to come together to hold unofficial markets for buying and selling livestock: these were known as *trysts*, and the most famous, the Falkirk *Tryst*, survived till 1901. In 1972 the *Scotsman* carried a reference to 'Tarnyt *Tryst*, Brechin's annual fair.' As a verb, in most senses *tryst* is now localised or dialect Scots, but the sense of meeting, or arranging to meet, is still general Scots. People *tryst* to meet at a particular *trysting* place, or they may *tryst* (meet) with others by arrangement. One curious localised sense is to order something in advance: clothes may be bought either ready-made or *trysted* (made to order). *Tryst* was first recorded in Scots in 1349. It comes from a Middle English word, which in turn came from a medieval Latin word for a place where hunters lay in wait for their quarry.

tume, toom, tim Empty, vacant. Colloquial Scots. An old Scots proverb held that 'a *toom* purse makes a blate (timid) merchant.' As many things can be *toom* in Scots as can be empty in English – a *tume* bottle or jar, a *'toom* hoose (house)'. A riderless horse has a *toom* saddle. A foolish person may be spoken of as *tume-heidit* (headed)), and there is no reason to fear the Greeks if they come *tume-handit* (not bearing gifts). Also used as a verb for to empty. '*Tim* the water oot of the pail.' In Banff in 1970 men were seen '*teemin* (north-eastern form of *toomin*) the dustbins.' Recorded in Scots since the early 15th century. From northern Middle English and, ultimately, Old Norse.

tyne To lose. Colloquial Scots. At one time *tyne* had the same range of meaning as English *lose*, but its range and its frequency have both been reduced. Nevertheless in recent times people have *tint* their purses, their keys, or their way. A Scottish lorry-driver, stopping in Chipping Campden to ask the way, admitted, 'God, I'm fair *tint*' (*Guardian* letter, 1987). Recorded since the 14th century; from Old Norse, through northern Middle English.

uplift To take up, collect. General Scots. The most common object of *uplifting* is money: someone may be sent to the bank to *uplift* the wages to be paid out, or an agent may be authorised to *uplift* all the debts due to a firm. A bus will stop to *uplift* waiting passengers, and a van may *uplift* packages to be delivered elsewhere. A slightly different usage, now less common, is to dig up or harvest such root crops as potatoes or turnips.

upsides To *be upsides wi* someone is to get even with him, to gain revenge: 'I'll be *upsides wi* you yet.' Recorded since the 18th century. Colloquial Scots.

upstanding On one's feet. Formal Scots, used only on very particular or ceremonial occasions. An after-dinner speech may end, 'I ask you to be *upstanding* and to drink the health of our guests.' A similar request may be made to the congregation of a church to stand during a prayer or for the benediction. This usage dates from the 19th century, and may now be finding its way into standard English.

wait on To wait for. General Scots. A messenger may hand a note in at the door and *wait on* an answer. A friend may offer to *wait on* you while you do some shopping. In 1951 someone was *waiting on* an apology – and perhaps still is.

wale To choose or select. Localised Scots. Someone may be given the job of *walin* tatties (potatoes), sorting out the good ones from the bad, or selecting those of a particular size. The *wale* of anything is the pick (of the bunch). Someone offered first choice of the prizes to be awarded will be able to get the *wale o* them. *Wale* has been recorded in Scots since the 15th century. It came through northern Middle English from Old Norse.

wallie Ornamental; made of porcelain or china. Colloquial Scots except in the phrase *wallie dugs*, which is general Scots. When Burns's Tam o'Shanter noticed among the dancing witches 'ae (one) winsome wench and *walie*', he saw her as a fine, well-built girl. That sense of *wallie* is now almost obsolete, but from it has developed a fascinating group of related usages. Of these the first was in *wally dug*, an 'ornamental dog' made of porcelain, usually one of a pair decorating the ends of a hearth or mantelpiece. Since these were made of porcelain, people began to think that *wally* meant porcelain, china or glazed earthenware. When a tiled entrance passage to a tenement came to be fashionable, it was called a *wally close*: to live in a *wally close* was regarded as socially desirable, if expensive. Street sellers used to go from door to door offering for sale a selection of *wally* objects – *wally* bowls and the like. Even when they were broken *wally* articles had their uses – children used the fragments as *wally money* in their games. At one time false teeth were made of porcelain, and so *wallies* was used as a plural noun for false teeth – a sense it has retained. It could also stand for *wally money* – hence the comment, 'he can't play for *wallies*', he is no good at all. *Wallie* was first recorded in Scots in the 16th century, in the sense of fine or beautiful. Its origin is unknown: it is perhaps connected with WALE (XV, to choose).

wee Though now widely used in all parts of the British Isles, *wee* was originally Scots, and is generally regarded as a characteristically Scottish expression. The most common sense today is small, tiny. 'When I was *wee*, I used to . . . ' is a common opening in reminiscence. 'A *wee thing*' is a small child, or sometimes a small person. *A wee bit* is often used to mean slightly (as is *a little*). 'Are you tired?' 'Aye, *a wee bit.*' For *wee hauf*, see HAUF (XIV); *wee heavy*, see BEER (IV); *wee sma oors*, see SMA OORS (XI). *Wee* was first recorded in Scots in 1375 as a noun in the phrase *a lytill we* (a small distance): it was not used as an adjective till the middle of the next century. It derives from an Old English word for a weight.

weel Scots form of English *well*, and used in the same ways. Colloquial Scots. Absence from school can be explained by the fact that 'ma mither wisnae (wasn't) *weel.*' 'Och, *weel*' is a slightly more ponderous version of 'Oh, well.'

wersh Used nowadays in two apparently opposite senses, both referring to the sense of taste. For centuries *wersh* has been used of foods that lack sharpness of taste, that tend to be insipid. 'A *wersh* kind o' dinner' damns with very faint praise. '*Wersh* beer' is flat, and *wersh* porridge lacks salt, though some hold that 'lumpy porridge is worse than *wairsh* porridge' (1972). On the other hand, since the beginning of the present century, *wersh* has been used of things that are too sharp in taste, or sour. Medicines often taste *wersh*: so does home-made wine that has gone wrong. A friend, presenting me with a jar of rowan jelly, said apologetically, 'I'm afraid it's a bit *wersh*' (1983).

In these senses, *wersh* is colloquial or occasional Scots. In the last century several older senses have become obsolete, or have retreated into dialect use. '*Wersh* land' used to be poor or unproductive land; a person who looked *wersh* was sickly or weak looking; *wersh* music was dull or uninspiring. *Wersh* was first recorded in Scots in the 15th century. It derives from a Middle English word meaning sickly or insipid, and may be related to *weary*.

wheesht, whisht Be quiet! Sh! General Scots. In the form *whist* once common in English, but now only dialect. Most commonly heard in 'Haud yer *wheesht*!' – literally, 'Hold your peace!' or colloquially, 'Shut up!'

widdershins, withershins In the opposite direction to the usual one; more particularly, anti-clockwise, in the opposite way to that followed by the sun. Now dialect, and occasional or literary Scots. To do something *widdershins* suggested in the doer a perversity, a desire to defy usage, that might bring with it evil consequences or ill-fortune. That is why witches always danced *widdershins*. The *Second Statistical Account of Scotland* noted that fishermen leaving for a day's fishing feared that 'they'd have bad luck if they were to row the boat *widdershins about.*' An accidental *withershins* movement was also considered a bad omen, and might bring ill luck in its train. First recorded in Scots in the 16th century; also known in English, but chiefly in dialect. From a Low German word for in the opposite direction.

wally dugs (XV)

For Further Reading

Reference

Daiches, David, ed.: *A Companion to Scottish Culture*, London, 1981.

The Concise Scots Dictionary, A new comprehensive one-volume dictionary of the Scots language, Aberdeen, 1985. Much valuable introductory material.

A Dictionary of the Older Scottish Tongue from the Twelfth Century to the End of the Seventeenth, Chicago, Oxford and Aberdeen, 1931–. Six volumes completed, from A–R.

The Scottish National Dictionary from the Eighteenth Century to the Present Day, Edinburgh and Aberdeen, 1929–76.

Periodicals

Lallans. The Magazine for writing in Scots.

The Scots Magazine Articles on many aspects of Scottish life. Some use of Scots language.

Tocher. Tales, Songs, Tradition. Selected from the archives of the School of Scottish Studies. Includes items in Scots.

Some books on or in Scots

Aitken, A.J. and McArthur, Tom, ed.: *The Languages of Scotland*, Edinburgh, 1979. Considers 'English in Scotland' as well as Scots.

Hanley, Clifford: *The Scots*, Glasgow, 1980. Entertaining personal view of the Scots and their culture.

Kay, Billy: *Scots; the Mither Tongue*, London, 1988.

— ed.: *Odyssey*, Edinburgh, 1980. —. *A Second Collection*, Edinburgh, 1982. Contains interviews with speakers of Scots from a variety of backgrounds.

Lorimer, William Laughton: *The New Testament in Scots*, Edinburgh, 1983. A translation that will test to the full any reader's knowledge of Scots.

Munro, Michael: *The Patter. A Guide to current Glasgow usage*, Glasgow, 1985.

Murray, Mary: *In my ain Words; an East Neuk* [Fife] *vocabulary*, Anstruther, 1982.

Index by sections

a, aw XIV
ablow XIV
abune XIV
advocate VII
ae XIV
afore XIV
aiblins XIV
ain XIV
airt XI
aleevin XIV
ane XIV
arbiter VII
argie-bargie VI
ashet XIII
ask for V
assoilzie VII
athegither XIV
Athole brose IV
aucht XIV
auld XV
auld lang syne XI
ava XIV
awa, away XIV
awfae XIV
ay, aye XIV
aye, ay XIV

ba, baw X
back XV
baffie III
bailie VII

bairn I
baith XIV
balmoral III
bampot I
bannock IV
bap IV
barley X
barley bree IV
barrie XV
bass XIII
bauchle III
bawbee XV
beal III
bed X
beer IV
behouchie I
bejant VIII
belt VI
Beltane IX
ben¹ XI
ben² XIV
besom, bizom XIII
bide XV
bidie-in I
big XIII
bing XII
birk XI
birl VI
black bun IV
blackmail VII
black-strippit ba IV

bladderskite I
blaeberry XI
blaes, blae XII
blate II
blether V
bletherskate I
blooter VI
bluebell XI
body I
bogie X
boke, bock III
bonnet III
bonny III
bonspeil X
Borders, the XI
bothy XIII
brae XI
bramble XI
braw III
bree IV
breeks III
breenge VI
bridie IV
brig XIII
brither I
broch XIII
brock XI
brogue III
broo VII
brose IV
broth IV
bubble II
bubbly jock XII
bucket XIII
buckie XII
bum V
bunker X
bunnet III
burgh VII
Burns night IX
bursary VIII
but and ben XIII
butterie IV
by-ordinar II
byre XII

ca XV
caber X
ca canny XV
caddie X
cairn XIII
cairngorm III
canny II
cantrip VIII
capercailzie XI
carfuffle VI
carnaptious II
carpet bowls X
carry out IV
carse XI
cat's lick XV
cauldrife XV
causey XIII
caution VII
ceilidh IX
chanter IX
chap XV
cheep V
chiel I
children's hearings VII
chitterin(g) bit(e) or piece IV
chore II
chuckiestanes X
chum VI
clachan XIII
claes III
clamjamfry, clanjamfry XV
clan I
clarsach IX
clarty XV
claymore VI
cleek XII
cleg XI
clishmaclaver V
cloot III
close XIII
cludgie XIII
clype V
cock-a-leekie IV
college VIII
collie XI

collie-buckie X
collieshangie VI
collop IV
common good VII
Common Riding IX
conceit II
coo XII
cookie IV
coorie VI
coronach V
corrie XI
corrie-fisted III
couple XIII
Court of Session VII
couthie II
cowp XV
crabbit II
crack V
craig XI
cranachan IV
craw XI
crawstep XIII
creel XII
croft XII
crowdie IV
cry V
cuddie XII
Cullen skink IV
culpable homicide VII
cundy, condie XIII
curling X
cuts of beef IV

dae XIV
daft II
darg XV
daud XV
dauner, dander VI
dean VIII
deave V
decree VII
defamation VII
defender VII
deid XV
deil VIII
den¹ X

den² XI
d(e)ochandorus IV
dice III
dicht XV
diddle IX
diet XV
dinger VI
dirk III
disjaskit II
dispone VII
disposition VII
disruption VIII
divot XI
dochter I
dominie VIII
donnert II
doo XI
doocot XIII
dook XV
doon XIV
doot, doubt XV
Doric V
douce II
dour II
dram IV
drap XIV
drappit egg IV
dree XV
dreich XV
drive X
drookit XV
drop scone IV
dross XII
drouth II
drove road XI
drystane XIII
dub XI
dump VI
dumplin(g) IV
dunt VI
dux VIII
dwam III
dyke XIII

easy-osy II
Edinburgh Rock IV

ee I
eediot, eejit I
eerie VII
efter XIII
eident II
eightsome IX
elder VIII
eldritch VIII
end X
entry XIII
ettle XV

fae XIV
fair XIV
Fair, the IX
faither I
fank XII
fankle XV
fantoosh II
far enough XV
farl IV
fash XV
feart II
fecht VI
feckless II
ferlie XV
feu VIII
fey VIII
Finnan haddie IV
fire-raising VII
first-foot IX
firth XI
fish supper IV
fit I
flannen III
flat XIII
flee XI
fleein II
flesh IV
fling IX
flit VI
flyte V
foostie XV
footer II
for XIV
forby XIV

forenoon XI
forfoch(t)en II
forrit XIV
fou II
foursome IX
fower XIV
fowk I
frae XIV
freen(d) I
fulmar XI
fur XIV
furth XIV
fushionless II
fykie II

gab I
gae VI
Gael I
Gaelic V
gall(o)us II
galluses III
galore XIV
games X
gang VI
gansey III
gantree XIII
gar XIV
gathering IX
gean XI
General Assembly VIII
General Council VIII
gey XIV
gie XV
gigot IV
gillie I
gin XIV
gird and cleek X
girdle XII
girn II
glaikit II
glamour VIII
Glasgow Fair IX
glaur XI
glebe VIII
glen XI
glengarry III

gley III
gloamin(g) XI
gob I
golf X
gollop II
gomerel I
goose IX
gowan XI
gowk XI
graip XII
graith XII
Grand Match X
grannie XV
gravat III
green X
greet II
grue II
guddle X
Guid Book VIII
guiser IX
gunk XV
gutser I

haar XI
hae XV
haggis IV
hail XV
haim XV
hairst XII
hairy I
haiver V
Halloween IX
halve XV
hap XV
hard stuff IV
harl XIII
hauf XIV
haun I
heather XI
heckle V
heelster-gowdie XV
heeze XV
heid I
hen I
hen-toed III
herd XII

heritable VII
hersel I
hert I
heukbone IV
High Court VII
Highers VIII
high heid yin I
Highland XI
Highland fling IX
Highland schottishe IX
high school VIII
high tea IV
himsel(f) I
hirple VI
Hoast III
hoch IV
hochmagandy II
hog(g) XII
hoggar III
Hogmanay IX
hole X
holograph VII
hooch V
hoolet XI
hoot(s) XIV
hoshen III
hotchin XV
house XIII
howe XI
howf XIII
howk XV
howtowdie IV
huidie XI
humph XV
hunker I
hunner XIV
hurdie I
hure I
hurl VI
hutch XII

ilk XIV
ilka XIV
Immortal Memory IX
inby XIV
indictment VII

ingan XII
ingle XIII
interdict VII
iron X

jag XV
jalouse II
janitor I
jaw-box XIII
jeelie IV
jessie I
jiggin IX
Jimmy I
jing-bang XV
jink VI
Jock Tamson's bairns I
joiner XII
jotter XV
jouk VI
joukerie-pawk(e)rie II
Justiciary, High Court of VII

kail XII
Kailyard school V
keek XV
keelie I
keepie-up(pie) X
Kelvinside accent V
ken XV
kenspeckle XV
keys X
kilt III
kip XV
kirk VIII
kirk session VIII
kirn IX
kist XIII
kittiwake XI
kittle II
klondyke XII
knock XIII
kyle XI

lad, laddie I
laich XV
laird I

laldie VI
Lallans V
lament IX
Lammas IX
land XIII
landward XV
lane XIV
lang syne XIV
lass, lassie I
laverock XI
law lords VII
lazy-bed XII
learn VIII
leed V
leet V
len XV
lenth XIV
lesion VII
lib XII
libel VII
licence VIII
lichtlie V
lift XI
line V
links X
linn XI
lintie XI
lippen XV
loch XI
lockfast VII
loon I
lord VII
Lord Advocate VII
Lord High Commissioner VII
Lord Lyon King of Arms VII
Lord Provost VII
lowp VI
lowse XV
luckenbooth brooch III
lug I
lum XIII

machair XI
main-door XIII
mains XII
mair XIV

makar V
malt whisky IV
man I
manse VIII
march VII
mart XII
mask IV
maukit XV
maun XIV
maw XI
meal IV
meat IV
meikle XV
mell XII
menage X
mercat cross XIII
merchant XII
message(s) XV
messan I
mickle XV
midden XII
midgie XII
mind XV
mingin XV
minister VIII
minor VII
mirk XI
misca V
missives VII
miss onesel(f) XV
mither I
mixter-maxter XV
mod IX
moderator VIII
mon I
moolie II
moorfowl XI
moothie IX
morn XIV
Morningside accent V
moss XI
moveable VII
muck XV
muckle XV
muir XI
mull XI

Munro X

na, nae XIV
neb I
neep XII
Ne'er Day IX
neuk XV
never XIV
next XI
nieve I
no XIV
noo XIV
nor XIV
Norn V
not proven VII
numerals XIV
nyaff I

oatcake IV
och XIV
Old Firm X
oo III
oor XIV
ootby XIV
opencast XII
ordinary VIII
orra XV
outwith XIV
ower XIV
oxter I

Paisley III
pallally X
pancake IV
pan drop IV
pan loaf IV
pape VIII
paraphrase VIII
park XII
parkin, perkin IV
partan XII
pauchle XV
pawkie II
peat XI
pech II
peelie-wally III

peenie III
peep XV
peerie X
peever X
pellock XII
pend XIII
perjink II
pernicketie II
pertinent VII
petticoat tails IV
pibroch IX
pickiemaw XI
pickle XV
pickmaw XI
piece IV
pie-eyed III
pig XIII
pinkie I
pipes IX
pirn XII
piskie VIII
plaid III
plat(t) XIII
play oneself XV
plook III
plowter II
plump XI
plunk V
pochle XV
poind VII
poke XV
pokey-hat IV
policy XIII
pony XI
pope's eye (steak) IV
porridge IV
pottit heid IV
pouch III
precentor VIII
precognition VII
preen XV
prelims VIII
presbytery VIII
press XIII
Principal VIII
probationer VIII

procurator fiscal VII
provost VII
ptarmigan XI
public school VIII
puckle XV
puddin IV
puddock XI
puggled II
pulley XIII
pupil VII
pursuer VII
putt X

quaich XIII
quine 1

ra XIV
radge II
raggle XIII
raid VI
rammy VI
ram-stam II
rant IX
rax VI
real Mackay XV
rector VIII
red biddy IV
redd XV
red-handed II
reek XV
reel IX
regionalisation VII
Register House VII
relevant VII
reset VII
richt XIV
rickle XV
Riding of the Marches IX
rift II
rink X
roll IV
rone XIII
roof XIII
room XIII
round steak IV
roup VII

rowan XI
rowie IV
Royal and Ancient X
rummle VI
rump steak IV
runt 1

sair XV
sapple XIII
sapsy II
sark III
sasine VII
Sassenach I
sax XIV
scaffie I
scart VI
scheme XIII
sclaff X
scone IV
scoor-oot IX
Scots V
scree XI
scrieve VI
sculduddery II
scunner II
sea maw XI
see (oneself) doing XV
seevin XV
semmit III
Senatus VIII
servitude VII
seven-a-sides X
shank end IV
shauchle VI
shaws XI
shed XII
sheltie XI
shenachie I
sheriff VII
sherrakin V
shilpit III
shinty X
shog VI
shooglie VI
shore XIII
shot XV

shote XV
shoulder steak IV
shuil XII
sicker XV
siller XV
single end XIII
skail VI
skean-dhu III
skeerie II
skelf XV
skellie III
skelp VI
skew XIII
skink IV
skinnymalink(ie) I
skip X
skirl V
skirlie IV
skite VI
skitter XV
skoosh XV
slaister II
sleekit II
slider IV
slogan V
sma oors XI
smeddum II
smirr XI
smokie IV
smoor XV
smowt XII
snash V
sneck XIII
snell XI
snib XIII
snifter II
snod III
solan (goose) XI
solicitor VII
sonsie III
soop X
soor-dook IV
soor plooms IV
sort XV
souch V
southron I

spail XV
spalebone IV
spate XI
speir V
sporran III
spug XI
spurtle XII
squeegee XV
stair XIII
stance XV
stand XV
stank XIII
stave XV
stick II
stinkin Willie XI
stirk XII
stone X
stookie I
stoor XV
stot XV
stot stirk XII
stoun(d) XV
stovies IV
stramash VI
strath XI
strathspey IX
stravaig VI
stushie, stashie VI
stymie X
suit III
sup IV
superior VII
sweetie IV
sweir II
swick XV
swither II
sword dance IX
syboe XII
synd, syne XV
syne XIV
synod VIII
syver XIII

tablet IV
tam o'shanter III
tartan III

tattie, tawtie XII
tattie scone IV
tawse VI
tee X
teind VIII
tenement XIII
tent XV
term, term–day VII
teuchter I
thae XIV
the XIV
theevil XII
thegither XIV
thirled II
thistle XI
thole XV
thon XIV
thrang II
thrapple I
thraw X
thrawn II
tig X
tim XV
tocher XV
toddle VI
tolbooth XII
toom XV
toorie III
tot I
tousie III
Trades Holidays IX
trauchle VI
trews III
tron XIII
tryst XV
tume XV
twa XIV
twal XIV
twa-three XIV
tweed III
tyne XV

uncanny VIII
unco XIV
unco guid VIII
Uphellya IX

uplift XV
upset price XII
upsides XV
upstanding XV
uptake II
usquebaugh IV

vennel XIII

wabbit II
wait on XV
wale XV
wallie XV
wame I
warlock VIII
waukrife II
waulk XII
waur XIV
wean I
wee XV
Wee Free VIII
weel XV
weird VIII
well-fired IV
wersh XV
wha(t) XIV
whaup XI

wheech, wheek VI
wheen XIV
wheesht XV
whiles XIV
whin XI
whinge V
whin(stone) XI
whirligig XIII
whisky IV
whit XIV
wi XIV
widdershins, withershins XV
wife I
willie-waught IV
wulk XII
wur, wir XIV
wynd XIII

yammer V
yatter V
yett XIII
yin XIV
yon XIV
yonder XIV
youse XIV
yowe XII

Scottish Interest Titles from Hippocrene. . .

SCOTTISH PROVERBS

Compiled by the Editors of Hippocrene
Illustrated by Shona Grant

Through opinions of love, drinking, work, money, law and politics, the sharp wit and critical eye of the Scottish spirit is charmingly conveyed in this one-of-a-kind collection. The proverbs are listed in the colloquial Scots-English language of the turn-of-the-century with modern translations below. Included are twenty-five witty and playful illustrations. There is something for everyone in this collection.

130 pages • 6x 9 • 25 illustrations • 0-7818-0648-8 • $14.95 • W • (719) • May 1998

SCOTTISH LOVE POEMS

A Personal Anthology
edited by Lady Antonia Fraser, re-issued edition

Lady Antonia Fraser has selected her favorite poets from Robert Burns to Aileen Campbell Nye and placed them together in a tender anthology of romance. Famous for her own literary talents, her critical writer's eye has allowed her to collect the best loves and passions of her fellow Scots into a book that will find a way to touch everyone's heart.

220 pages • 5 ½ x 8 ¼ • 0-7818-0406-x • $14.95pb

Language Guides ...

SCOTTISH [DORIC]-ENGLISH/ENGLISH-SCOTTISH [DORIC] CONCISE DICTIONARY
Douglas Kynoch

This dictionary is a guide to the Scots language as spoken in parts of the northeastern corner of the country and northern England. Beginning with a brief introduction to spelling, pronunciation, and grammar it presents a two-way lexicon of North-East Scots with 12,000 significant entries.

186 pages • 5½ x 8½ • 12,000 entries • 0-7818-0655-0 • $12.95pb • (705) • September 98

SCOTTISH GAELIC-ENGLISH/ENGLISH-SCOTTISH GAELIC DICTIONARY
R.W. Renton & J.A. MacDonald

Scottish Gaelic is the language of a hearty, traditional people, over 75,000 strong. This dictionary provides the learner or traveler with a basic, modern vocabulary and the means to communicate in a quick fashion.

This dictionary includes 8,500 modern, up-to-date entries, a list of abbreviation and appendix of irregular verbs, a grammar guide, written especially for students and travelers.

416 pages • 5½ x 8½ • 0-7818-0316-0 • NA • $8.95pb

ETYMOLOGICAL DICTIONARY OF SCOTTISH-GAELIC
416 pages • 5½ x 8½ • 6,900 entries • 0-7818-0632-1 • $14.95pb • (710)

In the Kitchen . . .

TRADITIONAL FOOD FROM SCOTLAND: THE EDINBURGH BOOK OF PLAIN COOKERY RECIPES

A delightful assortment of Scottish recipes and helpful hints for the home—this classic volume offers a window into another era.

336 pages • 5½ x 8 • 0-7818-0514-7 • W • $11.95pb • (620)

CELTIC COOKBOOK: Traditional Recipes from the Six Celtic Lands: Brittany, Cornwall, Ireland, Isle of Man, Scotland and Wales

Helen Smith-Twiddy

This collection of over 160 recipes from the Celtic world includes traditional, yet still popular dishes like Rabbit Hoggan and Gwydd y Dolig (Stuffed Goose in Red Wine).

200 pages• 5½ x 8½ • 0-7818-0579-1 • NA • $22.50hc • (679)

Ireland

THE ART OF IRISH COOKING
Monica Sheridan

Nearly 200 recipes for traditional Irish fare.

166 pages • 5½ x 8½ • 0-7818-0454-X • W • $12.95pb • (335)

New!

ENGLISH ROYAL COOKBOOK: FAVORITE COURT RECIPES
Elizabeth Craig

Dine like a King or Queen with this unique collection of over 350 favorite recipes of the English royals, spanning 500 years of feasts! Start off with delicate Duke of York Consommé as a first course, then savor King George the Fifth's Mutton Cutlets, and for a main course, feast on Quails a la Princess Louise in Regent's Plum Sauce, with Baked Potatoes Au Parmesan and Mary Queen of Scots Salad. For dessert, try a slice of Crown Jewel Cake, and wash it all down with a Princess Mary Cocktail. These are real recipes, the

majority of them left in their original wording. Although this book is primarily a cookery book, it can also be read as a revealing footnote to Court history. Charmingly illustrated throughout.
187 pages • 5½ x 8½ • 0-7818-0583-X • W • $11.95pb • (723) • May

Wales
TRADITIONAL FOOD FROM WALES
A Hippocrene Original Cookbook
Bobby Freeman
Welsh food and customs through the centuries. This book combines over 260 authentic, proven recipes with cultural and social history
332 pages • 5½ x 8½ • 0-7818-0527-9 • NA• $24.95 • (638)

TRADITIONAL RECIPES FROM OLD ENGLAND
Arranged by country, this charming classic features the favorite dishes and mealtime customs from across England, Scotland, Wales and Ireland.
28 pages • 5 x 8½ • 0-7818-0489-2 • W • $9.95pb • (157)

All prices are subject to change. To order Hippocrene Books, contact your local bookstore, call (718) 454-2366, or write to : Hippocrene Books, 171 Madison Ave. New York, NY 10016. Please enclose check or money order adding $5.00 shipping (UPS) for the first book and $.50 for each additional title.